JEWELS
FROM
E.M. BOUNDS

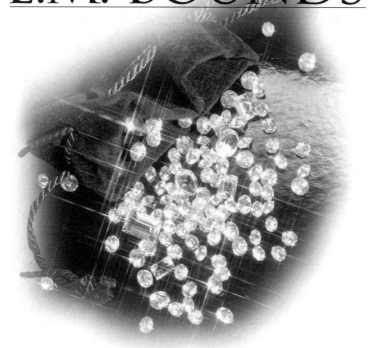

E.M. BOUNDS

BRIDGE
LOGOS
FOUNDATION

Alachua, Florida 32615

Bridge-Logos
Alachua, FL 32615 USA

Jewels From E.M. Bounds
by E. M. Bounds

Dr. Darrel King researched, compiled, and edited this material. He is the Director of the E. M. Bounds School of Prayer, Conyers, Georgia.

Edited by Beverly J. Chadwick

Printed in the United States of America.

Library of Congress Catalog Card Number: 2010927427
International Standard Book Number 978-0-88270-995-6

Unless otherwise indicated, Scripture quotations in this book are from the *King James Version* of the Bible.

G163.316.N.m1005.35230

CONTENTS

VOLUME II: OUR SPIRITUAL WALK

VOLUME III: LEADERSHIP GOD'S WAY

FOREWORD

E. M. (Edward McKendree) Bounds has left a legacy of Spirit-inspired sermons as relevant today and all future tomorrows, as they were when he first spoke them. His scriptural, powerful, and heartfelt teachings on foundational themes, such as the great need for prayer—both prayer for individual needs and corporate prayer for the Church—are so stirring you may forget you are reading them because what he is saying makes you feel that you are sitting in his congregation absorbing the truth of his words as they flow into your spirit.

His sermon topics include revival, prayer meetings, Church spiritual growth, family and personal growth, discipline, purpose of the local church, spiritual principles, preaching, spiritual leadership, thought life, evangelism, praise and worship, Heaven, the Christian home, the Holy Spirit, sin, self-denial, and faith, just to mention a few.

Because E. M. Bounds had children himself, his sermons are written with the whole family in mind. His concerns for the spiritual welfare of Christian families echo those of God himself. Without a doubt his teachings were wrapped in love and given as gifts to the whole family of God.

As you read these sermons, you will find that each one is a journey into God's will for your life, the lives of your loved ones, family, friends, and those God brings into your life as you walk this journey of faith with Him.

Beverlee J. Chadwick, Editor
Bridge-Logos Foundation

BIOGRAPHY OF

EDWARD MCKENDREE (E.M.) BOUNDS

August 15, 1835–August 24, 1913

"What the Church needs today is not more machinery or better, not organizations or more novel methods, but people who the Holy Spirit can use—people of prayer, People mighty in prayer. The Holy Spirit does not flow through methods, but through people. He does not anoint plans, but people—people of prayer."
E. M. Bounds

E. M. Bounds once wrote, "Elijah learned new and higher lessons of prayer while hidden away by God and with God...." Clearly Bounds must have understood the ramifications of "new and higher lessons," because he, too, was a man hidden away by God and with God. He was a son, a husband and father, a gold miner, a lawyer, a pastor, a Confederate Army chaplain, a writer, a community leader, and a friend and neighbor. But the enduring legacy of E.M. Bounds is that he was first and foremost God's man. He was a man of prayer.

Edward McKendree Bounds was born on August 15, 1835, to Thomas J. and Hatty Bounds in Shelby County, Missouri. His middle name, McKendree, came from the famous Methodist circuit rider, Bishop William McKendree, who planted churches from the Atlantic coast to Missouri. The name was a prophetic choice, for Edward would grow up

1

to serve God in a quiet, powerful ministry that still resonates today through his writings.

Bounds may have started his life with a pastor's name, but his early career did not reflect a pastor's path. His father died of tuberculosis when Edward was only fourteen years old. Even though his father left the family well provided for, the tales of the California gold rush were too much for his older brother Charles. Together they heeded the call: "Go west, young man, go west!" They left their home in Missouri and traveled to Mesquite Canyon in California to seek their fortune in mining and panning for gold. But the promise of wealth soon faded into backbreaking work and crushing disappointment. Not only that, but living among miners wrenched the boys from their tender Methodist upbringing in Missouri into the grimy, gritty moral degradation of Western boomtowns. Surprisingly, they lasted four years. Edward and his brother might not have struck gold, but he set his sights on greater treasure. He turned to the God of his youth.

Very quickly Edward started reading his father's law books and excelled in this study. He was the youngest man ever admitted to the bar in Missouri. His services flourished in the Mississippi River town of Hannibal, but his spirit longed for something more fulfilling.

That "something else" soon revealed itself. The Great Spiritual Awakening of 1854–58 reached northern Missouri. The Methodist Episcopal Church South in La Grange, Missouri, sponsored a brush arbor meeting with Evangelist Smith Thomas. Edward was there. That night, enfolded in the preaching and praying, his spirit was ignited and more: His heart was moved to answer God's call for full-time Christian ministry. After only five years in practice, he locked the door of his law firm and walked away—straight into the service of God. He enrolled in Centenary Seminary of the Methodist Episcopal Church South in Palmyra. Two years later he graduated and was ordained in 1859.

His first pastorate was in Monticello, Missouri, and in October 1861, he moved to Brunswick, Missouri. His idyllic life as a country pastor with a red brick church was to be short-lived. The Civil War, which had seemed so far away from the daily life of peaceful Brunswick, roared into Missouri.

On May 10, 1861, Union troops imprisoned the State Guard in St. Louis and captured the Arsenal. Their rampage took the life of a seventeen-year-old boy who was deliberately drowned by Union soldiers in the Grand River. Reverend Bounds officiated at his funeral. Later Bounds would personally witness the brutal execution of ten more innocent civilians and officiate at their funerals as well. His despair grew. When he was asked to sign the Oath of Allegiance to the Union and post a $500 bond, he had no moral choice but to refuse. His conscience would not permit him to support the federal government that had butchered the Constitution as well as the citizens who lived within its protection, and condone the atrocities he was witnessing. His courage would have consequences.

On November 14, 1862, Union troops thundered up on their horses, stormed the church where Bounds worked quietly, and took him into custody. Obviously a man of peace, his only crimes were that he hadn't signed the Oath of Allegiance or posted a bond. In punishment, he was beaten and thrown into federal prison at St. Louis. To describe conditions as harsh would be an understatement. This horror might have destroyed a lesser man, but Bounds embraced prison as a wonderful opportunity to serve God, by ministering to the Confederate prisoners who shared his dank existence. The reputation of this godly man spread quickly. Early the next year, Bounds was sent to Washington, Arkansas, in a prisoner exchange and released. He was ordered to stay out of Missouri as long as there was conflict there.

Bounds walked out of prison and continued walking— over 100 miles to Pinebluff, where he purchased a mule and continued his journey another hundred miles. His single-minded mission was to join the Confederate Army and defend his beloved Missouri—not with a rifle, but with prayer. On February 7, 1863, he joined the Confederate Army, Company B of the Third Missouri Infantry, where he served as a chaplain.

Against the dark and bloody backdrop of the Civil War, in a country torn apart by moral and political issues so inflammatory that they pitted brother against brother on the battlefield, a gentle man of God rose.

The Missouri troops were merged with General John Bell Hood's Army of Tennessee before the Battle of Atlanta. After the defeat in Atlanta, General Hood moved his troops back to Nashville, thus the Battle of Franklin.

Chaplain Bounds asked to be assigned to a front line. He wanted to be with those in greatest need, the ones who he could point to God. At first, Bounds found it difficult to preach to battle-weary veterans who were accustomed to chaplains who would preach about faith at night at the campfire, but run home when the fighting broke out the next day. Bounds, however, was a "battle-weary veteran" in his own right. As a fatherless boy, he had been toughened up by the rough and tumble California miners and later by harsh conditions in prison in St. Louis. Additionally, his faith wasn't one of speech. It was one of practice. From the first volley fired to the last, Bounds stood side by side with his fellow soldiers, shouting encouragement and praying for their safety. The men were won over.

Their affection was apparent in the fact that they teased him. Bounds was short in stature: just over five feet tall. With a full pack bowing his slim shoulders, he was nearly dwarfed by the load. His men good-naturedly nicknamed him "the walking bundle."

But any small bit of good-natured fun would soon vanish. Life changed forever at the Battle of Franklin, Tennessee. On November 30, 1864, Bounds' commanding officer, General

Hood, ordered his troops to attack entrenched Union forces under General Schofield in Franklin, Tennessee. Eighteen thousand Rebels stormed Union lines in a battle still etched in history as one of the most brutal and possibly ill conceived in the Civil War. Called "The Gettysburg of the West," Franklin was one of the few battles fought in the dark of night in the Civil War. It was also one of the smallest battlefields of the war (only two miles long and one-and-a-half miles wide). The main battle began around 4:00 P.M. and wound down around 9:00 P.M. In five bloody hours General Hood's army suffered over 6,000 casualties.

> [Franklin] is the blackest page in the history of the War of the Lost Cause. It was the bloodiest battle of modern times in any war. It was the finishing stroke to the Independence of the Southern Confederacy. I was there. I saw it. – Sam Watkins, 1st Tennessee Infantry

Chaplain Bounds stayed in Franklin with the wounded. He had also suffered head wounds during the battle. After General Hood's loss at Nashville he retreated back through Franklin. Though Bounds could have traveled with the retreating troops, he chose to remain with the wounded and suffered capture for the third time. For two horrific weeks following the defeat, the injured and exhausted Bounds helped dig battlefield graves and buried friends and comrades with whom he had served and to whom he had ministered. Still, his spirit would not be broken. While he dug and hauled corpses, he offered support to fellow prisoners of war, sang hymns out loud, and quoted Scripture. At the end of two weeks, Bounds and the wounded were placed on a train and taken to prison in Nashville. Many did not live through the trip, yet Bounds was with them praying and helping. He stayed in prison until the surrender at Appomattox,

Virginia was completed. Still Bounds could not return home to Missouri because the scattered fighting continued.

Early in 1865, Bounds returned to Franklin. With prayer, fellowship, sharing, and preaching, the church and community started healing from a most tragic experience. Even the Union forces were accepted into community life.

Pastor Bounds often walked by battlefield graves with pieces of wood marking each gravesite with a name. These boards were being destroyed by the weather and many of them could no longer be read. He made a list of all the fallen comrades from Missouri that had shed their blood in Tennessee, and carried this list until his death.

After a discussion of the need to preserve the graves of those who died in battle, John and Caroline McGavock gave two acres of land adjacent to the family plot. This became known as the Carnton Cemetery, which is the nation's only Confederate Cemetery. Under Bounds' direction and with the McGavock family's generosity, 1,481 Confederate soldiers were exhumed from the shallow graves of the prison camp and given proper, individual Christian burials. One hundred seventy-seven of these men are from Missouri. Bounds even raised enough money to pay local men to care for their graves. Brother Bounds had their names published in the newspapers of Missouri in his efforts to try and locate the families of these courageous men.

While in Franklin, although Bounds concentrated on the exhumation and burial of his men, he couldn't escape noticing that a pall hung over the entire town. Perhaps they were exhausted and shell-shocked from all the death and destruction of the Union invasion. Even though it was a dominantly Christian community, there was no spirit of joy. No love. No hope. There was also no Methodist minister to turn it all around—until Edward M. Bounds stepped up.

Bounds took over as pastor of Franklin's Methodist Episcopal Church. Of course, he had his usual duties as a pastor, his usual responsibilities to his congregation, but his eye was on the larger picture. He entreated God to show him a way to lift the sorrow and darkness that engulfed the entire town. Then one day God answered his prayer with an idea: Bounds would call the men of the town to join him in prayer every Tuesday evening in the town square and cry out to God for their city. Even if the idea might have seemed far-fetched and frankly much too simplistic to work, the men gave it a try. For months, every Tuesday evening, they would gather on their knees in the town square and pray that the sorrow and darkness would lift. Slowly, but surely, it worked because it was done God's way.

For over a year this faithful band called upon God until He answered. Revival came down without any previous announcement or plan, and without the pastor sending for an evangelist to help him. Not only did Franklin, Tennessee, begin to heal, but God began to touch hearts and awaken spirits all over town. Bounds' own congregation exploded from a few faithful believers to over 500.

Within two years, Bounds knew that his work in Franklin was completed. He had buried his friends, and he had been God's servant in lifting the town by bringing its people to their knees in prayer. God had given Bounds a commission for intercessory prayer, and gifts for building and reviving churches. Bounds was sure-handed and fervent, but was not always popular with other ministers. He said, "Revivals are among the charter rights of the Church. A revival means a heartbroken pastor. A revival means a church on its knees confessing its sins—the sins of the individual and of the Church—confessing the sins of the times and of the community."

W. H. Hodge, the pastor who would later become his trusted friend and assistant, and who is responsible for putting most of Bounds' writings into print, remarked, "His constant call for revival annoyed those who believed that the Church was essentially sound...." Undaunted, he prayed without

7

ceasing for the sanctification of preachers, revival of the Church in North America, and the spread of holiness among Christians. Bounds spent a minimum of three to four hours a day in concentrated prayer. "Sometimes the venerable mystic would lie flat on his back and talk to God, but many hours were spent on his knees or lying face down where he could be heard weeping...."

Hodge generously offers a private glimpse into Bounds' prayer life. He writes:

> I have been among many ministers and slept in the same room with them for several years. They prayed, but I was never impressed with any special praying among them until one day a small man with gray hair and an eye like an eagle came along. We had a ten-day convention. We had some fine preachers around the home, and one of them was assigned to my room. I was surprised early next morning to see a man bathing himself before day and then see him get down and begin to pray. I said to myself, "He will not disturb us, but will soon finish." He kept on softly for hours, interceding and weeping softly for me and my indifference, and for all the ministers of God. He spoke the next day on prayer. I became interested, for I was young in the ministry, and had often desired to meet with a man of God that prayed like the saints of the Apostolic Age. Next morning he was up praying again, and for ten days he was up early praying for hours. I became intensely interested and thanked God for sending him. "At last," I said, "I have found a man that really prays. I shall never let him go." He drew me to him with hooks of steel.

When Bounds' intercessory work in Franklin, Tennessee, was complete, he moved on to Alabama—first Selma, then

Eufaula. While in Eufaula, Alabama, Bounds came face to face with a community saturated with hate. Assault and robbery were a daily occurrence. Much of the bitterness was coming through the newspaper. Bounds soon had a column in the local paper which brought a healing Spirit. The church began to grow. They moved into a public building, and then started to build a new worship center with the tallest steeple in the South. Next, Brother Bounds took a church in St. Louis, Missouri.

One day while conducting a funeral, Bounds looked upon a woman he said was "the most beautiful woman in all the world." Her name was Emmie Elizabeth Barnett.

On September 19, 1876, Brother Bounds and Emmie Barnett were married in the church he helped build in Eufaula. The service was conducted by her father, Dr. A. W. Barnett, who was also a medical doctor. The marriage brought forth four children with three surviving. Emmie became ill and returned to Eufaula where her father treated her during her illness. On February 18, 1886, ten years after their marriage, Emmie was called home to her Lord. Brother Bounds was brokenhearted, and he was left alone to raise three children.

It was hard for Bounds to return to St. Louis even with the support of his family and church. He struggled without Emmie. He made frequent trips to Washington, Georgia, because while on her deathbed, Emmie shared with her husband and family that she wished Brother Bounds would marry her cousin, Hattie Barnett, from Washington and together raise their children. He found happiness again, and on October 24, 1887, Brother Bounds and Harriet Alexandra Barnett were married. Dr. A. W. Barnett, father of his first wife, performed the wedding ceremony. He and Harriet were blessed with six children. Sadly, Edward Jr., his son with Emmie, became ill and died. Then Charles, Bounds' infant son with Harriet, died.

On June 7, 1890, Reverend Bounds accepted the position as assistant editor of the Methodist Episcopal Church South's official publication, *The Christian Advocate,* and moved his family to Nashville, Tennessee. But his uncompromising views on holiness and the role of pastors put him into philosophical conflict with the members of the National Conference. He simply could not support the discussions he was being asked to help promote. Within four years, he resigned rather than compromise.

And I will give you pastors according to mine heart, which shall feed you with knowledge and understanding. (Jeremiah 3:15)

He refused severance pay and quietly left *The Christian Advocate* and moved his family to Washington, Georgia. If the Bounds' family's financial future looked bleak, it was for only a moment. Bounds might have essentially severed ties with his own Methodist Episcopal Church, but he had attracted the attention of other denominations that shared his uncompromising stance. He immediately began to receive invitations for speaking engagements in ministry. Wherever he preached, crowds of people who were hungry for truth gathered, and revival ignited their spirits.

For the last nineteen years of his life, E. M. Bounds devoted himself to intercessory prayer. He was deeply burdened because of the backslidden condition of the Church, the corruption and self-interest of his fellow ministers, the moral decay of the government, and for the lost souls of his people. He spent a minimum of three to four hours each morning in prayer. In fact, with regard to Bounds' commitment to intercessory prayer, there is a good story that Bounds scholars tell. It seems that at the end of the day, when the rest of his neighborhood would fall into slumber, Bounds would frequently, quietly slip out of his home and wander the lamp-lit streets until he finally selected a house. He would stand in the street in front of the house, where he would devote himself to impassioned prayer on behalf of the occupants unaware. Local police on patrol were so accustomed to finding this quiet man walking the streets at night they no longer bothered to "check him out." They knew this man in the shadows was not an intruder or a voyeur or a criminal. No, it was merely Brother Bounds, praying for people who probably never even knew he was there in the night.

After the 1904-1905 Spiritual Awakening, the churches around the world were looking for programs to bring about another awakening. Brother Bounds and others were saying, "It is God—not programs—that will make this happen." Bounds read the book, *God's Plan for Soul Winning* (prayer bands), by Thomas Hogben from London, England. After meeting with him regarding prayer, Bounds started "The Great While Before Day Prayer Bands" and began writing his great books on prayer.

Although Bounds was a very human man with very human triumphs and tragedies, his legacy—the gift he left to all who would come after him—is that he was a man of prayer. Filtered through the perspective afforded us by history, it's interesting, even perplexing, to note that he never attracted a large following during his lifetime. In spite of his scholarship, faithfulness, authorship, and unusually heroic and colorful life in forty-six years of ministry, he was largely unknown. Today, most evangelicals regard E.M. Bounds as an important authority on prayer, but during his lifetime, only two of his eight books on prayer were even published. Among his works are *Power Through Prayer, Prayer and Praying Men, The Essentials of Prayer,* and *The Possibilities of Prayer.*

E.M. Bounds died on August 24, 1913, at his home in Washington, Georgia, at the age of seventy-eight. Just as surely as his soul entered immortality, his work endures—a triumphant partnership between a glorious God and a faithful, humble servant.

Dr. Darrel King

PHOTO GALLERY

Portrait of E. M. Bounds.

E. M. Bounds at age 24. Photo is from his seminary class book of 1859.

The youthful Bounds and his elder brother Charles left their home in Missouri and traveled to Mesquite Canyon in California to seek their fortune in mining and panning for gold.

E.M. Bounds served as a Confederate Army Chaplain during the Civil War.

The harsh circumstances Bounds encountered early in his life prepared him to minister to the battle-weary troops in the final days of the war. He stood side by side in battle with his fellow soldiers, shouting encouragement and praying for their safety, winning the men over completely.

13

The Confederate troops suffered a bloody defeat at the Battle of Franklin, Tennessee. As a result, Bounds was captured and held as a prisoner of war for a short time.

The Federal Army commandeered the Carter family home as its headquarters. At that time, the Carter Farm consisted of 288 acres on the south edge of Franklin. After the battle, the parlor of the Carter House was converted into a Confederate field hospital.

The Confederate cemetery in Franklin, Tennessee, is located near the hills of the Carter Farm on a small parcel of land donated by a local farmer, McGavock.

The Carter House was purchased by the State of Tennessee in 1951 and first opened to the public in 1953. Today, it's a Registered Historic Landmark dedicated to all Americans who fought in this battle ... among them E. M. Bounds.

The last photo of E. M. Bounds was taken in 1912 at a campmeeting in Indian Springs, Georgia. He was seventy-seven years old.

ON MISSION

A CALL TO PRAYER
Prayer for Missions and Missionaries
September 13, 1890

THE MISSIONARY AGE

This is the missionary age. Protestant Christianity is stirred as never before in the line of aggression on pagan lands. The missionary movement has taken on proportions that awaken hope, kindle enthusiasm, and demand the attention, if not the interest, of the coldest and most indifferent. Our own church has caught the contagion, and the sails of her missionary movement are spread wide to catch the favoring breeze. The danger is imminent, that the missionary movement will go ahead of the missionary spirit. This has always been the peril of the Church; losing the substance and spirit in the shell and parade of the movement, and putting the force of effort in the movement and not in the spirit. The magnificence of the movement may not only blind us to the spirit, but the spirit that should give life and shape to the movement may be lost in the wealth of the movement, just as a ship carried by favoring winds may be lost when the winds swell to a storm.

DR. OLIN, MISSIONARY

Dr. Olin, a missionary of over forty years ago, was a man who had the rare and matchless combination of great intellectual ability with profound apprehension and a grasp of great spiritual principles. He said this regarding "whether the offerings of the Church to the missionary treasury, inadequate

17

and scanty as they have been, have not yet been greater than their faith, more numerous than their prayers; whether the missionary movement is not far in advance of the missionary spirit."

I do not hesitate to declare, this is my most solemn and mature conviction, this is the true and chief source of our difficulties. The novelty and even the sublimity of the enterprise, the new and strange facts brought to light in missionary reports; the stirring appeals of the press and platform, and the extent and glitter of our machinery stretching out through all the land have one and all had the effect of waking up an interest in this cause that is widely different from a true Christian sympathy for perishing sinners, or a pious concern for the honor and will of the Savior.

WORDS AND PRINCIPLES APPLICABLE NOW

If these words and principles were true and applicable at that time, then they are doubly applicable to us now.

The spirit of missions is the spirit of prayer. Prayer is the chief factor in the genuine missionary movement. Prevalent, united prayer is the agent that moves the world toward God and moves God toward the world. Jacob's wily shrewdness of invention and schemes failed him in the presence of Esau's revenge, but he reached and changed Esau when he reached God by prayer. What we need in our missionary movement, now more than anything else, more than all things else, is the spirit of fervent and effectual prayer.

The inquiry is made at our meetings: "Are the collections for missions full?" A more pertinent question would be, are our prayers for missions full? Do we pray up to the full measure of gospel privilege, fervor, and anguish? The inquiry is making the rounds in regard to our new leaders, are they platform men [good speakers]? A more important question would be: Are they prayer closet men? Men's words in the pulpit will be feeble, and their effects fleeting, if their words are not surcharged [filled to capacity] with power and permanency by much prayer closet work as well as much study work.

PRAYER: THE PRIMARY NEED

As much as we need men and money in this work, we need God more, and prayer brings God into it; and He never comes alone, but always brings the men and money with Him. When God comes, there is a mighty quickening; purse strings are loosened, and men are willing and prepared to go.

However, we may expand other conditions; God magnifies one, and bases the whole result of the conquest of the world to Christ on this one of prayer. *"Ask of me,"* [says God,] *"and I shall give thee the heathen for thine inheritance, and the uttermost parts of the earth for thy possession"* (Psalm 2:8). God is sovereign and has original rights and the power of disposal in this matter, and we ask and persevere in asking of God in the name of Christ and for Christ's glory, this is scriptural. Prayer is mighty because it links itself to Christ and our plea depends on the power of His name and the merits of His death and intercession. Prayer is mighty because it is the action of faith in God's word, and in God's oath [solemn promise] to His son.

Prayer projects God into our affairs in full force. He does not intrude himself. He does not come uninvited into our holiest efforts, nor into the work that does so greatly concern Him. His presence must be sought, pursued. Our plans, to have God in our plans, they must be inspired, sustained, and conclude in unceasing prayer.

The fervent, effectual prayers of God's people would exalt and purify the motives of those who go to the mission field. A short-lived enthusiasm would play no part in this call. Low, questionable motives would be lost in the constraining love of Christ. The church on her knees, with tearful, outstretched hearts to God, would secure the right kind of men and implant the right kind of motives to move them in their going; for God would elect the men and kindle in them the irrepressible desire to go. A church mighty in prayer would secure the money. Only God can break the love of money that restrains the giving of the church. If the church would set its heart on God by mighty prayer, He would scatter these fortunes and pour them through a thousand hills to carry the water of life to the perishing nations. Prayer will not only secure the right kind of men and money, it will make the men and money effective.

MISSIONARIES BACKED BY A PRAYING CHURCH

Without the missionaries being backed by the faith of a praying church, their going will be only another maneuver, the marching up the hill with ten thousand men and the marching down again. The money given will be as powerless in saving results as granite, if it is not fertilized by prayer. The Church has been fixing her eye and heart so strongly on her growing material resources that she has forgotten the nature, the secret, and the power of prayer. To forget these is to forget God. To restrain prayer is to restrain God. The history of the Church, the marvelous career of the missionaries, and the Word of God, all declare the praying Church to be the aggressive missionary of the Church.

REVIVAL PREACHING
The Golden Opportunity
January 31, 1891

REVIVAL: THE SPIRITUALLY GOLDEN OPPORTUNITY FOR PRAYER AND PREACHING

It is a great mistake to suppose, as is sometimes done, that preaching can properly be dispensed with at any stage of a revival meeting. In fact, there is no other occasion that offers such opportunity for expounding and enforcing the gospel. In revival meetings, people are most inclined to hear. Indifference is dispelled; and prejudice ceases. The Word falls on attentive ears and quickened consciences. The same utterances that at ordinary times would awaken no interest and create no concern, often produce the most wonderful results during periods of religious excitement.

A TIME TO PLANT THE HOLY DOCTRINES OF GOD'S WORD

The time to plant the great doctrines of our holy religion in men's minds is when men are most open to receive them. The wise preacher will recognize this fact, and, instead of allowing himself to waste his opportunity in mere gospel talks, without unity and without point, he will deliver spirit filled, thought provoking messages. It is natural that the subject of revival preaching should consist largely of direct, personal appeals to a better life. By a true instinct, the preacher feels what is needed at such a time is an earnest and affectionate appeal. He knows many of his hearers are not far from the Kingdom of God; and he longs to speak the decisive word that shall cause them to take the last step in the right direction. We have often heard devout men in the midst of great spiritual upheavals, deliver the gospel call as if they had been commissioned

21

straight from Heaven, and their lips touched with holy fire for the task. When the whole atmosphere is thus pervaded with an unusual moral earnestness, no man will dare to deliver an abstract or unpractical sermon. The mere thought of such a thing would be sin.

REVIVAL PREACHING SPEAKS TO THE ROOT PROBLEMS OF THE CHURCH

We have, nevertheless, thought there is a tendency among some preachers to curtail the themes of revival preaching even beyond the proper limits. It is sometimes the case that a direct appeal will do no good unless the ground has been laid for it in advance. In every community and congregation, there are points when special instruction and exhortation is needed. The lack of this will block the way to a successful revival with absolute certainty.

If there is wrangling and disturbances among brethren, let the sin and folly of them be faithfully pointed out. If Christian parents regularly neglect family worship, let them be taught they are endangering the salvation of their own souls (not loss of salvation) and that of their children. If covetousness is eating away at the life of the church, or if worldliness and frivolity are destroying its power, let the trumpet give no uncertain sound on these subjects. The best revival with which God ever blessed our ministry began with a sermon on the duty of honoring parents.

We look back to it now, after the lapse of twenty years, with feelings of genuine gratitude to God. One of our ablest young ministers told us a most remarkable work of grace once followed a series of plain, straightforward sermons he delivered in a Southern town on business honesty. We might illustrate our thought still further, but it is not necessary. Let everyone think about the matter for themselves and adjust their methods with a view to the best possible results. Intelligent use of opportunities is what is demanded.

PLANS, WORK, CONSECRATION
Spiritual Life and Growth
February 14, 1891

It is a serious mistake to put great activity in place of acceptable service, or to put great planning and great working for God in the place of consecration. These fatal mistakes are being constantly made, and will be the sources of endless confusion, guilt, and shame in the day of final accounts. Christ declared, *"Many will say unto me in that day, Lord, Lord, have we not prophesied in thy name, and in thy name cast out devils, and in thy name done many wonderful works? And then will I profess unto them, I never knew you; depart from me, ye that work iniquity"* (Matthew 7:22-23).

These great workers for Christ had the flavor and appearance of His name, but the hidden and mainspring motive was self. They were successful workers, applauded workers; however, self was at the bottom, self appropriating the glory. In striking contrast with the animating principle of this class of workers is the principle that controlled Christ. *"I came down from heaven,"* He said, *"not to do Mine own will, but the will of Him that sent me"* (John 6:38, NKJV).

This truth cannot escape the thoughtful student of God's methods. God's great men have not been men who have originated great plans for God, but rather men, who, like Christ, the great model, have laid aside their own wills, however wise and good, and submitted themselves to follow so these mighty and renowned workers for God have felt the

23

pressure of God's hand. They were flexible to its slightest touch, listening to His softest whispers, and obedient to His every call.

SUBMISSION TO GOD'S WILL

This submission to God's will is much more than the passive principle of determination which submits by endurance to the chastening of God. This submission is an active virtue; it works, as well as suffers, under the sweet supremacy of God's direction. It bears the rod, but works under the rule of the same divine will when the rod is not seen, feared, or felt. The consecrated life adores the fact that God is sovereign. It is His business and wisdom to plan and arrange His own work, settle His methods, and choose His agents to carry out His purposes. The efficiency and success of these agents does not depend on the maturity of their plans, or on their contrivance and skill, but on their submission to God's will, and their fidelity in executing God's plans.

MOSES

Moses did not originate the plan of delivering the Jewish people from Egyptian bondage, but he manifested his fidelity by following the plan shown to him on the Mount. The plan was God's; the obedient, compliant instrument was Moses. Martin Luther did not plan the Reformation; he followed God in the dark, as each step was illuminated by the direction of God's way. John Wesley did not map out a plan for the Wesleyan movement; he could not do this; but he followed God's light and God's voice, saying, "This is the way, walk in it." Paul's inquiry at his conversion, *What wilt thou have me to do?* "(Acts 9:6) struck the keynote for his whole life of service.

JOHANN AUGUST WILHELM NEANDER

Johann August Wilhelm Neander, in his book, *The Life of Christ*, states this well:

The greatest achievements of great men on behalf of humanity have not been accomplished by plans previously arranged and digested. On the contrary, such men have generally been the unconscious instruments working out God's purposes, at least in the beginning before the fruits of their labors have become obvious to their own eyes. They served the plan of God's providence for the progress of His kingdom among men by giving themselves up enthusiastically to the ideas which the Spirit of God had imparted to them. Not infrequently, has a false historical view ascribed to such labors after their results became known, a plan which had nothing to do with their development. Nay, these mighty men were able to do their great deeds precisely because a higher-than-human wisdom formed the plan of their labors and prepared the way for them. The work was greater than the workman, they had no presentiments of the results that were to follow from the toils to which they felt themselves impelled.

This view of our relationship to God and His work hides vanity and pride from the workers, and gives the glory to God, a lesson of spiritual wisdom necessary for all ages and for every Christian. Consecration in this light is not such a mysterious thing, it is the simplest, the lowliest, but the plainest way. The work of God is one; our conversion was secured by submitting to God's plan, and this strait gate opens the whole way of acceptable and consecrated service, the pathway of submissive obedience, the pathway of studying God's plan and following it.

This lowly path where self finds its grave was marked by all God's royal workers as well as by the lowliest and most obscure. God plans His own work for each life. To find God's plan and to follow it is the highest style of consecration. We must not curiously seek to know all the steps of the plan, but follow it as God unfolds one step at a time. Follow, though we may not see the traces of His leading, but feel only the pressure of His hand in the blinding darkness.

TOTAL SURRENDER OF OUR WILL TO GOD'S WILL

To surrender our life purpose to God's will; to put forth all our energy in doing that will, and walking in God's ways, this and this alone is consecration. Christ, though He was a Son, learned this obedience, not by great activity, but by great suffering. In this, the servant will not be above his Lord. Active submission to, and working out God's will is consecration, and ends its career with the most magnificent of all endings, *"I have glorified thee on earth: I have finished the work which thou gavest me to do"* (John 17:4). O may we so triumph when all our warfare's past.

THE MOURNER'S BENCH
Repentance and Salvation
February 28, 1891

THE CHRISTIAN EXPERIENCE OF REPENTANCE

The mourner's bench, as used by many churches, was a prudential means of much value. It separated and distinguished the penitent from the careless crowd. It induced decision and action, the movement to it was in the interest of confession and public declaration. It centered and intensified the faith, prayers, and sympathies of the church. The mourner helped the church as much as the church helped the mourner. But the mourner's bench was more than a prudential means, much more than a happy device. It was the embodiment of a principle, the assertion of our views of a doctrine, the declaration and distinction of a character. It asserted with emphasis the necessity and nature of repentance. It located and signalized it. It took repentance out of the realm of sentiment, or dry theology, and put it as a potent fact in the Christian experience.

Thus, making it dependent for its existence, not on the human will, resolution, fixed purpose, however strong, nor on reformation, but a grace wrought in the soul by the Holy Ghost, preceded by a pungent conviction for sin. As Paul's three days and nights struggle distinctly marked his transition state and gave impulse and vigor to his after life, so the mourner's bench was a period of darkness, struggle, and conflict never to be forgotten. The nature, results, and memories at the mourner's bench became an epoch period in one's life and affected the quality of the afterlife.

EFFECTS OF THE MOURNER'S BENCH EXPERIENCE

The mourner's bench represented the Church's idea of salvation in its beginnings, continuance, and ending—a conflict and a triumph. The germ of the Christian movement was in it. The desire to destroy the wrath to come, the presence and enormity of sin, and the hold it has on the human heart by original and habitual tendencies and desires. The fearfulness of wrath, the struggle to escape it, and the hope of the salvation, all belonged to the mourner's bench. It christened religion as a mighty, conquering force, and set up its banners on its first field of triumph.

A SERIOUS MATTER
The Greatest Time of Peril
March 7, 1891

Straws show which way the wind blows. We are not blind to the advance of the times; to its material shift, or to its spiritual activity. But Satan is not dead, nor are his agencies withdrawn or prostrate. In seasons of great spiritual activity he is the fully active and his methods are the most insidious and deceitful. We cannot afford to waste time or strength in glorying over what has been done, when so much remains to be done. Nor are we to be deluded by a show of genuine success into lessening our vigilance or slowing our effort.

We give God thanks for the advance secured, but show our gratitude and express our praise by keeping up the hottest fire on the enemy during the calm, when he has ceased activity, or while he is in full retreat. We see many things to encourage, us in God, and we would see everything to encourage us in God, even though every encouraging thing was black as midnight and all the points of observation and command were possessed by the enemy. But this battle for God will not be fought by men of the dreamy eye, or by those who shut their eyes, but by men who can see under the surface of things, are aware of their source and flow, and are not afraid to know the facts and face them.

SUCCESS: THE TIME OF GREATEST PERIL

The time of our greatest peril is when we are bewildered or demoralized by success. There are many points of great danger to Christianity, and many of those points seem to be good at first glance. The Devil's most cunning schemes are not in his open attacks but in his covert ones. He does his master work by infusing a secret poison into the good, thereby inventing methods of evil.

We emphasize and focus on one point; the system of public school education, a system much lauded and with great promise of good by assuring instruction and intelligence to the masses. But, neither instruction, nor intelligence, will necessarily advance morals or piety. Knowledge without piety is vanity. To instruct children in secular education and ignore Christianity and morals is to rear a nation of infidels, or atheists. But, it is said there are two saving points. We are told the teachers will impersonate the Bible and impress in the most vital way morals and piety on their scholars.

This is a very important point, and most beneficial results may be expected from the teacher of strong individuality and of personal piety. But the charge is being made in the normal schools, that teachers are so directed in their methods as to destroy much of the hope in this direction. Dr. Hall, president of Clarke University says:

> More and more everywhere, the value of a national system of instruction depends on the quality and quantity of the professional training of teachers, and if confidence in the system is shaken, here is where we must first look. Unhappily, however, experience abundantly shows no part of an educational system is so prone to deteriorate, and to become not only unproductive but dangerous.

He goes on to indict the normal schools for "routine teaching, method cramming, which Ziller called 'the specific and fatal disease of normal schools,'" and other faults too complex to be here cited; the upshot being that "the live teacher" is being exchanged for an automation, and his "leading" for a blind following of "methods." The educational journals teem with essays on "character building," which is to be conducted on purely ethical lines, by prescript rules, requiring no individuality in the teacher and respecting none in the scholar.

If this be true, the evil will spread and the faith based on the teacher as possessing personally the system of morals and religion that is to be impressed on the young mind is worthless, because no mechanical teacher will ever plant spiritual truths. There must be conscience and heart, a sublime fixed purpose, and the pressure of a divine obligation.

THE TEXTBOOK

The other point that has been made and much relied on for conveying a large body of religious truth to the children of the land is the textbook. The number and variety of religious articles in these books would in a measure, atone for the exclusion of the Bible. The textbooks in the reading department have been mainly relied on for this important feature. The old edition of the McGuffey series had a large amount of religious matter in it, but this new series has been modernized under the ideas now dominant; to get rid of religion in secular schooling. The results in this series and in other new reading school books are thus summed by Professor Swing of Chicago:

Thirty-three years ago, *McGuffey's Reader* contained 101 pieces in prose and poetry, thirty-three of which were religious. In his *Sixth Reader*, published recently, only seveneen of the 133 pieces pertain to religion.... The religious sentiment is weakened still further in a recent *Fifth Reader* that has only four religious pieces in 100; and, in a popular *Fourth Reader* there is no religious piece. In an elegant *Fifth Reader*, of a great publishing house of today, five out of ninety chapters pertain to religion.

It seems to us, that so many tendencies of this kind should open the eyes of the most stupid to see the trend of things, and awaken us to the fact that literature, education, and business are being fortified against religion. These things should have no power to dampen our faith, but rather, to arouse us to vigilance and effort. He who expects the tame, conservative, or strong spiritual efforts of half a century ago will meet and overcome the energy and activity of the foes of Christianity of this day, is in the worst state of delusion.

DIVORCED FROM THE WORLD

We must have redoubled spiritual power. The mightiest aggressive forces known to the gospel must be put in play. The individual Christian must be lifted to a higher plane of personal experience, personal devotion, and influence. He must be so charged with spiritual forces, that others will be affected by his presence and touch. The home and church life must be entirely divorced from the world, and permeated with tenfold more spiritual power. Holiness must be sought with a unity, fervor, and fixed persistency we have not known.

Christ must be enthroned in the heart and life above business and home, and with an unrivaled and unprecedented power. Our homes, our churches, our Sabbath schools, and our Epworth Leagues [an organization formed in 1889 of young people of the Methodist Episcopal Church in Cleveland, Ohio. The purpose was the intelligent and vital piety among the young people of the church], must claim and devote our children to Christ in a way that practically insures their salvation and their strength for Christ. This matter of religion must be watched and worked at as the chief and sum of all good. And then, despite all the wiles and depths of Satan, this age will shine as the richest gem in Christ's crown.

AN ANOINTED CHURCH
The Church's Spiritual Unction
June 20, 1891

The anointing of the Holy Ghost under the old dispensation was a rare gift, the special privilege of the favored few. The Christian dispensation in the universality and commonness of this gift is in contrast with the earlier and dimmer dispensations. The prophetic eye noted this contrast and declared:

> *"I will pour out my Spirit upon all flesh and your sons and your daughters shall prophesy, and your young men shall see visions, and your old men shall dream dreams: and on my servants, and on my handmaidens I will pour out in those days of my Spirit."* (Acts 2:17-18)

These words had their fulfillment on the day of Pentecost, and are to have repetition and full illustration throughout the history of the Church.

The Church in its organized capacity can no more perform its functions as the Body of Christ without this anointing than the pulpit can carry out its functions without its anointing. As Christ was anointed for His life and work by the Holy Ghost, so the pulpit and the Church, each in their sphere and according to their functions, must be consecrated and qualified.

POWER OF THE HOLY GHOST

The Church can only be committed and held to its high and holy work by the power of the Holy Ghost. It is easy for the individual Christian to be diverted from the main issue. It is just as easy for a church to miss the whole reason for its existence. A church may fritter away its opportunities and privileges in frivolous or worldly activities; it may never rise above the low level of material aims, and be essentially earthly and sensual. Its assemblies may have no more regenerating grace than a lodge, no more spiritual force than a club, and no more unction than a banking company. Its pleasant entertainments and activities may have a flavor of religiousness, while it is wholly devoted to the world and to the temporal and fleshly. To bring the Church to its serious work of reproducing the life of Christ, and completing His work of spreading scriptural holiness over these lands, it must be set apart and enabled for that work by the power of the Holy Ghost. This power comes on the Church as a company of believers, that in its organized capacity and aims it may be true to Christ as His body, doing His work under the mastery of His Spirit as well as through the power of His name.

THE HOLY GHOST ANOINTING

This Holy Ghost anointing does not flow into the Church through its sacraments, but comes as it waits before God in earnest prayer and supplication until the windows of heaven are opened and deluging showers are poured from on high, till the rivers run in dry places, the parched land becomes a pool, and the thirsty land becomes springs of water.

This does not mean every member is true to God. A Judas or an Ananias and Sapphira may be found in the most elect company. Nor does it mean the control and direction of the Church is for holiness and for God. It means the great body of the Church has received individually, for personal and organic uses, the great gift of the Holy Ghost. It does mean the force and trend of the Church is along the line of fidelity to Christ, and that in a prayerful, happy, and strong way it has taken up His work with His Spirit and aim. It does mean by this anointing that the Church is elevated above all human institutions, is completely divorced from the world and married to Christ, and every heart beats in unison with Him.

33

The coming and continuance of the Holy Ghost on the Church is the seal of Heaven as to its fitness and ability to do its appointed work. If these sealing, filling and overflowing times do not come to the Church, it is wholly unfit and without ability to do its work, however beautiful and well suited it may seem to human eyes.

THE ANOINTING GIVES UNCTION

This anointing gives unction to the Church. Unction is the element that keeps the emotions susceptible, the spirit of devotion alive, and the sympathies tender. This protects the Church from being hardened by selfish, worldly, or secular influences, and maintains the smoothness, harmony, softness, and polish of its movements.

This anointing empowers the Church and makes it the mightiest and most effective organization. The apostle compared it to the human body with every member placed and fitted for its work by the sovereign will and wisdom of the Spirit, each to fill their allotted place and perform their individual functions for the healthy development of the members and for the good of the whole. The organization of the Church was as complete the day after Pentecost as it ever would be, and through the Church's life, unity, fellowship, and energy have been developed for centuries.

The anointing gives to the Church the qualifying force of a fullness of spiritual life. Spiritual life; simple, attractive, and overflowing, is the conspicuous result of the Pentecostal anointing. Everything is stirred, joyous, and brotherly. Not by enforced activities, nor by the diplomacy of committees, but by the full and energetic tide of spiritual life. All the great deeps are broken up, the rocks are reduced to powder, and the floods are at high tide. No deadness, no dullness, nothing is stereotyped, and everything is hearty and free. Songs, prayers, exhortations, contributions, and fellowship are the spontaneous outbursts of full, glad hearts.

THE REVIVAL
True Revival
August 1, 1891

TRUE REVIVAL

The revival is not an episode. It is not an irregular, abnormal thing. True revival is part of the Church work and life. The revival grows out of the right spiritual development of the Church. It is part of the Church. Without the revival the Church is incomplete. The revival, to be valuable and lasting in its effects, must be the fruit of the pastorate. The revival is the spiritual sequence of spiritual work.

The pastor has prayed, worked, looked, and waited for it. Right at this place we must make and stress a point. Too often, the revival is the result of the special service of some other preacher than the pastor; and this other preacher's work had a plainness, directness, and power which not only went far beyond the pastoral direction which the church has had, but which stands out in striking contrast, if not in direct opposition, to the whole trend of the pastorate. From such a condition several things will result. The visiting brother has to expend his force, exhaust his strength and time in getting the church into the spiritual attitude which secures the revival. The daily work and toilsome routine of the pastorate should put the church in revival attitude. The special service, instead of being an exhaustive drill on scattered, untrained spiritual forces, ought to be but the marshaling and gathering of these forces, and their precipitation, with all the foretelling of victory on the hosts of sin and hell.

But if the special services do get the unready forces into line and into action with a victorious front and a successful conflict, the gracious results cannot be garnered and preserved by a pastorate whose spiritual energy was so weak or ill defined it could neither prepare for nor lead to the victory. It takes the same kind of spiritual qualifications to keep the revival in staying power as it does to secure its coming.

A revival secured by a spiritual pressure and elevation to which the regular pastoral work is a stranger, and to which the regular pastorate is not the sure leader, will, when left to the care of such a pastorate, fall down to its sickly, sluggish pace, and very soon not only will all traces of the work wrought by the revival be lost, but a worse state than that before the revival will ensue. The harvest will not be gathered, and the grain will rot. The revival, to be abiding in its fruitage, must spring from the regular work of the pastor. It comes, if it comes to bless and stay, as the legitimate result of his faith and convictions, and is the predecessor of his high-toned spiritual work. The whole pastorate, if it be a true pastorate, will be pitched on the revival key, and every effort will be but an added note to the full harmony and crowning work of the revival.

THE TRUE PASTOR SOWS THE SEEDS OF REVIVAL

The seeds of the revival are sown daily by the true pastor. Watered by his tears and prayers, they grow under the emphasis of the invisible and Divine Hand. Thus conditioned, the helping brother, his methods and spirituality, will not be something in contrast or in opposition to the trained and expectant life of the church, but in full harmony with it. His presence will be to help bear the strain of the increased and urgent labor of a glorious harvest.

REVIVAL PREACHING, SINGING, AND EFFORTS SHOULD BE DAILY WORK

It is a most damaging idea that revival preaching, revival singing, and revival effort must be something entirely different from the regular and daily work of getting souls to Christ, and discipling them for work and for Heaven. Nothing novel, sensational, or sentimental is needed; all additions of this kind hinder and mar the genuine work. Nothing need be added but the increased prayerfulness, increased faith, and increased effort that are demanded by the special effort.

The church and pastor, who have the seriousness, sweetness, richness, and power of Christ in their daily life, in progressive, transitional force, are the ones upon whom these advanced and supernal seasons of great grace come in mightiest force. These revivals would come as naturally, strongly, and sweetly as spring comes, as richly as harvest comes, and as grandly, refreshingly, and majestically as the storm comes, if we would always press the matter along spiritual lines the results would be well garnered.

But to run the regular pastorate on the plane of entertainment, or sensation, or by worldly or political methods, by inducing these hook or crook ways of using the revival as an increased sensation, or as the extension of an exhausted entertainment, is to mock the whole weighty and serious business of eternity. To bring a true, spiritual revival into such a pastorate is to introduce a pleasant but delusive episode, an episode as fleeting as Ephraim's religion, transient as the morning cloud, as short-lived as the early dew; something that has "gone glimmering through the dream of things that were, a schoolboy's tale, and the wonder of an hour."

37

THE PRAYER MEETING
The Spiritual Power Tool
September 19, 1891

THE CHURCH NEEDS PRAYER MEETINGS

The Church needs a prayer meeting. One of its vital prerequisites is a meeting for prayer, where the praying people may join together and voice their united prayers to God in an audible and a spiritually agreed manner. The prayer meeting has been called the pulse of the Church, but it is more. It is the heart of the Church, the seat and source of its life. In many places the prayer meeting does not exist.

LOSS OF THE PECULIAR FUNCTIONS OF A PRAYER MEETING

Many churches have never had an established prayer meeting as a custom or vital force. In many of the churches where it has been an established and longstanding institution, it has lost the peculiar functions of a prayer meeting. A devotion or sermon has been substituted for it. One or two prayers are said at the beginning, along with some songs as interludes, and the rest of the time is consumed by the devotion. These may be good, very good, but a sermon does not meet the objects of a prayer meeting.

OBJECTIVES OF A PRAYER MEETING

The objective of a prayer meeting is the gathering together of God's people in the attitude of prayer, praying persistent agreed upon prayers of great value and force and producing the result of answered prayer. However, if other activities as good as they may be, are introduced into the prayer meeting, then the benefits accrued from them are not secured by this kind of meeting. If the disciples in that upper room at Jerusalem had turned their praying into our modern pleasant devotional meeting, the Day of Pentecost to the Christian Church would scarcely have been realized to this good hour. Whatever benefits may attend the meeting in the way of entertainment or edification, it cannot claim it has the energy to create a distinct spiritual gain, or vitality enough to introduce a new dispensation of grace and power.

A SERMON, SONG, OR DEVOTION IS NOT A SUBSTITUTE FOR A PRAYER MEETING

We are not objecting to the sermon. It has its uses and its place, but it is not to be a substitute for the prayer meeting. We emphasize it is not the same as the prayer meeting, nor to be compared to the value of it. The intensity, agreement, fervor, and pertinacity necessary to secure the ends of prayer are not to be gained through a sermon. Let us retain the sermon for its special purpose of teaching and edifying the Body of Christ.

THE TRUE PRAYER MEETING

As for the prayer meeting, let it be a meeting for prayer, distinctly and emphatically; a time and place where prayer is to be made.

Where burdened hearts may come and unload their burdens and be helped by the added sympathy and faith of their brethren.

Where the united, repeated petitions of God's people may be voiced, and amplified.

Where faith will be inspired by contagious touches, and fired by added flames.

Where holy boldness will be increased by a holy unity.

Where languor will be aroused and inflamed by the presence of zeal, and faith nerved to a holy violence by alliance and confederation.

And where the agreed ones shall present their united petitions, and with all the force of spiritual harmony and union, plead the promises, and urge their pleas.

PRAYER MEETINGS BENEFIT THE SUNDAY SERVICE WITH THE FRAGRANCE OF PRAYER

There is something of a silent waste in the place that ought to be fruitful and vocal with prayers and praise. Family altars are the exceptions rather than the rule. Closet places for prayer and the individual engagement of soul to the place of secret prayer, we fear is to be classed also as the exception rather than the rule. If our prayer meetings are taken from us by a pleasant substitute, then the house of prayer is by us almost forsaken. If our family altars and our closets no longer witness our prayers and if the Wednesday night is filled up with sermons and gospel songs, then the Sabbath preaching service will have neither the color nor fragrance of prayer in it.

Prayer and worship meetings were not united, but each remained specifically what its name indicated. Except for the opening prayer, no prayer was ever made at the worship meetings, and the Scripture was not read at the prayer meetings.

At the prayer meeting, the leader announced the opening hymn and everyone rose to their feet and sang it. After that, everyone knelt and the leader prayed, after which any one prayed who felt moved to do so. All prayers were voluntary. After a prayer or two, they again rose to their feet and stood while a familiar hymn was sung. Anyone might start a hymn, or if he could not sing, he would choose it and someone else would start the tune. It was always understood that the one who selected the hymn would lead next in prayer and someone else would follow. No time was lost in waiting, and the prayers were never very long, but full of the Spirit.

PRAYER MEETINGS FULL OF THE SPIRIT AND MIGHTY FORCE OF PRAYER

We must have prayer meetings in the Church that will put in full play all the mighty force of prayer. Give us real, genuine, hearty prayer meetings, meetings of those whose souls are knit into oneness by the Divine Hand and souls who are burdened with intense desire. Meetings where the tide of song and the stir of exhortation will conspire to the ends of prayer, and swell by confluent streams the current of holy petition. Give us genuine, hearty prayer meetings. Our God is the God that hears and answers prayer.

GOD'S HOUSE IS A HOUSE OF PRAYER

God's house is the house of prayer. God's people should be eminently the people of prayer. God's people should often assemble themselves in God's house for prayer, avowedly and specifically to pray, not as a form, but in an earnest, expectant attitude. Prayer moves the arm that moves the universe, and while we are to do many other things, the one great thing for us to do is to move that arm, and we must have an aggregation of faith to do it. The agreed ones must be together in prayer.

WHERE THE REVIVAL BEGINS
Starts with the ...
December 19, 1891

IS THE CHURCH NO LONGER REVIVAL ORIENTED?

A prominent church periodical gave a full section to answer the question, "How Should We Promote Revivals in our

Churches?" It added a stirring editorial under the heading, "Is the Church No Longer Revivalistic?" The necessity for the inquiry is ominously suggestive. This knowledge ought to be instinctive in our churches. It ought to be bred in our blood and bones. The article emphasized the question of revivals, for that question lies at the very heart of Church purity and thrift. The revival fire is the divine fire in the Church of God. The ability of the Church to secure these seasons of great blessing and grace is the true test of her spiritual condition. The inability or ability of any church to exert the spiritual energy necessary for a revival is just simple proof of the presence or absence of God's Spirit in that church. The revival is not a foreign or accidental thing to the Church. It is something that must occur in every true church of God. Not to have these seasons should be the cause for heart searching and contrition before God, for a church to be divested of them is to lose that which, has been, and must ever be, her chief excellence and distinction. It may be stated as a spiritual axiom, these seasons of surpassing spiritual power belong to the history and experience of every individual and of every church in which the Spirit of God dwells as a saving, sanctifying force.

REVIVAL BEGINS WITH THE PREACHER

The revival must begin with the preacher. It is a rare thing for the church in spiritual experience and expectation to go beyond the preacher. He, as a rule, gauges, in fact, almost limits the Spirit's operation in his charge. The revival must first be in the preacher. Its fire burns in his bones, its quickening must stir his whole being. It is the goal to which his faith and efforts press. His faith must hold it in keeping while it comes forth.

SOME PREACHERS CAN BE A
HINDRANCE TO REVIVAL

The main hindrance to the revival is the preacher, who is often in his everyday life and everyday experience of administrations far below the revival mark. Revival is above his ordinary reach. To many, the revival is looked on as an extraordinary occasion having no connection with the ordinary course of religious effort. To some, it is considered an exceptional condition of things let down from heaven, or manufactured by some expert for the occasion and having no reference to the past or present. The truth is, while the revival is an extraordinary season, it has the most sensible connection with the past and the most important relation to the future of the individual and the church.

REVIVAL IS THE FRUIT OF SEED SOWN

The revival is the fruit of the seed sown a long time in secret and with tears. The revival is the spiritual result of causes which have been long at work. The preacher is to sow the revival seed, and he must put in action the causes which are to result so gloriously. The preacher must embody the revival. He must live the revival life of closeness to God; of travail for the souls for men; of self-denying faith; of fervent, prevailing prayer. The preacher must carry the key that unlocks the storehouse of God and opens up all the treasures of grace. The article makes this statement of preachers across the line:

> But the most lamentable and portentous evidence of a transformation is observed in the minister. In him is exhibited a strange look of faith in his ability to secure and direct a revival. The fathers were eager and confident for an assault upon sin and sinners. The minister then believed in God, and in himself as helped of God, to begin and carry on a revival. If a revival

43

is desired today, the first movement involves that of
seeking an evangelist or some outside help. Our mail is
burdened with requests for evangelists and revivalists.
This desire, in itself, is a confession of a lack of faith,
and of spiritual impotency.

This looks like a picture drawn from what we have seen
on this side of the line, for preachers are very much akin and
alike. The revival, if it begins at all, must have its head and
center under God in the strong spiritual forces that live and stir
in the preacher. Spiritual forces that live and stir in his daily
life, live and stir in his study, live and stir in his closet, live and
stir in the homes of his people, and live and stir in his pulpit.

SERIOUS BUSINESS
Revival
January 7, 1892

GENUINE REVIVAL

The true revival is no holiday pastime, no pleasant spiritual
episode. The genuine revival is serious and radical work.
A genuine revival of religion extending throughout the entire
Church, in which the membership is quickened into new
spiritual life and hundreds of souls, added daily, such as are
being saved, is greatly needed at this time. It is needed in view
of the perils that confront us in our approaching ecclesiastical
deliberations. It is needed in view of the waves of worldliness
that now sweep over the Church. It is needed in view of the
subtle clouds of skepticism that are already settling down on
the minds of ministers, Sunday school teachers, and young

people, and threatening to obscure the clear light of divine revelation.

SEEING AND FEELING THE NEED OF REVIVAL

We have taken a good step when we can see and feel our need of a revival of spirituality. We fear that many have not advanced to this first step. It is good, too, if this sense of the need for revival presses on us from a clear view of the many forms and floods of worldliness that are flowing in on us, and it is not wasted with the man who is too blind to see this. The Church cannot prosper in the most peaceful times, nor meet her feeblest foes without revival. She will be calm in the happiest hours like "a painted ship on a painted ocean."

THE CHURCH WITHOUT REVIVAL

Without revival, she will backslide and will never be so well situated spiritually. The Church must have revival or die spiritually. She must have revival or she will save no souls. Her sacraments cannot save. She has no priestly hands to impose priestly absolution. The Church must have the genuine article or nothing. Her revivals have educated her to the highest form of spiritual life and made her adept in the soul saving trade. To lose the revival is for her right hand to lose its ability.

But to have the revival is a most serious business in our present state. It does not come for the saying. If anyone desires to know what a heavy job he has on hand, let him try to secure a revival in the average church. Let him discard all methods that tend to create a sensation, or stir things up by means of charismatic leadership, machinery, or manipulation. Let him reduce the whole movement to a spiritual basis and labor to secure a revival in the church, as the product of the relation of the church to God. If the one who undertakes such a discrediting task does not find himself like a sparrow alone upon the housetop, he must be accounted as one of the most favored of men.

REVIVAL IN THE LOCAL CHURCH

The revival means serious work by the church. It means more than an interested church, focused on just seeing preachers gather people in. The stewards will always be interested in seeing men of financial ability coming in. The church doors will always be open to those who have influence and who come to join. But, true revival means a great deal more than concern for additions to the church roll, much more than increase of social or financial ability. It means a church is weighed down with interest and agony as Christ was weighed down. It means a church is in sorrow for sin, as He was in sorrow; a church in prayer, as He was in prayer.

REVIVAL SOUGHT FOR THE WRONG REASONS

Revivals sought for the wrong reasons will be like spasms, spurts, a surface stir, of an induced or manufactured interest, genuine or counterfeit; but whether genuine or counterfeit, equally worthless. These may be secured without this depth of interest, without this radical process, but they are not worth the money we pay for them, not worth the little spiritual outlay we make.

The true revival should begin with the preacher, but the church must be with the preacher in the beginning or very soon thereafter. In one sense, and in a very strong one, the revival must begin with the church. If the preacher begins it without the hearty and profound sympathy of his church, it will soon end if they do not rally to him. The revival which comes with power and stays must begin with the church. It must go deep into the church life, transform, elevate, and mightily quicken. It must go deep, and with sharp incisiveness divorce the church from its sins and from the world.

A revival means a heartbroken pastor, and it means a heartbroken church membership. A revival means a church on its knees, confessing its sins and the sins of the individual and of the community; the sins of the sinners and the sins of the saints as well. If revival is to begin in the church, the church must enter into closer relationship to God. The travailing spirit must be present. The intense desire for God's glory must move it. The church must sit down with the sinner in dust and ashes, must in its penitence represent the sinner, and seek God with a broken heart. And while crying to God for mercy, the sinners must unite themselves in interest and sin, and cry: "Have mercy on us."

THE CHURCH IN THE ROLE OF A SPECTATOR

The church too often assumes the role of a spectator, interested it is true, but still a spectator. The preacher and church too often turn the whole matter over to an evangelist or visiting preacher, and if he, perchance, has in him the force of God, some good may be accomplished. If he is a professional revivalist, an interest will be manufactured, and a well executed counterfeit of a genuine revival will be passed off on them. As a result, neither preacher nor church will have discernment enough to discover its corruptness; and when by sad experience they find out about the bad fruits, they will make a wholesale discredit of all revival efforts.

PREPARATION FOR REVIVAL

The great preparation for the revival ought to be in the hearts of the church leaders. These individuals should be the first ones involved in this good and great work, but they are too often content to see that the assessments are well up. And if an extra effort must be made to save souls, they leave it to the poorer members and humbler ones to see to the business. The leaders have no time nor taste for the exactions of this work; however, it is time we were seeing to it. Other churches have accepted the revival feature as the aggressive force of the church; as distinctive of spiritual operations, as the feature linking us to Pentecost. To let the revival flame grow feeble on our altars, while others are kindling it to a brighter glow and a more intense flame, is to surrender our glory to them and to fall to the rear in ignoble ease and spiritual senility. It will not do to say we have changed the phase of our work; that we are solidifying, edifying, polishing. The church that lacks the spiritual force for a thorough revival clearly lacks the edifying, solidifying elements. Nothing edifies, matures, and unites like a revival. The preacher whose ministry does not culminate in a revival does not finish in anything else essentially spiritual.

THE CHURCH WITHOUT REVIVAL AND SOUL-SAVING IS A FAILURE

The ministry that does not deal in the fullness of revival and the work of soul saving is a failure. The church or the pastor waiting for the coming of an evangelist is most unhealthy. It is an open confession of weakness and of total unfitness to do the very work God put them there to do. A work that they can do better than anyone else, if they are not a sham and their existence and profession a farce. We do not underrate the benefits a godly preacher can give, one who is called in to help in the exhaustive work of the revival. But this is quite different from sending for an evangelist to do the work as a job, while the church and pastor have only a reversionary interest in the enlarged church roll and their reputation for having had a revival.

GOD-GIVEN REVIVALS THAT GLORIFY GOD

We need revivals that spring out of the strong spiritual life of the church and the pastor; the source of which is the connection of pastor and church with God. Revivals that are not gotten up, but prayed down. Revivals that God brings and not the evangelist. Revivals that make saints of sinners, and make saints more saintly. Revivals that fill God's saints with His glory, and fill God's house with prayer and praise. Revivals that restore the mourner's bench and crowd it with mourners, and revivals whose converts are *"trees of righteousness, the planting of the LORD, that He might be glorified"* (Isaiah 61:3, NKJV).

A SELF-DENYING MINISTRY
The Principle of Self-Denial
March 10, 1892

SELF-DENIAL IS A PRINCIPLE AND VIRTUE OF CHRISTIAN MINISTRY

Self-denial is the right-hand virtue of the Christian ministry; and a sanctifying, vitalizing force. The word self-denial is a common use. We can scarcely touch the verbiage or the frontiers of Christ without meeting it, but the principle of self-denial, we fear, is as rare as the word is common. Self-denial as a principle in its profound depths, solemn surrenders, painful crucifixion, and its happy rehabilitation of character, is a great stranger to many who accept the term but toy with its meaning.

SELF-DENIAL IS FORGETTING AND RENOUNCING SELF AND ITS INTERESTS

Self-denial is the absolute forgetting and renunciation of ourselves and our interests. It is the withdrawal from fellowship with self. The minister should professionally insist every man who pretends to patriotism should: talk and vote in the interest of pure politics, fair taxation, the improvement of the civil service, the increase of knowledge among the people of sanitary and hygienic law, the reconstruction of tenement houses, the classification, education, and wise care of convicts, a just distribution of wealth, free public libraries, industrial education, compulsory education, the care of the homeless and orphaned, the extension to all classes of the full benefits of our present civilization, the education of the people to high ideals of manhood, womanhood, and political responsibility.

The Methodist Recorder [a newspaper produced by the Methodist Church in London], speaking of the phase the question has assumed there, makes it one of:
- decent homes for the people,
- a sufficiency of pure water,
- no smoke,
- no sewer gas,
- no deleterious drink or unwholesome food,
- the cutting off from all places of public amusement all demoralizing sights and sounds,
- the regulating and the conditions of production and distribution,
- of trade and commerce,
- of capital and labor,
- of service and leadership, so as to abolish all the evils connected with these.

SABBATH DAY AFTERNOON

It is no use disguising facts. A new fashion has sprung up in the Church and is running like wildfire. It seems to be taken for granted in some quarters that Sunday afternoon may be utilized for semi-political purposes, and in some instances, for playing with the edged tools and explosives of Socialism. According to our old-fashioned belief, those activities are not in harmony with the mind of Christ or the principles of Christianity. The wind is being sown, and we shall reap the whirlwind. We are quite aware that anyone lifting up his voice on behalf of ideas, principles, and habits dear to the Apostle Paul, and other ancient people, must expect to be denounced as a reactionary, or to be jeered at as an old fogy.

THE CONSEQUENCES

This plausible and popular demand will work the most radical and engaging consequences, even more than the claims of eternal life; the cost will be of a much greater importance and practical affair than the resurrection. Personal holiness will be trivial, and mythical. The tremendous truth that life is a state of trial will be ignored, then forgotten, and then scouted. All the great facts of revelation will be retired and silenced in the presence of the ever-stirring, ever-present and ever-pressing material questions.

THE PREVENTION

The only possible way to keep the great facts of revelation alive in the hearts of the people is by preachers who will shut themselves up to the ceaseless reiteration of these all important truths. Preachers who can discount the urgent interests of this life, which tend so strongly to remove the impressions which the higher and eternal make, and subordinate the claims of the fleeting present to the endless future. For this new idea will certainly take the eye off of God and fix it on man, make Earth first and Heaven last. Thereby making man and the Earth the biggest, and God and Heaven the littlest.

NOT THE MISSION OF CHRIST OR THE CHURCH

If this enlarged social and political sphere is the true one for the Church, then the Jews understood Christ's mission better than He did by demanding a Messiah who would enter at once into their social and political betterment; but this is the very thing He refused to do. If this earthly phase of Christ's Messianic work is the true one, then Christ's rebuke of Peter was unpardonable, for Peter's plan was the first edition of this one. If Jesus is "the great divine social philosopher," then His system is one of philosophy, but a philosophy is the very thing Paul declared Christianity was not and never could be.

SPIRITUAL SUCCESS OF A MINISTRY IS DEPENDENT ON THE NARROWNESS OF ITS COMMISSION

The most effectual way to revolutionize and dethrone religion is to abate the intense spirituality of its ministry, and there is no surer process to abate ministerial spirituality than by widening its functions and taking in all the social and political currents that are set afloat by the restless and ever varying social demands of the age. This suicidal demand puts the preacher on a stormy ocean, at the mercy of the waves, without chart or compass. The intensity and spiritual success of the ministry depend on the narrowness of its commission, not on its wideness. To widen is to lose in the shallows, sands, and morass. Paul compressed his commission in its narrow limits, and kept it there by solemn resolution, in the face of social and political questions as pressing and absorbing as any that ever convulsed a people or engaged the philosopher or philanthropist.

THE PANACEA FOR THE AFFLICTIONS OF BODY, POLITICAL, AND SOCIAL ISSUES IS PERSONAL HOLINESS

Jesus Christ healed many bodily infirmities as the attestation to His Messiahship but fled with haste from all social or political complications. He had higher and holier demands than to tinker with Jewish politics or socialistic questions. Pentecost, which ushered His system into fullness of execution, gave no lessons in politics, arranged no programs for social reform, endowed no political economist, and issued no dispensary for civic evils. The execution of their commission by the apostles proves how far that commission transcended all the fading dreams of humanitarianism, or the delusions of social millenarians. Jesus and the disciples stood in boldness, readiness, and efficiency to their ministry. Repentance toward God and faith in the Lord Jesus was their demand in response to the social and political clamors of the age. Personal holiness was their panacea for the ills which afflict the body, politic or social.

CRIPPLING POLITICAL AND SOCIAL ISSUES
DURING THE REFORMATION

Political complications and dabbling into social questions crippled the Reformation and stripped it of half its spirituality and forceful permanence. Political philosophers who have neither sympathy with, nor apprehension of, the spirituality of the Wesleys do not hesitate to say they saved England from the upheaval and revolutionizing social forces which devastated France. They did it simply and only by the severe and ardent spiritual narrowness with which they executed their apostolic commission. Their sermons were no mixture of the pulpit and the forum, no stump political speeches in disguise. They put no social schemes to the front or to the rear, only those which sprang up as the incidents to holy hearts and holy lives.

THE POWER OF REGENERATION AND
SANCTIFYING GRACE

Dr. Clarke, whose great learning and great intellect eminently fitted him to deal with the stirring social problems of that day, as a sensible Christian, spurned all the charlatan methods of philosophy and politics, and applied himself to preaching with increased force and frequency the Church doctrine of Christian perfection. If preachers would cease to pose as philosophers, political economists, and social reformers, and preach and practice personal holiness as Wesley and his coadjutors did, the whole problem of social and political evils will be solved, so far as they are soluble. For, notwithstanding our civilization prophets, the resurrection trump will find greed and oppression glutting themselves with lawless gain, and that trumpet will only be able to bring full relief to their oppressed victims. This whole matter of bettering the world is not one of question or methods of political or social reform, but of the power of regenerating and sanctifying grace in the individual, and the training and perfecting in holiness the character by the agency of a holy ministry.

The important function of pastoral visiting, by which the preacher in the privacy and sanctity of the fireside comes into tender sympathy with the spiritual struggles of his people, is to be lost in the wide dead sea of vital statistics and political economy.

In pastoral service he must visit from house to house, not merely in official service, but with the scientific enthusiasm of an original Investigator, permeated with the good will of a philanthropist who has large views and great hope. He should study the population of his own community; the various classes represented there; from what countries they came; what opinions they hold; what ecclesiastical and political convictions limit and restrain them. It will not do here to depend on supernatural illumination. Prayer will not steer a ship. He must investigate as one left alone by the heavenly powers to find his own way.

THE CHRISTIAN PASTOR NEEDS DIVINE ILLUMINATION

The Christian ministry turned into a bureau of politics and filling itself with a whole range of duties where it is independent of God, cannot claim, it does not need, "divine illumination." Think of it, if such a condition can be imagined without stark atheism. Christian preachers filling themselves with plans and work outside the sweep of prayer! These brethren will have to bring their new ministerial function into the region where "divine illumination" reaches, or near enough to God for prayer to serve some good purpose, before it can lay any claim to our favorable or even patient consideration.

THE CHURCH FOR GOD
Evangelism
May 5, 1892

THE CHURCH AND ITS RESOURCES

It cannot be denied, the Church has sufficient raw material in it to Christianize the world.

It cannot be denied, the Church has men enough in it to carry the gospel by rapid transit to the ends of the earth, and money enough to pay their passage and support these missions.

It cannot be denied, the Church is committed to the high end of sending the gospel to all nations.

Yet, it cannot command the means that are nominally in its hands for the specific uses to which the Church is pledged; because the great bulk of her men and their money are diverted to worldly ends.

THE CHURCH AT THIS TIME

The Church, in its present position, will scarcely carry the gospel to the world in commanding power. There is quite a difference between sending a gospel to the heathen and sending the gospel to them in a form that will save. The difference between sending a single missionary to declare war, and sending a representative backed by an invincible and conquering army and a thoroughly aroused and war-clad nation is very great. The difference between an army of possession and a raid may seem slight, but in permanent results they cannot be compared. As the Church is now constituted, it can no more conquer the world than a freight train can execute the most brilliant aggressive race.

HOW CAN THE IMMENSE RESOURCES OF THE CHURCH BE USED FOR THE CHRISTIANIZATION OF THE WORLD?

We believe this end could be best secured in many a church if we stopped funding them and closed their doors awhile to take stock, ascertain assets and liabilities, and find out their spiritual solvency or bankruptcy. Others might be put on the docks for spiritual repairs, as their sailing in their present case is perilous to crew and passengers. We are sure an encampment for reorganization and thorough drill would add greatly to the spiritual force and fighting qualities of the average church.

The cry has been made for preachers to take hold of this generation. Our cry is for preachers who can take hold of the Church for God. If the preachers will take hold of the Church for God, the Church will take hold of this generation and take hold of the world for God. If the Church has pastors who will take hold of it:
- as Harms took hold of the German village of Hermansburg and vicinity,
- as Baxter took hold of Kidderminster,

- as Fletcher took hold of Madeley,
- as Brainerd took hold of the Indians,
- as Knox took hold of Scotland,
- as Martyn took hold of India,
- as Wesley took hold of England, and
- as Luther took hold of Germany

the problems will be solved, the question answered, and the conquest of the world to Christ would be only a matter of time, and of short time at that.

The church is to be directed and handled by the preacher. He is put there by God for that purpose. Though the church may be asleep, in bondage, or may be misguided, the preacher is the agent by which the sleep and bondage are to be broken and the church made to feel its responsibilities and meet them. The preacher is to the church what the General is to his army. It is the highest and first duty of the preacher to train and prepare his church for the war and its battles. The preacher can no more fight the battles of the Lord alone than the General can wage a victorious war without his army.

THE TRUE INTERESTS OF CHRIST

The true interests of Christ at this present time demand far more than recruits, the manual of arms is much more in order now than a call for volunteers. A corps of good drillmasters will render better service than any number of recruiting officers. Edification and not evangelization, is the crying need of the Church of today. We need to have solid, spiritually sifting, spiritually bold, and spiritually edifying preachers, not evangelists. This is what we must have despite popular clamors or superficial waves. We need men who are wise enough, brave enough, and thoroughly trained in spiritual tactics to prepare our Christian army for the conflict. It will tax to the utmost, all the skill, energy, and patience we can command from God to develop the spiritual resources of the Church and lay hands on its men, money, and time, and put them under tribute for Christ. Incidentally, this can be done in any age, and with any church that has not wholly gone over to the enemy.

EVANGELIZATION AND EDIFICATION

Some of the apostles and their co-laborers were committed to the work of evangelization, but they only sowed the seed, and established a plant. The edification of the evangelized ones was the process by which the community was reached and won to God. The Church, planted and trained, was the salt impregnated into all the ways of social and business life, and touched them with its pungent, life-giving contagion at every point. The Church is the light that is to shine and attract, and he who removes its eclipse and brings its full-orbed light to shine on the world has done the best work for the Church, for Christ, and for the world. Edifying the Body of Christ and getting them into the militant attitude and under the battle fire is a slow, painful process. It is often a thankless task with many conflicts, friction or curse, but this is the divine plan.

TAKING HOLD OF THE CHURCH

To take hold of the church means much more than good or popular preaching. Spiritual preaching is not an end, but a means to this great end. Pastoral visiting is not an end, but only one of the essential conditions to this end. The taking hold of the church for God involves that deep, pervasive influence and authority only the true man of God can secure by his fidelity to God, to God's truth, and by his tireless efforts in seizing and directing all the sources of spiritual control. He, who holds the church for God must give himself up to God and to the church with a consecration that knows no limit, has no flaw; with a zeal that consumes him; with a faith that can remove mountains and laughs at impossibilities, with unceasing labors and limits, save with life.

EDIFYING THE CHURCH

Pleas are made against coddling believers which have some force in them. We do not belong to the spoiled and pampered generation, but we do believe in edifying the church till it stands as an imposing building, whose beauty and sublimity wins every eye and impresses every heart. We do not believe in scolding. Bad temper never made sinners saints, nor saints saintlier; but we do believe in disciplining the church till every step is in time, in tune to the music of the gospel and till its consecration to God is deeper than its consecration to business, or to money; till its heart is set in Heaven and not on Earth, till it stands in its true unearthly and heavenly attitude, looking heavenward, *"fair as the morn, clear as the sun, and terrible as an army with banners"* (Song of Solomon 6:4).

THE CHURCH HELD FOR GOD
Fulfilling Its Purpose
June 16, 1892

A cursory glance at the history of the Church or the slightest acquaintance with spiritual operations will reveal the fact the Church can easily be turned aside from its high goals. Over and over again, unconsciously and by imperceptible degrees, the Church has been wholly diverted from the object for which God established it.

THE CHARTER MISSION OF THE CHURCH

The charter mission of the Church is to represent Jesus Christ in the world, and to execute and complete His work of gathering out of the world a people for His eternal glory. It is the preacher's responsibility to see that the local church holds itself strenuously and singly to this purpose. The purity and power of the Church, the salvation of the individual, and the glory of God are all bound up in the fidelity of the Church to its Heaven appointed mission. A local church may have a show of prosperity in many ways, an increase of members, enlarged contributions, show great advance in church secularities, denominational solidity and activity, and yet in its heart and life it is alien from its great design.

We may state as a fact: no church will be for God singly and truly whose preacher is not for God singly and truly.

We may state another fact: a church which is not for God will not tolerate a preacher that is for God. It will very soon change itself or change its preacher.

It is the high and solemn duty of the preacher to hold the church for God, at any cost. By all sacrifices and labors this must be done.

THE PREACHER THAT HOLDS THE CHURCH FOR GOD MUST HAVE A STRONG HOLD ON GOD HIMSELF

The preacher that holds the church for God must have a very strong hold on God himself. He must have the tenacious and unrelaxed hold on God that Jacob had in his all-night wrestling and his princely prevailing. He must have the grasp of an all-conquering, never-despairing faith, yielding to no pressure or force, and accepting no denial. He must have the hold on God that Moses or Hezekiah had, to turn aside the purposes of God, and snatch hope and life from the very jaws of despair and death.

SOME PREACHERS TAKE HOLD OF A CHURCH, BUT NOT GOD AND HIS WILL FOR THE CHURCH

A preacher, by popular ways, may take hold of the church at many points and bring it forward in the scale of church appointments and raise it high in ecclesiastical consideration, though God is not to be found in the whole range of this reputable, churchly operation. It requires no hold on God for the preacher to secure these ends. But to increase the piety of the church, lift its eye and heart from Earth to Heaven, and clothe it with the alluring beauty of holiness, he must possess a stalwart hold on God. Popular talents cannot do this, however great they may be, but only by one whose personal hold on God is strong. If the preacher's hold is not anchored in God, the robust earthward trend of things will set both him and his church adrift.

COURAGE AND BRAVERY ARE REQUIRED FOR THE PREACHER

The preacher who holds the church for God must be a brave man. Courage of the highest order is requisite. *"Be not afraid of their faces"* (Jeremiah 1:8), was the Lord's charge to the timid Jeremiah. There is much in men's faces to intimidate the preacher, especially in those that represent wealth, social position, or other influences. These are strong times. The materializing forces are so opulent, and the worldly and secularizing forces so engaging and aggressive, that no fearful or timid hand can hold the church for God. Fear will be awed and overridden, worldly prudence will be compromised, cowardice will surrender, and faintheartedness will despair. Nothing but godlike courage can hold out for God, and save the church for Him.

THE APOSTLE PAUL URGENTLY DEMANDED
THE BRETHREN TO PRAY FOR HIS BRAVERY

Paul was urgent in the demand for his brethren to pray constantly that he might be brave. The church cannot be held for God unless sin is reproved with loving sharpness, severe impartiality, and conspicuous personality. It takes courage of the highest form to look into the faces of those in the pews, where sin is veiled behind the screen of wealth, eminent social position, or personal friendship. It takes courage to say to these royal sinners, "thou art the man." It takes courage to strike with the hand of reproof the sources from which meat and bread come to a wife and children. But a pastor cannot hold the church for God without sin being reproved and the sinner rebuked. Only courage can do this and this kind of courage is a different thing from self-assertion, rudeness, or self estimate. These may relieve from timidity or cowardice; they may induce outspokenness and reproof, but they are not courage. Neither is passion courage. Passion will give freedom to utterance, frankness to statements, and will make personal arraignment of offenders, but all this may be nothing but the free and hot deliverance of a scold.

THIS KIND OF COURAGE DEFINED

The courage by which the preacher takes hold of the church for God is divested of self, free from passion, clothed with humility, and comes in the garb of gentleness. Nevertheless, it is girdled with unwavering firmness, and its gentle touch and voice has underneath them the everlasting adamant of God.

No preacher can take hold of the church for God who does not take hold of the individual for God. He cannot hold the church for God by any social compact or organization. He must come into the individual life and all the force of his drawing for God must center on the individual. To reach the individual, pastoral visiting is absolutely necessary. By visiting, the preacher comes to know his people in person, in their everyday surroundings. He knows them as they are and where they are. He links himself to them for God through all the tender and intimate relations of the hearthstone. The holding of the church for God means simply the holding of the individuals for God. This cannot be done, except by the personal contact of the preacher in all the abandon of the perfect and sacred intimacy and inquiry of the home life. The preacher must know the people in their homes, if he would know them for God and hold them to God.

THE PREACHER HOLDS THE CHURCH FOR GOD BY THE WORD OF GOD

The preacher that holds the church for God must hold them through God's Word. Eloquence, ability, and genius may please, fascinate, and hold them, but the holding will not be for God. The preacher must make all his issues, found all his demands, base all his utterances, sharpen all his reproofs, inspire all his exhortations from the Word of God. He will hold the church most strongly for God who holds himself most truly to the Word of God.

"FOLLOW MY SERMON" DOES NOT HAVE THE SAME AUTHORITY AS "FOLLOW MY LIFE"

The preacher who would hold the church for God must hold himself for God in all ways and at all points in the strongest way. His example and spirit, his whole life must be for God. The mightiest agent for God is a holy ministry. The preacher must be one who lives, walks, and talks with God. He must shows his people the narrow way to heaven and true loyalty to God by walking in that way and giving constant exhibition of that loyalty. The people will feel the smallest force of the most biblical preaching if the preacher *does not* press his sermons home by the purity, elevation, and strenuous force of his personal piety. Pulpit preaching does little for God without the preaching of a holy life. "Follow my sermon" does not have the same authority as "follow my life." The life will be followed despite the sermon. High preaching and low living is a fatal defect in any pulpit. To preach like an angel and live like a sinner makes not angels, nor saints, but sinners.

A TYPICAL MOVEMENT
God Directed and Authorized
June 23, 1892

GOD'S ORDER MUST DIRECT
ALL OUR MOVEMENTS

God has His order and this order must direct all our movements. David committed a fatal mistake in moving the ark because he failed to follow God's order. We should not only study what we are to do for God, but determine and follow God's way of doing it.

In the enthusiasm engendered by a great movement, the wealth of materialism, and in the push and hurrah of excited and showy activities, we are liable to disregard the divine method. Spiritual forces are modest and retiring, and have no self-assertion. And they are the very forces which will be forgotten in a bustling, hurried age.

PREVALENCE OF THE CURRENT
MISSIONARY MOVEMENT

The missionary movement prevails in this age. It is irresistible in its impulse. Satan is too wise to attempt to resist or abate the impulse, but he will try a wiser thing; his purpose will be to impregnate the movement with the worldly spirit of the age. If he can secure the confusion of the movement, it will serve his purpose better than to stop it. Satan much prefers to have a worldly Church than no Church at all. No greater calamity can befall a religious movement than to substitute the strong and evident world-ruling forces for God's spiritual agencies. God's purpose can only be secured by following His order. Times and conditions change, but if we paid more attention to God's plans, we would not so often be the sport of times and conditions, and would be able to defy or control them. The missionary movement inaugurated by God and recorded in the thirteenth chapter of Acts deserves our most prayerful consideration as the typical missionary movement. The record is *"As they ministered to the Lord, and fasted, the Holy Ghost said, separate me Barnabas and Saul for the work whereunto I have called them"* (Acts 13:2).

THE CONDITION OF THE CHURCH AT THAT TIME

The condition of the Church claims our notice. It was in a flourishing state spiritually. A great revival had visited them; many people had turned to the Lord. They were active and earnestly serving God, cleaving to Him with purpose of heart. They were executing the work of the Lord in brotherly communion, divine fellowship, and with the strong underlying forces of self-denial as evidenced by their fasting. In divine order they were both ministering and fasting. The divine approval is on the fasting as well as on the ministering. The ministering represented the spiritual energy of their service, while the fasting showed the spiritual energy of their self-denial. The Church was spiritually cast for a forward movement, and it was in a condition to support the movement. The sovereignty of the Holy Ghost was declared and accepted. He designated specific individuals to do their appointed work. The movement did not find its basis in the hasty impulses of new converts, in the activities of the age, in the enthusiasm of fiery zealots, nor in the matured plans of their leaders. The movement was ordered by the Holy Ghost and is under His sovereign control.

THE CHURCH'S RESPONSIBILITY WAS SUPPORT AND FELLOWSHIP WITH THE NEW MISSIONARIES

The early Church had its part to do in the support and fellowship with the new missionaries. What they did about the collection we cannot say; about this all important point there is a conspicuous, remarkable silence. Money played no part in the movements of this age and these spiritually heroic men. What the Church did do is distinctly stated: *"And when they had fasted and prayed, and laid their hands on them, they sent them away"* (Acts 13:3).

SENT WITH PRAYER AND FASTING

They sent them not with feasting and speechifying but with prayer and fasting, the same principles on which the Holy Ghost based His call sent them on their mission. Prayer and fasting are as eminent in this transaction as the collection is with us. If we had more of the prayer and fasting spirit and principles in our church life and mission work, we would not need to make money so preeminent. If we focused on prayer and fasting, we would have all the money we needed without the money preeminence, without the money worldliness, and without the money rule.

The Holy Ghost puts His sanction on the conditions for fasting and prayer, fasting having the precedence in the statement. Fasting symbolized their state of self-denial, prayer their devout reliance on God. These conditions *"ministering to the Lord in fasting and prayer"* indicate a high state of spirituality. Fasting and prayer are emphasized and joined together by the Holy Ghost, who dare disjoin them or discount either. They spring from the same divine authority, and are recognized as equally binding and beneficial.

MISSIONARY WILLIAM CAREY AND THE GREAT MISSIONARY MOVEMENT

The most successful missionary operations are those that are patterned after this first movement in simplicity and spiritual authority. A few Baptist preachers one hundred years ago covenanted to spend one day in each month in concert as a day of fasting and prayer for God's work. The great missionary movement, and the great missionary, William Carey, came out of this covenanted fasting and prayer time. How was this work accomplished?

It is not by the sending of a number of men to pagan lands.

It is not by establishing many missionary stations.

It is not by the amount of church enterprise.

It is not by ecclesiastical wide-awake aggressiveness.

It is done by the sending of men under the direction of the Holy Ghost.

It is done by men whose faith has been nurtured in the atmosphere of self-denial.

It is done by and in the abounding fullness of the Holy Ghost.

It is done by the support of a home church that is responsive to every demand of the Holy Ghost.

It is done by the vigor of those whose faith has been trained in the school of fasting and prayer.

Barnabas and Paul *"being sent forth by the Holy Ghost departed."* Thereby, the Church of Christ began its missionary work. Happy and blessed the Church, and glorious the results, if her missionary movements had always been projected by such simple unworldly and spiritual forces. *"Not by might nor by power, but by My Spirit, says the LORD of hosts"* (Zechariah 4:6). This is the lesson of this missionary movement, the most

67

important of all lessons for the Church to learn. Seemingly, however, one the most difficult for her to learn, and one that she has ever to learn anew.

GOD REVEALED IN US
God's Work Within Us
July 21, 1892

CHRISTIANITY IS THE REVELATION OF GOD IN US

Religion is the revelation of God in us. Christian experience is not the presence of sweet emotions, neither is it simply the implantation and culture of certain principles. Emotions and principles are results, not causes; just as fruits are not their own cause, but the harvest of the tree that bore them. Christian experience is the conscious presence and dealing of God with the heart. The revelation of God in Paul changed his career, transformed his character, and gave resistless impulse to his life. A personal Christ revealed and realized in us is the only basis for the hope of glory, the only light that shines away our darkness and gives knowledge of the glory of God. This unfolding or revealing of God to the soul may be greatly varied, often repeated, and largely increased, limited only by the finite capacities of the soul. These capacities may be increased to an almost indefinite extent. There is really no limit to the unfolding of God to a soul that is ever seeking after Him with an ever-increasing, insatiable desire.

TO THE CHRISTIAN, THE REVELATION OF GOD IN US IS A SPIRITUAL ADVANCEMENT

To the Christian whose religion is worth anything to himself, to God, or to the Church, this revelation of God must be definite, enlarging, as real, and as evident as his life. The growth, intimacy, sweetness, and power of this revelation form the sum total and advance of spiritual life. We do not grow by evolution, but by revelation; the subjective only grows by the enlargement of the objective. Our spiritual advance and vigor are not the rekindling of the old and wasted fires, but the securing of new fire and more fuel from God. Paul's prayer for the Ephesians shows how our religion depends on the increased revelation, the implanting and filling of God.

> *That he would grant you, according to the riches of his glory, to be strengthened with might by his spirit in the inner man; that Christ may dwell in your hearts by faith, that ye, being rooted and grounded in love, may be able to comprehend with all saints what is the breadth, and length, and depth, and height and to know the love of Christ, which passeth knowledge, that ye might be filled with all the fullness of God.* (Ephesians 3:16-20)

THE MAKING OF A SAINT

This repeated and enlarged revelation of God to the soul is the way the saints of old were made, and it is the only way to make the saints of the present. Our leanness and barrenness comes in right at this point. Our lives are marked with no jubilees of God's revealing himself in us. No bright, inspiring eras mark our spiritual history; no red letter days marked on our spiritual calendar.

A dead level, and often barren waste stretches between the oasis of our conversion and the sandy present. It seems evident to us that there are possibilities, privileges, and duties at this point of securing the full revelation God promised in the Bible. A revelation that we have not yet attained, and one toward which we have no earnest desire and fixed purpose to obtain. We need the revival of religion; the study of its nature as revealed in the Bible, and as illustrated in the saintly ones who have lived and died. What they have experienced of God would be a source of information and quickening as to the possibilities of a soul to receive God, and the effects of that revelation as the only way to produce saintly character. We will give examples of a few of these to stir up our pure minds by way of remembrance.

WILLIAM CARVOSSO

William Carvosso was one of the early saints, few sunnier, more devout, stronger, or more active Christians than he has adorned the Church in any age. He was remarkable for his Christian experience, his initiation into, and knowledge of, the secret things of God. He says:

I have sometimes had seasons of remarkable visitation from the Lord. I was one night in bed so over powered with the glory of God that had there been a thousand suns shining at noonday, the brightness of that divine glory would have eclipsed the whole. I was constrained to shout aloud for joy. It was the overwhelming power of divine grace. Language fails to give but a faint description of what I then experienced. I can never forget it in time or to all eternity. Many years before, I was sealed by the spirit in a somewhat similar manner. While walking I was drawn t o turn away from the public road to pray. I had not long been engaged with God, before I was so visited from above and overpowered by the divine glory that my shouting could be heard at a distance. It was a weight of glory that I seemed incapable of bearing in the body, and I therefore cried (perhaps unwisely), "Lord, stay thy hand."

We will take another illustration from Lady Maxwell. She moved in the first circles of rank and fashion (while Carvosso was from the people). She was endowed with rare intellectual gifts, noble, refined and cultured. "Early on Sunday morning," she says, "in secret prayer, God the Father and the son drew very nigh. A sense of the divine presence so penetrated my inmost soul as to arrest the whole powers of my mind. I felt so surrounded with Deity, so let into Jehovah as no word can express. The eternal world felt very nigh. I seemed by faith to come to mount Zion, the heavenly Jerusalem, and my spirit felt to mingle with its inhabitants." She went to church, "when the visitation greatly increased, it was glory all past expression I seemed to sink deeper into the boundless ocean of pure love." Later in life she makes this record:

> My fellowship with Jehovah has sensibly increased of late. At times I am favored with such lettings into Deity, as far exceed my barren powers of expression. The Lord condescends to give such glorious views of the Christian privileges, and by the light of a luminous faith enables me to realize future and unseen things. O what height and depths I see before me! What as yet unexperienced degrees of nearness to and close walking with, and rich enjoyment of the sacred Three; but more especially with Jehovah. I feel such a sinking into Him, such as conscious union with Him as He lays me in the dust before Him and keeps me there. I never had till late such piercing convictions of my nothingness. Language fails to express what I feel of this. All my powers seem gathered up and centered in God, who allows me a holy familiarity with himself that stamps a conscious dignity on the soul, and seems to fit me for present duty however above my natural abilities. This assistance is afforded in a way that proves its divine origin; keeps me little in my own eyes, disposed to

give the glory where it is due. I do reap much benefit by living by simple faith; it, indeed, brings deep peace and present power.

REVEREND GEORGE BOWEN

Reverend George Bowen, editor of the *Bombay Guardian*, "discovered there was an experience to which he had not attained, and in which it was possible permanently to abide." When he came into this fuller revelation of God, it came to him as almost new; so far did it transcend what he had received. Learned, gifted, famed, but "all his literary ambitions and pursuits, all his linguistic attainments, all his social reputation he not only laid on the altar, but seemed to forget that he ever had such attainments and objects. From that time his labors were so abundant, his life so eminently holy, that he was called the white saint of India.

MRS. JONATHAN EDWARDS

Mrs. Jonathan Edwards was a remarkable illustration of how much a soul may experience with God. Her husband requested she draw up a statement which covered many pages. So filled was she with God, and so powerfully drawn toward Christ and Heaven, at times she would unconsciously leap from her chair, and it appeared as if she must ascend hither. Her visions of God took away her strength.

The whole world, with all its enjoyments, and all its troubles, seemed nothing. I seemed to be drawn upward, soul and body, from the Earth toward Heaven, and it appeared to me I must naturally and necessarily ascend hither. This was accompanied with a ravishing sense of the unspeakable joys of the upper world. It was a sweetness which my soul was lost in. I never felt such an entire emptiness of self-love, or any regard to any private selfish interests of my own. It seemed that I was entirely done with self. I lay awake most of the night. God seemed close by with a constant, delightful sense of His presence and nearness. My soul remained in a kind of heavenly Elysium [a place or condition of ideal happiness]). The road between my soul and Heaven seemed opened wide, and the consciousness I had of the reality and excellency of heavenly things was so clear, and the affections they excited so intense, it overcame my strength, and kept my body weak and faint the great part of the day. I could not sit still, but walked the room for some time in a kind of transport.

These extracts are from different parts of her statement. At the time of this wonderful revelation of God she had been growing in grace, and was enduring a mighty conflict with sin and living above the world. We are in full sympathy with the views of President Edwards [elected president of Princeton College, September 29, 1757] in regard to God's dealing with his wife. He says:

If such things are enthusiasm and the offspring of a distempered brain, let my brain be possessed evermore of that happy distemper. If this be distraction, I pray God the world of mankind may all be seized with this benign, meek, beneficent, beatific, glorious distraction. What notions have they of religion who reject what has here been described?

These persons did not work themselves into a good feeling by singing, handshaking, or by any emotional, physical, sympathetic, or contagious methods. They were noted for holiness of character, eminent in self-denial, and deadness to the world. These repeated and powerful revelations of God in them implanted and matured the magnanimous, heroic, and sacrificial principles of faith in them. It also brought into full bloom all the sweet and gentle graces that make the spirit divine, and filled their lives with zeal and holiness.

Our spiritual barrenness and want of heavenliness are explained by our lack of this vision of growing intimacy and fellowship with God. These revelations always create an experience that results in spiritual overflows of seasons of joy unspeakable and full of glory, transformation of character into perfect saintliness, and creates the constraining force and readiness by which the mightiest works for God are done. Not only do we fall short of the full vision of God, but the quiet assurance which makes a perpetual Sabbath is not ours. We are not locked into the calm and sunny havens of love. Neither does there seem to be much longing for favoring breezes to gently carry us into that happy anchorage.

OUR FIGHT AND WEAPONS
Sin and Spiritual Weapons
July 28, 1892

THE WEAPONS OF OUR WARFARE ARE SPIRITUAL NOT CARNAL

Our war is against sin, our weapons are spiritual, not carnal, God prepared and not invented by man. The churches of this country are awakening to the alarming condition of things. They have been solacing themselves with the outward appearance, with a delusive peace and a fancied great advance. Where we ought to find an Eden of righteousness we find Satan, through the very forces which we vainly imagined were spiritual allies, is running the matter. *The Epworth Herald* [newspaper of the Methodist Episcopal

Church headquartered in Chicago, Illinois] alarmed at the peril to the young people. It says:

> The Church is waking up on the evils of the day. She feels herself, as never before, the sponsor of public morals. The public is dealing out broadsides on what a few years ago would have been considered questions for politicians alone. It begins to feel, as a colleague said a few weeks ago, "that if all the preachers in this country would let alone metaphysics for a week, and if all the *isms* and *ologies* would take off their coats and pitch into the scamps, official and otherwise, in our communities, they would do more to save the young men than by any other process." We must lay hold of evil in the concrete. We must not only declare principles, but apply them. We must not only deal with sin, but with sinners. We must stop shooting the enemy at long range. We must get down where he is and take him by the throat. While distinctively religious work is our first business, to make society moral is our second.

IN ACCORD WITH THE NEED FOR REFORM, NOT THE PROPOSED SOLUTION

With this spirit and much in the same strain from other sources, we are in hearty accord, earnest and stirring appeals become similar to the times, perils, and the interest involved. But the point to which they look for the remedy is not at all in keeping with the gravity of the disease as they make it out. They are demanding the functions of the Church and of the ministry be widened: that the spiritual weapons given us in God's word will not serve us in this crisis and that we must go off into all kinds of schemes, reformatory, political, social and sanitary, to do the work. We believe in reforms, we are for pure politics, and sanitary and civil improvements have their uses and their place. But, we do protest against the widespread and to us alarming, opinion that to fight sin we must leave our pulpits, lay aside our Bibles, abate our praying, and pull off God's armor. There has been failure in these spiritual weapons, but the failure is not in the weapons themselves, but in their nonuse and misuse.

HAS THE BIBLE CALL TO WARFARE AGAINST SIN FALLEN ON DEAF EARS?

The extract we have quoted says: "Religious work is our first business; to make society moral is our second." The religious work that does not make society moral is a sham. The divorce between religious work and religion is one of the prolific sources from which our appalling situation has sprung. We have stressed religious activity at every point. We have thrown out as an incentive to this activity every human stimulant, until there is not only a divorce between religious work and religion, between morality and religion, but we have ignored the presence and nature of sin, and the great Bible call to warfare against sin has fallen on deaf or frivolous ears. The only thing the Christian and the Church have to do is to fight sin; sin in us, sin in the Church, and sin in the world.

THE CHRISTIAN IS A SOLDIER

The Christian is a soldier by birthright, by profession, by training, by oath. But instead of training as soldiers and marshaling us against the enemy, we have heard the call to petty activity and have fitted our hands with a world of petty doing. We have been too busy to pray. Too active for meditation. We have no time to be alone with God and for fasting, and all the stalwart soldierly principles have been despised as antiquated. The non-military theater of our bustling, busy, prayerless, weak, and non-spiritual doing has been the richest soil for sin to vegetate and mature in.

THE PASTOR PREACHING AGAINST SIN FROM THE PULPIT HAS AN UNLIMITED REACH

The preacher does not need to go outside the pulpit to attack sin. All the rich, tender, and omnipotent graces that qualify him for that divine position are the most fitting and most powerful equipment for fighting sin. There is no sin in any relation of life, business, politics, society, or public sentiment that cannot be reached by the pulpit. Its commission is against sin. Its war, that knows neither truce nor peace, is against sin. Sins that reach to the throne or descend to the beggar. Sins that are covered by church, fashion, custom, and by law. Sins secret and timid, or open and defiant. To expose and reprove these sins is the business of the pulpit. If it does not do this, its occupation is worse than gone and it ought to have *Nehushtan* [The bronze serpent destroyed by King Hezekiah because of inappropriate worship of it, instead of God, 2 Kings 18:4] written all over it. The Word of God in the hands of a God-called and God-empowered preacher is the most powerful weapon in the universe.

> *For the word of God is quick and powerful and sharper than any two-edged sword, piercing even to the dividing asunder of soul and spirit, and of the joints and marrow and is a discerner of the thoughts and intents of the heart. Neither is there any creature that is not manifest in his sight, but all things are naked and opened unto the eyes of him with whom we have to do. For the weapons of our warfare are not carnal, but mighty through God to the pulling down of strongholds; casting down imaginations and every high thing that exalteth itself against the knowledge of God and*

bringing into captivity every thought to the obedience of Christ. (Hebrews 4:12)

We do not underrate law and all subordinate protecting and regulating agencies, however:

- no legal enactment by earthly legislators,
- no commanding and imperative reforms,
- no measures of political sagacity or purity,
- no social measures of the loftiest benevolence,
- no organizations with the counsels of old heads and the blood of young hearts

none of these can do anything in the way of combating the swarms of monster sins that have been warmed and fattened into life by the rich soil of our civil civilization in comparison with a holy ministry armed from head to foot for God. All the angels in heaven could not do it near so well, and all the devils in hell, and all the rotten, reeking civilizations of the world cannot brood a host of villainies that this ministry of ours, exercised with fidelity, fullness, and with all its limitless potencies, cannot combat and destroy.

WE MUST FIGHT SIN IN EVERY ASPECT OF LIFE

Our appalling condition arises from the fact that a majority of the churches and preachers *have not* been fighting sin. We have so failed in this that to fight sin has become exceptional and regarded as abnormal, a sensation, an interlude, or a byplay. We must fight sin, fight it daily, hourly, fight it on Sunday and follow the fight up through all the week; fight sin in business as well as in church, fight it in the heart as well as in the life, fight it in the pew as well as in politics.

We need preachers who will fight sin, always and everywhere. Fight it with all long-suffering and doctrine. Fight it with all the motives that come from our dying probationary state, by all the motives that flow down from and cling to the

Cross of the dying Son of God. Fight it by all the solemnities of the Judgment Day, by all the fears of an eternal hell, and by all the hopes of an eternal Heaven.

"GIVE ME 100 PREACHERS, WHO FEAR NOTHING BUT SIN AND DESIRE NOTHING BUT GOD"

We need preachers who believe in the Bible and in God and Christ with a mighty faith. Preachers who have been made brave and eloquent, gentle and strong by the power and ever-abiding fullness of the Holy Ghost. It was true of the gospel when Wesley said it, and it is as true now as then, "Give me 100 preachers, who fear nothing but sin and desire nothing but God. Such alone will shake the gates of hell and set up the Kingdom of Heaven upon the Earth." Whatever good subordinate agency reforms may do, how much the strong arm of the law can benefit in this war, there must be no going out of the pulpit, no subordinating it. The pulpit stands unrivaled in power to combat the ills that curse our world. It is God's plan, God's voice, God's throne on Earth, and when it fails the cause of holiness, morals, and reform; the good alike of God and man, all fail. The Church of God and His pulpit are not playthings, not pleasure-seeking silken yachts for silvery streams, but they are God's steel-clad war vessels, made for every ocean, made for every war for God and the good, and made to stand every storm.

It may do some good for the New York preachers to expose political corruption. But the Wall Street bankers that sit in their satin pews and hear with great satisfaction these denunciations are the very ones whose boundless greed and world-wide reaching wrongs have made this greed possible. If the New York clergy will clean out Wall Street seated in their pews, the associated greed will go as well. A large church in New York held its official denominational meeting at the home of one of these Wall Street railroad magnates whose name the public judicial records has made immortal in infamy. Those drawn to that home sanctify its infamous greed in the name of religion and the lure of ten thousand dollars to church extension weakens all the sinews of war in the fight against corruption. It is a more fearful menace to righteousness and law than all the seducing of corrupt politicians.

THE SPIRIT OF CHRIST
Obtaining a Christlike Spirit
September 1, 1892

To work for Christ is not very difficult. Many good, but not very high, motives may impel us to good works. Many wrong and ruinous motives may generate the greatest enthusiasm and the most tireless diligence. We may by our capacity and efforts do most marvelous things and secure the most marvelous results. However, all these mighty works and their marvelous results only bring us into greater discredit with Heaven. All our doing may seem to be for Christ, may shine with the appearance of piety, accompanied by slogans and sanctified by "in His name," yet only be services of delusion and utter confusion when the solemn reckoning for eternity is made.

WORKING THE WORKS OF CHRIST MUST BE DONE WITH THE SPIRIT OF CHRIST

We must not only work the works of Christ, but we must do these works with the spirit of Christ. To do the works of Christ without the spirit of Christ is to do them to the glory of the Devil. We may illustrate: we knew of a great worker, tireless and sacrificing in her activities and doings, and yet she would not speak to a very pious member of her family because of some petty jealousy, pique, or prejudice she had against her; and this was her daily habitual attitude while she was found daily on her round of religious work. This worker seemed to have the martyr spirit, but not the spirit of Christ.

ELEMENTS OF A CHRISTLIKE SPIRIT

Many elements are involved in the Christlike spirit. The thirteenth chapter of First Corinthians holds this spirit in its analyzed compounds. The fruit of the spirit, love, joy, peace, long-suffering, gentleness, faith, meekness, temperance, shows us the simple ingredients of this rich compound. As the motor to all our movements, the inspiration of all our activities, we must have the spirit of Christ. The spirit in which He was sweetly swathed, the impulse that moved Him through His entire divine career, must bind and move us. The *unchristlike* spirit comes in upon us unawares, by temptation, habit, lack of the Holy Ghost, by a feeble and defective piety; and by allowing a root of sin, self, or the world to remain in us unconsciously affecting all our acts. Our whole life of religious activity may be projected without the spirit of Christ animating us. Our indignation against wrong may awaken a zeal kindled at earthly altars. Our whole lives may be in a flame for doing religious work, no spark of which ever came from the altar of Christ.

ZEALOUSNESS IS REQUIRED TO DO GOOD WORKS

Work is to be emphasized. Our vocation binds us to be zealous in good works. The world is crying out for good doers. Christ died to purchase a people who would be consecrated to doing good. In religion there is no excellence without great labor. Work perfects faith. Christ went about doing good, and all who belong to Him will walk in His footsteps. The health and vigor of piety cannot be maintained except by diligence in

81

good works. To do Christian work in the spirit of Christ is the employment of the heavenly life on Earth as well as in Heaven. The loftiest archangel can rise no higher in his service than this.

OBTAINING A CHRISTLIKE SPIRIT

The preparation to do the work of Christ is far more arduous, painstaking, and painful than to do the work. To obtain the spirit of Christ is the greatest of all these works. When the spirit of Christ possesses and animates, all else is easy. The current of the brook flows not downstream more naturally or more musically than does the spirit of Christ doing the work of Christ. It is not the amount of work, nor even the amount of sacrifice involved in the work, that give it value. The spirit in which the work is done puts gold into the work. The spirit of Christ sweetening all our efforts is the only thing that will commend them to God's favor and secure them against the fire and ruin of the last day.

LAYING OUR ALL ON THE ALTAR

It is not enough for the feet to be weary in going, not enough that the hands be stiff or tremulous with overwork, and not enough that the body be bowed from cross bearing and the fatigues of weary ministering; for the spirit of the fainting spiritual toiler must go out as a rich perfume to sweeten all the doing. The spirit consumed as Christ's spirit was consumed by a holy zeal, the flame subdued, but its intensity increased by the meek and lowly spirit. The spirit of Christ in the worker must be the altar on which the offering of works is laid. The spirit must be laid at the feet of Christ in fullest consecration as the first of all our works; with all its bitterness sweetened, all its fierceness tamed, all its turbulence and haste calmed; and passion purified of all its Earth heat and dross. Ambition, self, and all that is low or sinister must be forsworn forever in the bitterness of a Gethsemane agony and nailed to the Cross. While the spirit, stripped, scourged, and chastened, comes into its real Christlike life, with the ability to walk in the laboring steps of Christ, and to reproduce His life of heavenly doing. Then it becomes the passion of a divine life to work like Christ did because it has renounced, suffered, and loved like Christ did.

GUARD THE HOME
Making Your Home a Spiritual Haven
September 15, 1892

THE WORLD, THE FLESH, AND THE DEVIL

The Church has made a condensed summary of its foes in the form of a trinity, the world, the flesh, and the Devil. The world stands in the front as being the channel through which others war against the Church. The Devil would make a poor endeavor out of tempting and ruining men if he did not have the world with all its amazing seductions to operate through. And the lusts of the flesh would die from weakness if they did not have the world to feed on. The world has countless forms in which it presents itself, but it changes these forms and hues with the chameleon's facility.

The world affects all classes. It has a lure for everyone. The bait is fitted to the taste and the condition. The world engages the elderly and holds them with a mighty force to the very jaws of death. The young are ensnared by the world's guileful charms. One powerful agency through which it works on the young is by what it terms good society. To live out of society is to be like a hermit martyr. Young people naturally love society, they flock together and in this association they find their life. The world has exercised its wiliest and most alluring ways to make society fascinating and to impregnate it with all deadly influences.

HOW THE WORLD AFFECTS CHILDREN

Our children are surrounded with this atmosphere that the world has so heavily charged, from their earliest years. The distinguished preacher, the late Dr. James Alexander, noticed that as he grew older and more spiritual, and had more experience and observation on the ruinous nature of the worldly conformity of society, became alarmed at the magnitude of evil and put himself on record as follows:

As I grow older as a parent, my views are fast changing as to the degree of conformity to the world which we should allow our children. I am horror-struck to count up the profligate children of pious persons, and even of ministers. The door at which these influences enter which countervail parental instruction and example, I am persuaded, is yielding to the ways of good society. By dress, books, and amusements, an atmosphere is formed which is not that of Christianity. More than ever do I feel our families must stand in a kind, but determined opposition to the fashions of the world, breasting the waves, like the Eddystone lighthouse [famous lighthouse built on rocks in England]. And I have found nothing yet which requires more courage and independence than to rise a little, but decidedly above the par of the religious world around us. Surely the way in which we commonly go on is not the way of self-denial and sacrifice and cross-bearing of which the New Testament talks. Our slender influence on the circle of our friends is often to be traced to our leaving so little difference between us and them.

The New York Observer draws this graphic picture of the whirlpool into which the young people are drawn by the present day society, and their present day habits.

> With the freedom to travel, to visit, to seek pleasure on Sunday, vanish the regular, serious, restful occupations of the sacred day. No hours of the Sabbath are devoted by the household to its highest and most precious interests. During the rest of the week the assimilation of the young people with the un-Christlike world around them becomes easy and complete. They visit the favorite haunts of the gayest and most reckless without compunction. They exercise no discrimination in regard to any dance, play, or entertainment that is under the patronage of the society they follow and enjoy. This mode of thinking and living makes the place of prayer, the fulfillment of duties, the endurance of trial and other daily requirements of godly and unselfish living, intolerably irksome. Where, now, is the spiritual life and moral power of the self-indulgent pleasure loving household? What books are read during the week besides the weak and worthless of novels? Are these the young people upon which the churches, the missionary enterprises, the benevolent institutions, and the educational establishments are to depend for their efficient support and conduct during the next generation? This is not the school in which strong minds, tender consciences, pure hearts, unselfish spirits, and devoted lives are prepared for the noble offices of the Redeemer's Kingdom.

A RELIGION OF NO DEPTH

This is no pleasant condition. Our religion does not seem to reach the foundation of things. It plays around the surface or mingles gaily with a thousand worldly combinations. In the meantime, while we are going through with our religious entertainments like children gratified with the show of things, the world has possession of church and home, sanctuary and altar, pulpit and pew, business and society.

NEEDED: CHRISTIAN HOMES HEDGED BY PRAYER

Religious homes are the only remedy for this state of things.

- Homes where God really rules, where loyalty to Him is law.
- Homes hedged by the most thorough and prayerful religious training, buttressed by the gentlest, yet firmest, religious discipline.
- Homes filled with the perpetual fragrance of the evening and morning incense.
- Homes radiant with the brightness of a glad experience of an indwelling Christ.
- Homes where order and law are found but where parental example is more potent in its brightness and strength than either law or order.
- Homes where religion is the chief duty, the chief excitement, and the chief joy.
- Homes that make conscience the business of being religious.
- Homes out of which *"our daughters may be as corner stones, polished after the similitude of a palace,"* and in which *"our sons may be as plants grown up in their youth"* (Psalm 144:12), and shall come forth *"rejoicing as a strong man to run a race"* (Psalm 19:5) and shall speak with the enemy in the gates.

A STRONG CHURCH
Functioning in the Power of God
October 6, 1892

THE ELEMENTS OF CHURCH STRENGTH

We are constantly hearing and seeing that the true elements of a church's strength are greatly misunderstood, and this misunderstanding is working great mischief. To mistake the elements of a church's strength is to mistake the character of the church and also to change it. The strength of a church lies in its piety, all else is incidental.

In popular language, a church is called strong when its membership is large, has social position, financial resources, ability, learning and eloquence fill the pulpit, and when the pews are filled by fashion, intelligence, money, and influence. An estimate of this kind is worldly to the fullest extent. The church that thus defies its strength is on the highway to apostasy.

The strength of the church does *not* consist of any or all of these things. The faith, holiness, and zeal of the church are the elements of its power. Church strength does not consist of its numbers or its money, but in the holiness of its members. Church strength is not found in these worldly attachments or endowments, but in the endowment of the Holy Ghost on its members. No more fatal or deadly symptom can be seen in a church than this transference of its strength from spiritual to material forces, from the Holy Ghost to the world.

THE POWER OF GOD IN THE CHURCH IS THE MEASURE OF ITS STRENGTH

The power of God in the Church is the measure of its strength, and the estimate which God puts on it, and not the estimate of the world; it is the measure of its ability to meet

87

the ends of its being. Dr. Olin put this matter so strongly and so well, we quote his words and make them our own:

The church illuminates the world by the manifestation of its piety, but this manifestation can never exceed its real piety. Its power to fulfill its most peculiar and essential function may therefore be accurately measured by the faith, zeal, and holiness of its members. A church may be what the world calls a strong church in point of numbers and influence. A church may be made up of men of wealth, of intellect, of power, highborn men of rank and fashion; and being so composed may be, in a worldly sense, a very strong church. There are many things such a church can do. It can launch ships and endow seminaries. It can diffuse intelligence, can uphold the cause of benevolence, and can maintain an imposing array of forms and religious activities. It can build splendid temples, can rear a magnificent pile and adorn its front with sculptures, lay stone upon stone, and heap ornament on ornament, till the costliness of the ministrations at the altar shall keep any poor man from ever entering the portal. But, I will tell you one thing it cannot do, it cannot shine. It may glitter and blaze like an iceberg in the sun, but without inward holiness it cannot shine. Of all that is formal and material in Christianity, it may make a splendid manifestation, but it cannot shine. It may turn almost everything into gold at its touch, but it cannot touch the heart. It may lift up its marble front and pile tower upon tower and mountain upon mountain, but it cannot touch the mountains and they shall smoke; it cannot conquer lands for Christ; it cannot awaken the sympathies of faith and love; it cannot do Christ's work in man's conversion. It is dark in itself, and cannot diffuse light. It is cold at heart and has no overflowing and subduing influences to pour out upon the lost. With all its strength that church is weak, and for Christ's peculiar work, worthless. With all its glitter and gorgeous array, it is a dark church and cannot shine.

THE CHURCH IS AFFECTED BY THE MATERIAL PROGRESS OF THE AGE

We are being seriously affected by the material progress of the age. We have heard so much of it and gazed on it so long that spiritual estimates are tame to us. Spiritual views have no form or comeliness to us. Everything must take on the rich colorings, luxuriant growth, and magnificent appearance of the material, or else it is beggarly. The most perilous condition the church has to meet is when the meek and lowly fruits of piety are to be discounted by the showy and worldly graces with which material success crowds the church. We must not yield to the flood. We must not for a moment, nor the hundredth part of an inch, give place to the world. Piety must be stressed in every way and at every point. The church must be made to see and feel this delusion and snare, this transference of her strength from God to the world, this rejection of the Holy Ghost by the endowment of "might and power."

CONTRAST OF THE PIOUS CHURCH AND THE WORLDLY CHURCH

Dr. Olin, contrasting a pious with a worldly church, says:

On the contrary, show me a church, poor, illiterate, obscure, unknown, but composed of praying people; they shall be men of neither power, wealth, nor influence; they shall be families that do not know one week where they are to get their bread for the next; but with them is the hiding of God's power and their influence is felt for eternity and their light shines and is watched, and wherever they go there is a fountain of light and Christ in them is glorified and His Kingdom advanced. They are His chosen vessels of salvation and His luminaries to reflect His light.

THE SPIRITUAL ADVANCES IN A CHURCH CANNOT BE REDUCED TO A SECULAR STATISTICAL COLUMN

We are, as a church, more and more inclined not only to disregard, but to despise these elements of spiritual strength and set them aside for the more impressive worldly ones. We have been, and are, schooling ourselves into regarding as elements of a church's prosperity only those items that make showings in a statistical column. Things that impress an age given up to the materialization of secular facts and figures, such as vital spiritual conditions and gains cannot be reduced to figures, so they are left out of the column and its aggregates, and after awhile they will neither be noted nor estimated. If we do not call a halt and change our methods, the whole estimate of the strength of a church will be supremely worldly.

THE CHURCH'S STRENGTH IS IN THE VITAL GODLINESS OF ITS PEOPLE

However imposing our material results, however magnificent and prosperous the secular arm of the church may be, we must go deeper than these for its strength. We must proclaim it, and iterate and reiterate it with increased emphasis that the strength of the church does not lie in these. They may be but gilded delusions that we mistake for true riches, while we are vainly saying, "we are rich and increased in goods," God has written of us that we are *"wretched and miserable and poor and blind and naked"* (Revelations 3:17). If we are not sleeplessly vigilant, the downfall of our churches will be the costly spices and splendid decorations that will embalm and entomb our spirituality. The church's strength lies in the vital godliness of its people. The aggregate of the personal holiness of the members of each church is the only true measure of strength. Any other test offends God, dishonors Christ, grieves the Holy Spirit, and degrades religion.

CHRIST ON DISCIPLINE
Basic Principle of Christianity
October 27, 1892

DISCIPLINE IS A BASIC PRINCIPLE OF CHRISTIANITY

The base principle of Christianity is discipline. Discipline is not more vital to an army than it is to the Christian Church. The strength and maturity of the individual Christian, as well as the purity and efficiency of the organization, are dependent on the right uses and enforcement of discipline. The brotherhood must be protected and strengthened by the excision of its impenitent violators. The Church must be kept holy, without spot or blemish, by getting rid of the sin or by getting rid of the sinner. No principle is more strongly enforced in the Bible than this. Without discipline, piety vanishes into the air; spiritual robustness and health are lost in the thin diffusiveness of sentimentality. Neither heart holiness, life holiness, nor doctrine, will survive the decay of discipline. The city will perish when its walls give way. The river will dry up when its banks are removed.

THE PRESENT-DAY CHURCH OFTEN LOOKS ON DISCIPLINE AS HARSH AND LEGALISTIC

The present age is impatient with discipline. It feels it to be harsh, legal, and opposed to the nature of true religion. The enforcement of discipline is unpopular and declared to be at war with the high principles of our civilization, and not to be in keeping with the genius of the age nor with the spirit of Christ. As to the demands of our civilization and the genius of our age in regard to this question, we are not careful to inquire.

HOW DOES CHRIST ADDRESS THIS MATTER?

We pause to hear Christ speak. We bow to His authority. We submit without reservation to His Spirit. But we will not allow the perverted instincts of a perverted age declare or construe His Spirit. We will yield to His Spirit as interpreted by His Words. The Christ of the New Testament speaks on this important subject. He has no vicious sentiments to impair His allegiance to truth. He has no popular favors to win by surrendering vital principles.

Christ puts the New Testament law of disciples thus:

"Moreover, if thy brother shall trespass against thee, go and tell him his fault between thee and him alone: if he shall hear thee, thou halt gained thy brother. But if he will not hear thee, then take with thee one or two more, that in the mouth of two or three witnesses every word may be established. And if he shall neglect to hear them, tell it unto the church; but if he neglects to hear the church, let him be unto thee as a heathen man and a publican." (Matthew 18:15-17)

It is a most notable feature that Christ does not deal in this statement with the greater crimes that occur among church members, with offenses against God, those things which debauch humanity or outrage society. These are to be rigorously and summarily dealt with. He comes to those that an age like this age would esteem light and refuse or neglect to take hold of in a corrective or penal way.

CHRIST IS SPEAKING OF OFFENSES
AGAINST BROTHERLINESS

They are offenses against brotherliness. He is to be told of it face to face, the two alone. Such a step of fidelity on the part of the offended one can but be to him a great means of grace and could not fail in many instances to have the most salutary effect on the offender. If the brother is not mended, the fault atoned for; he is to be reproved before one or two brethren. Then, the Church is to hear it and give its direction. If he fails to regard the voice of the Church, he is to be put out of the Church brotherhood, and counted as a heathen man and a publican, the most thorough "turning out" possible. How far removed these directions of Christ are in spirit, fact, and in purity from those who have acted on the vicious idea that discipline is not to be maintained, nor penalties enforced. This wrong attitude against discipline has virtually cast Christ out of His Church and allowed the world and sin to come in and possess it. Instead of imitating Christ by enforcing discipline, we are violating His law, wounding Him in the house of His friends, and destroying His Church.

THIS WINTER
Revival of Christian Entertainment
November 17, 1892

TWO SPECIES OF REVIVALS

The custom in some sections of the Church is to hold the meetings for revivals in the winter. Winter is also the time when the Church entertainment flourishes. The revival and the entertainment are divergent. Their spirit and fruits are unlike. They have no affinities. If they run in parallels, they are parallels of contrast and opposition. In results they are like streams of hot and cold water poured into the same reservoir. The blending of the two destroys the essential nature of each. There is a class of revivals, religious stirs, superficial and short-lived, easy and quick to come, easier and quicker to go. There are genuine revivals and spurious ones. There are revivals that stay and others that do not stay. There are revivals which are the product of the Holy Ghost, and there are revivals manufactured by manipulation.

CHARACTERISTICS OF THE TWO
SPECIES OF REVIVAL

These two species of revivals, so widely differing in character and result, owe their difference mainly to the false or true principles into which the Church has been schooled. The entertainment impregnates the life of the Church with flippant and superficial principles upon which the spurious revivals feed and fatten. The superficial revival may visit a church whose spiritual fiber has become weak and flabby by habitual indulgence in the church festival; but the Holy Ghost cannot come into an atmosphere so spiritually depraved. Which shall it be this winter, the revival or the entertainment, fleshly indulgence or religion? Will our meetings be for worship or society? Shall we have devotion or fun? Shall self-indulgence or self-denial be the keynote for this winter? Will holiness or pleasure, Christ or the world, the flesh or the spirit, give direction to our meetings this winter? Shall prayer pervade and fill our churches, or the spirit of feasting and jollity? Shall God or our appetites rule? Will the Church adjust herself most seriously to her one serious work and strenuously pursue that work this winter and make no provision for the flesh? Will the Church this winter secure the presence of the Holy Ghost so fully that spiritual life, spiritual tastes, and spiritual energies will be planted in her converts? Or will the Church this winter so mix faith and the world, and so restrain the Holy Ghost that her converts will only be baptized worldlings?

TRUE REVIVAL

The true revival implants God in the soul with power, creates longings for Heaven, and gives a mighty impetus in the heavenly race. The fair, the festival, and the entertainment, lowers the spiritual temperature, quenches all holy flames, destroys all serious and high aims, cultivates earthly tastes and ties, foments the flesh, and fastens us on to the world with silver spikes. The true revival is the Church in her embattled and victorious attitude. She was born on the battlefield, and her kingdom and crown were won by fighting, and the revival has been the theater, the sign, and the right hand of her victories. With the Church, the revival is the pledge of her fidelity to her Lord and the one significant sign of His presence and favor. The Church is committed by her very being to genuine revival work, by her history, her traditions, her integrity, and by all tender, solemn, and gracious obligations. Will she waste her time this winter by throwing away the golden opportunities that open on every hand? Will she prove recreant to her trust; debauch her missions and the purposes of her calling by turning aside to the low and beggarly by going into the entertainment business? Will she exert her ingenuity to invent methods to please the worldly, and create and cultivate all fleshly tastes? However innocent in themselves these things may be, they cannot comport with the dignity and heavenly aims of God's Church. More than this, they make her wholly unfit her for the lofty and divine ends of saving and sanctifying men, and they belittle and degrade her sacred influence by diffusing the poison of frivolity instead of the fragrance of prayer through all her temples, thereby subverting her divine character.

REVIVAL AND THE ENTERTAINMENT BUSINESS ARE TWO OPPOSING POLES

The revival and the entertainment businesses are two opposing poles; oil and water are not more averse to union than they are. They have no point of cohesion. The revival must lose every divine characteristic before it can fall to the level of entertainment. The revival is of God, entertainment is of the flesh and the world; the one seeks to please men, the other is only intent on pleasing God. They are as dissimilar as day and night, as different as fire and ice. The revival keeps the Church to her main business and sends her along the highway of holiness with jubilant song and assured triumph. But the turning of the congregation of Christ into restaurant or bazaar keepers, entertainment managers, and circus clowns, where fun, frolic, the flesh, and the world hold carnival, is alien to every design of the Church, and in many ways and points at war with its purest sentiments. It violates the Church's most sacred vows and undermines its foundation.

BASIS OF THE OBJECTION IS SACRILEGE

We are not writing in the interests of old superstition. We do not place our objection to entertainment on the grounds they are unseemly in a house dedicated to God's worship, but that they are unseemly things for God's people to do. The violation of the sanctity of the place is a little thing, the violation of the sanctity of the person a great sacrilege. We have no undue reverence for the Church house. Its brick, stone, and wood, are quarried from earth and forest, from all common places. They have nothing in them sacred by right.

Their dedication and use for God's service gives them the show of sanctity, but it is only the outward show. They have never been received to God by transforming grace. They were fashioned, and put in place perchance by profane hands; but the real Church, the people who worship there, these are holy to the Lord far more so than the meeting house. These who joined themselves to the Lord by holy rites, holy vows, and holy blood, they are the Temple. They sanctify the wood, the brick, and the stone which compose their meeting house. The men, women, and children whose faith, prayers, sacrifice, and money have reared the meeting house, whose presence, prayers, and praise fill it, these are the holier. By all principles of reason and revelation, the congregation of Christ is more sacred than their meeting house.

Therefore, whatever tends in any way to violate the sanctity of the meeting house, will for a much stronger reason violate the sanctity of the society. It is a strange and pestilent perversion that some churchly people hold, that while the house of God is holy and should not to be defiled by routs, revels, fairs, or any of the various phases of the church entertainment, yet the membership to whom the meeting house owes its sacred character engages in these things without hindrance, and with no stain on their sanctity. This is the chief sham of a depraved superstition. The sanctity of the organization must far exceed the sanctity of the house, or else sanctity will exist only in name, rubric, and architecture, reverence will degenerate into superstition, and worship will be but a thing of place or occasion, and piety will freeze into formalism or be degraded to refined idolatry. The meeting house must be kept sacred, "set apart from all unhallowed or common uses, for the worship of Almighty God," always filled with glad and reverent praise, always filled with the incense of prayer and with the awe and felt presence of God. The organization should be always attuned to the divine harmonies, untainted by the low purposes of the entertainment, unprofaned by its worldly spirit and prayerless aims.

THE RESULT

God is ready, waiting to be gracious. All the infinite stores of His grace and power are at the command of His Church and for the glory of His son. The result of this winter's work will depend on the attitude of His Church. A heaven-sent revival will come when the Church turns away from the frivolous and worldly spirit of entertainment, applies herself with persevering prayer to her real work, rekindles the wasted fires of zeal and faith, clothes herself with sackcloth and ashes over the follies, feebleness, and sins of the past. Then with every divine and quickened energy the Church can assault the strongholds of sin with invincible might, and show God, angels, devils, and men, she is in dead earnest about saving men from sin and from an eternal hell. Her renewed purpose is to point men to holiness, an eternal Heaven, and hasten the coming of her Lord; she no longer intends to dissipate her strength and dishonor her vocation by her shams, shows, frivolities. Then the Church will be visited with such a revival as we have not seen in all these years, and the *"glory of this latter house shall be greater than the former"* (Haggai 2:9).

HINDRANCES TO THE REVIVAL
Flesh Led versus Spirit Led
December 8, 1892

LACK OF PREPARATION IN THE HEART OF THE PREACHER AND CONGREGATION

We have put the lack of preparation for the revival in the heart of the preacher, or in the heart of the congregation in the forefront of the hindrances to revival. This lack of preparation prevents the coming of a heart sought, prayed for revival, and if one does come, its proportions are dwarfed and its life destroyed. We often solace ourselves with the shallow and delusive idea that the failure in the coming of the revival is due to changed times and conditions, when the real cause is found in an unprepared preacher and an unprepared church.

SEEKING A REVIVALIST OR NOTED EVANGELIST

Waiting for an evangelist is prominent among the hindrances to the revival. The evangelist may be a faithful and efficient helper. His presence might be of much benefit; but these are all aside from the point we make. It has grown into a custom that few churches have faith enough to begin a meeting without the help of some noted evangelist. This is to lose sight of the great spiritual forces which are to control a revival. This transfers faith from God to the helping brother. If we can get a revivalist of reputation we will make the trial; if not, the occasion must be postponed to the more convenient season when we can secure the evangelist. The eye of the church is fixed on the coming of the evangelist, and not on God. Faith rests on the evangelist, and not on God; interest is centered on the coming of the evangelist, and not on the coming of God. The evangelist cannot always be secured. The demand for the revival is pressing at many points at the same time, and to postpone the revival until his coming is often to postpone it indefinitely, and in some instances to relinquish it altogether.

Spiritual movements are dependent for their success on the coming of God only. Faith must fix its eye on no other being but God. The Church of God cannot afford to wait for the coming of any person but God. He only is our hope, and our expectation is from Him. It is wholly legitimate for the pastor to get the best spiritual preacher he can to aid him in the work of the revival; but the less said about the helping brother to boost him to a place in their faith, and to display or manufacture a reputation for him, the better it will be for the real interests of the meeting; for faith in the preacher is not, except in counterfeit revivals, essential to the success of the meeting. Faith in God is the sole condition. Faith in the preacher hinders faith in God. It is true at this point, as elsewhere, *that the kingdom of God cometh not with observation*" (Luke 17:20). You cannot bring the revival in by parading the reputation of a man. The Church of God has forfeited her charter when she is waiting the coming of any man. The spirit of frivolity which prevails in our meetings hinders the coming of the revival, or dissipates its strength when it comes. The spirit of the revival is a bitter sorrow for sin.

THE SPIRIT OF REVIVAL

The spirit of the revival is the spirit of prayer. The spirit of the revival is the spirit of a fearful conflict with the powers of Satan. The spirit of the revival is deep reverence and holy joy. To inject the spirit of frivolity into the spiritual characteristics and divine elements will destroy them. The light and laughing spirit is a grievance to the profound interests of the revival. A grave and sober spirit is the only fit companion for that hour. Repentance for sin, its agony and gall, its sorrows of death, and its pains of hell, do not comport with any degree of fun. To be tearless in such an hour is almost a crime. Levity has no place in a revival any more than sin has a place in Heaven, or jokes and jollity have a place in the fiery indignation of the Judgment Day.

The tendency to intersperse these occasions with side-shaking jokes and foot stomping humor, or to plaster them all over with a light and humorous spirit, is vicious to the extreme. The Spirit of God is too serious a being to float in on the crest of a joke. The advent of God's Son was announced by a triumphant song, but that song was as sober and thoughtful as the woes and wants of humanity are profound. No room for mirth or trifling at that moment. At no other step of the marvelous march of the gospel is there any room for a fun provoking and frivolous spirit. The gospel is to be accepted in solemnity and tears, and in *"fear and trembling"* (Philippians 2:12), its eternal fruits are to be ripened.

TOO MUCH SINGING

Too much singing is another serious hindrance to the revival. Singing tends to destroy the spirit of conviction. Conviction rather suppresses the joyous feelings, and stills and silences the soul to prayer and tears. Some hymns may carry conviction to the untouched heart, but singing is more likely to touch the tender human cords and awaken sentiment or memory rather than conviction of sin with its guilt and shame. It is an axiom, that even when the most spiritually solid hymns are sung, too much singing damages conviction, this is most especially true of the light, insubstantial songs that are so popular in the revival meetings of the day. Fewer things will stop the deep work of the Spirit on the conscience than for a company of thoughtless, prayerless people, young or old, to lustily sing the light hymns and tunes which so well accord with their own lack of soberness, spirituality, and conviction. President Finney, whose deep experience, large observation, and clear insight into spiritual matters, and whose opinion carries great weight, bear his testimony in a strong and convincing way on this point. He says:

A great deal of singing often injures a prayer meeting. The agonizing spirit of prayer does not lead people to sing: I know what it is to travail in birth for souls, and Christians never feel less like singing than when they have the spirit of prayer for sinners. Singing is the natural expression of feelings that are joyful and cheerful. The spirit of prayer is not the spirit of joy; it is a spirit of travail and agony of soul, supplicating and pleading with God with strong sighing and groaning that cannot be uttered. This is more like anything else than it is like singing. I have known states of feeling where you could not distress the people of God more than to begin to sing. It would be so entirely different from their feelings. Why, if you know your house is on fire, would you just stop and sing a hymn before you put it out? How would it look when a building was on fire, and the firemen are all collected, for the firemen to stop and sing a hymn? It is just about as natural for the people to sing when exercised with a spirit of prayer. When people feel like pulling men out of the fire, they do not feel like singing. I never knew a singing revival to amount to much; its tendency is to do away with all deep feeling.

INDIFFERENCE OF THOSE IN AUTHORITY IN THE CHURCH

The indifference of the chief men of the church operates as a great hindrance. It is said of the Tekoites on the rebuilding of the walls of Jerusalem that *"their nobles put not their necks to the work of the LORD"* (Nehemiah 3:5). This is too often the case in the revival, and in fact, all phases of the spiritual work of the church. The leading men look after the finances of the church, and leave religious matters to the women and children. The faithful pastor and the praying ones often have to spend as much time and force to reach the business and moneyed circles of the church as would be sufficient to convert a town of sinners.

BE NOT DISCOURAGED DESPITE THE HINDRANCES

If one or all of these hindrances are in the way, and many others arise, they are not to be sources of discouragement.

Two are enough to begin the most marvelous revival, if God is one of the two. The revival is a serious and prayerful thing, and demands serious and prayerful work; but God can make the great mountain of hindrances become a plain before us, if we will get down to the revival work in all humility, with all prayer, and with an undaunted and invincible faith. Sin in the church must not be covered or apologized for. The issue with sin must be made with plainness and courage, with a broken heart and in God's name, and the chasm made between them and God must be bridged by grace and love. The pastor cannot do his work by proxy, nor shirk responsibility. He must bear the sins of his people; their coldness and hardness must burden his heart. He must meet the issue; bear the heaviest burden with ungloved hands and a loving heart. If the revival flame burns strongly in the pastor's heart, if he makes the issue with nothing of self, but only for God, he will not fail; sooner Heaven and Earth fail than he.

WITNESSING VERSUS BOASTING
True Witnessing
March 16, 1893

Witnessing and boasting, though somewhat alike, are as far removed as the North and South Poles. Witnessing is to speak out to the glory of God the things He has done for us and in us. *"Come and hear all ye that fear God and I will declare what He hath done for my soul"* (Psalm 66:16). This is the way the Psalmist bore witness for God. The foundation of witnessing is an experience of God's power realized in the heart; then out of its fullness of gratitude the heart speaks, and God is glorified.

THE ALL-IMPORTANT DIFFERENCE

Boasting resembles witnessing in that it talks; but the difference lies in the spirit with which the talking is done and the ends to be gained. Boasting is the talking of a proud or vain heart, and the ends are self-glorifying. Witnessing is the talk of a meek and lowly heart, abasing self and exalting Christ. Self inspires boasting, the Holy Ghost inspires witnessing. Boasting glories self, witnessing glorifies God. The difficulty of discriminating between the two lies in the inability to distinguish the motivating spirit. Boasting may often be set down to the credit of witnessing. Witnessing may often be dishonored by having the charge of boasting laid to it. We have no difficulty after the results are known to discover the boastfulness of the disciples when they each declared: *"Though I should die with thee, yet will I not deny thee"* (Matthew 26:35). Peter on this occasion was the spokesman, not of a crowd of fearless witnesses, but of a company of vain boasters. Not all declarations of fidelity are those of the braggart. There must be declarations the mouth must speak; for out of it, as well as out of the heart, are the issues of life; *"by it confession is made unto salvation"* (Romans 10:10).

WITNESSING IS NECESSARY FOR SPIRITUAL DEVELOPMENT

Many timid souls would be strengthened in the Lord by speaking; many burdened hearts relieved, many dumb tongues unloosed, and liberty and enlargement would result. Witnessing is necessary for the spiritual development of the witness as well as for the glory of God. Our Christian fathers contended most earnestly that to declare to the praise of God the measure of grace already received, was not only the condition of receiving more, but the imperative condition of retaining what we had.

A MARTYR'S SPIRIT, PURPOSE, AND WORDS

Strong expressions of fidelity may be the impulsive statements of untried or unreliable men; but strong statements may be the expression of a resolution as fixed and immovable as the sun. When Christ proposed to face His enemies and raise Lazarus, the appeal of Thomas, *"Let us go that we may die with Him"* (John 11:16), was no idle boast, but the fixed courage of despair. When Paul declared, *"I am ready not to be bound only, but also to die at Jerusalem for the name of the Lord Jesus"* (Acts 21:13), this was not the vaunting of a braggart, but the settled purpose of one who had counted the cost and made up his mind. These words were a martyr's spirit, a martyr's purpose, and a martyr's words.

When the Corinthians used their rich spiritual gifts for display, they became puffed up, vaunting boasters, destitute of love and full of self. When Paul inventories his loss, and declares, *"What things were gain to me, those I counted loss for Christ. Yea, doubtless, and I count all things but loss for the excellency of the knowledge of Christ Jesus my Lord"* (Philippians 3:7-8). This to a superficial critic looks like boasting, while it is the farthest removed from such a spirit. It is the outpouring of an earnest soul that stops at nothing, no crosses and no losses, to gain Christ. By a formal, worldly religion his statement, *"I am crucified with Christ; nevertheless I live; yet not I, but Christ liveth in me; and the life which I now live in the flesh I live by the faith of the son of God, who loved me and gave himself for me"* (Galatians 2:20), would be accounted boasting. But to a soul glowing with the fullness of Christ, it is but the fitting exhibit of a most important truth, and the testimony of a competent witness to a necessary and glorious experience.

SPIRITUAL POWER IN THE WITNESSING WORDS OF THE CHURCH

The Church must get away and keep away, as far as possible, from the spirit of boasting, but the fear of being called boasters must not close our mouths. What we have felt and seen must be told with confirmation strong as proofs of holy writ. Our victory *"is by the blood of the Lamb and the word of our testimony"* (Revelation 12:11). There are few things that abash and confound the Devil so completely and which he so cordially hates. Few things are as offensive to a worldly piety as a red-hot witness to Christ's power to fully save and to keep. The early Church was fully armed at this point. They were full-hearted, full-mouthed, and eager witnesses and the Word of the Lord, and being confirmed by their testimony it was spread and glorified.

Nothing can substitute for a good witness. Many a case has failed for lack of good witnesses. Justice, truth, and righteousness have suffered for lack of testimony. A holy life will do its part in voiceless witnessing, but it has a double voice when by the tongue it declares the secret of that life. When the words of witnessing open the hidden springs of a holy life, they refresh, chain, and convict by an increase of a hundredfold. Heaven has no silent tongues; Earth ought to have none. The stones will cry out if men are dumb. Infant tongues are stronger than the archangel's arm to glorify God and *"still the enemy and the avenger"* (Psalm 8:2).

HOLDING VERSUS SAVING
Spiritual Growth
March 30, 1893

ETERNAL PRINCIPLES

The change of essential principles may be so gradual as not to be evident. Fundamental ideas may be surrendered, grave errors introduced, and no evidence to the casual eye be given of any change. Great revolutions are often veiled under the most inconspicuous change of terms. In such cases the change in terms is so mild as to awaken no alarm and give no clue to the revolution inaugurated and hidden. The change of words is to be scrutinized by those who would keep pace with the threatened or accomplished changes in opinions and practices in the Church.

THE DIFFERENCE BETWEEN
SAVING AND HOLDING

These statements find their illustration in the two words that head this article. The term "saving" is a Bible term of very marked spiritual use and signification. It has been retired from its position and the term "holding" has been substituted for it in popular Church vernacular. The difference between saving and holding seems innocent and causes no concern, awakens no alarm, but they belong to two entirely different systems. Saving people includes holding them, holding them not simply to the Church or to Church society, but holding them to Christ and to the Church. Holding does not necessarily include saving. It may, indeed, have no reference to saving and as used, it ignores the principles and operations involved in saving. The popular Church inquiry is not, How can we save our young people and perfect them in spiritual character and

107

fruit? But the question of most engaging interest is, How can we hold our young people?

These two words represent two different departments. Saving has reference to sin and to Christ. It involves the method of forgiveness and cleansing. It includes the efficient and personal application of the gospel, the bringing of the soul to God and filling it with the whole range of spiritual graces. Holding has no reference to character, no necessary connection with Christ or sin. It has reference to attractive forces; creating an interest, securing the attendance. The primary end of holding is to keep the people in some kind of sympathy or connection with our church and to keep them from going elsewhere, without any reference to the agencies used. The main concern in holding is to secure the end of keeping the names on our church roll and their places in our congregation. The holding may be superficial or worldly.

TWO DIVERGENT METHODS OF OPERATION

These two words comprehend not only two distinct departments but, two distinct divergent and antagonistic methods of operation. Where the purpose to save gives inspiration and direction to church effort, the direction is in spiritual lines. The whole range of spiritual agencies are invoked and put into operation. The ends to be secured are serious and all important. The means are to be carefully selected and must be emphatically spiritual. Where the purpose is simply to hold, the methods are entirely changed, for holding does not look to the spiritual character of the people. Holding does not regard spiritual ends, does not seek to make Christians. It looks to numbers, social position; consults depraved tastes, worldly inclinations. Its purpose is to please, not to save. It wants the individual, not for Christ or for what the church may do for them in the way of purifying and helping heavenward, but for what the individual may do for the church in the way of giving it prestige and social power and adding to its working force, at least adding to its numbers.

One main cause of the evils of the entertainment business springs from this pernicious idea of holding as distinct from saving. We are sure that the entertainment business would never have been suggested to a prayerfully serious church solely bent on the high and holy aims of saving souls and fitting them for higher spiritual work here on Earth and for the fullest rewards of eternal life.

The whole line of agencies and operations put into the purpose of "saving," ministers to piety, but those that have "holding" for their end, minister to the flesh. Spiritual tastes and affinities are the only true churchly holding forces, and they are the mightiest way to truly hold the people, and if we keep on saving them we will hold them with an ever-increasing force. The Church is never more thoroughly disloyal to her Lord, never more apostate than when she adopts worldly methods to attract or to hold people to her.

THE CAMP MEETING SEASON
Spiritual Growth
July 20, 1893

The camp meeting has not lost its religious uses. It can never lose them. If rightly directed, the camp meeting may still be a great religious factor. The camp meeting, under strong spiritual direction, engaged in with simplicity and fervor, will yield a rich harvest of good. It is eminently the place to intensify and deepen the spiritual life.

The number of church houses, the convenience and frequency of the places and times of worship, have but little to do with the necessity of a camp meeting, and nothing to do with limiting its spiritual results.

If the old-time camp meeting spirit can be retained, we would have the old-time results greatly increased. The old-time camp meeting had retreating from the world's ways as its main feature. They left the world in all its forms behind; they withdrew from business, care, and everything else to be with God, and to worship Him. The present camp meeting carries the world with it. There is in it neither retirement nor separation from the world.

THE OLD-TIME CAMP MEETING

The old-time camp meeting was eminently simple, with one focus. They went out to worship God, and the spirit of worship prevailed in their motives and efforts. They were kind, hospitable, and cordial, but their purposes were not social, or recreational. The idea of diversion was intolerable and wholly alien to their thoughts. The spirit of the picnic transferred to this season was abhorrent to them. Weighty and serious business drew them to this woodsy temple of God. Simplicity reigned; all arrangements and plans were surrendered to the idea of worshipping God and securing His face and favor.

SPIRIT OF INTERCEDING PRAYER

The spirit of interceding, mighty, prevalent prayer was the spirit of the old-time camp meeting. All the air was charged with the reverent and uplifted spirit of prayer. If the camp meeting can be made the exponent of these spiritual forces, it will still be potent in its religious uses. But the world must be retreated from. Worldly church members cannot make an unworldly camp meeting.

The camp meeting must be the exponent of spiritual principles in their highest and purest form to make it successful as a spiritual agency. The one and only object of the camp meeting is to worship God, and it must rule as a commanding energy. We are to be there and to bring ourselves, our belongings and doings before God, that we may have a serious heart-searching, penitent, prayerful, triumphant, soul-saving time, retired from the world and alone with God.

THE CAMP MEETING CAN BE A MIGHTY SPIRITUAL FORCE

The simple truth is the camp meeting can be a mighty spiritual force if the men who direct it are men of spiritual might. The camp meeting will be in spirit, what the folks who make it are. If they are picnickers, the camp meeting will be a picnic. If they are worldly and dead, the camp meeting will be worldly and dead, without a stir of spiritual life. If they are program folks, the program will substitute for the Holy Ghost, and matters will run smooth and decently, in the allotted time according to the program, and the decently-coffined assembly will adjourn, well pleased with themselves and in high spirits, like the man who was in high spirits at a funeral, because he managed things.

Let us make our camp meetings spiritual, or else stop them. Without God's presence and blessing they are of no value.

AN IMPORTANT DISTINCTION
On Preaching
September 7, 1893

PREACHING DISTINCTIONS

We must never lose sight of the distinction between sensational preaching and preaching which creates a sensation.

SENSATIONAL PREACHING

Sensational preaching labors to create a sensation, always in stage attitudes, dealing in novelties and surprises, using any method, and or, device that will create a wave of excitement. If sensational preaching deals at all with solemn verities and divine truth, it does it in such a way as to destroy its lasting effect. Sensational preaching deals with the surface principles, and puts them in an exciting form.

PREACHING THAT CREATES A SENSATION

Preaching that creates a sensation may be of the most quiet and least exciting kind. Christ created a sensation by His teachings and works, and yet was ever trying to dispel the sensation as creating an unhealthy atmosphere, unfavorable to the deep and permanent work He desired to do. Robert Hall says of John Wesley, the greatest marvel about him was that being the quietest of men he kept everything around him stirring. The presentation of the gospel of solemn truths by a man who immerses them into the spirit of the people will often create the greatest sensation.

It may do to cover up our lack of zeal by decrying earnestness and spiritual power as sensational. Nothing can be further removed from the spirit of the gospel than sensational preaching; always working on the sensations, sympathies, emotions, or the nerves. Such preaching depraves spiritual taste, creates itching ears, and turns the gospel into sound and fury signifying nothing. With this in mind we must not weaken the gospel, or tone it down to a tameness that makes it insipid and nauseous. Neither must it be trimmed and polished so as to be without point, as glittering as an icicle, and as cold.

PAUL'S PREACHING TO FELIX

Paul's preaching to Felix was no sensational effort. A serious, brave man putting on the conscience of his auditors, the truths of righteousness, temperance, and a judgment to come. It created a sensation! Paul had a scene before Agrippa, but it was of no stage effect or sensationally manufactured, but the calm and unstudied utterance of a true man inspired and burdened by the great interests involved.

Of sensational preaching we cannot hear too little. But of the preaching that creates a sensation, profound, alarming, and spiritual preaching, we cannot have too much.

THE AGGRESSIVE POWER
Teaching Spiritual Principles
September 14, 1893

AGGRESSIVE FORCES OF THE GOSPEL

The aggressive forces of the gospel lie in the vigorous faith and spiritual power of the Church life. This is God's plan for conserving and aggressive work. The preacher may be the pioneer, and sow the seeds but the possession of the land, the stability of that possession, and its salutary and forceful influence, depend on the type of life that succeeds the first occupancy and first sowing. The main force of primitive Christian effort, after the planting of the Church, was directed to its purification and edification. The process was to plant and train a strong form of spiritual life in a community, and out of it there would flow regenerating and attractive forces into the home, business, and social life.

DONE BY THE TEACHING OF
SPIRITUAL PRINCIPLES

The minister worked through his church, not by stirring their activities and inflaming their vanity to working heat, but by injecting into them spiritual principles. These principles would press them out to press others in by so filling them with divine light and life that others would be drawn by its radiance and warmth, and by so filling them with divine energy that others would be compelled by its potency. The planting of a church in any community and its vigorous and healthy growth and edification, were the surest guarantees of the acceptance of the offer of life in all sweet and strong ways would be pressed on that community.

THE PROCESS NOT UNLIKE SEED PLANTING

This process was not in the nature of a boom, nor was it sensational. It was a growth, hidden, without hurrah, clamor, or publicity. The seed was sown, the leaven hidden, and the net cleaved its covered way through the turbulent waves of the great sea of humanity. The preacher was not the main force. He was the leader, the advance guard, while the church was doing the work. The church was the salt to save by its touch from the corruption of sin. The church, by the beauty, elevation, and sweetness of its holiness, was to be the *"city set on a hill"* (Matthew 5:14), to fill with its charm and to draw by its elevation and conspicuousness. The preacher is to work mightily, but his main force is to be spent on his church; the preacher is to project Christ on the world through the spiritual body Christ so wonderfully and fearfully makes. The preacher who fails to greatly edify his church fails at a vital point. Converts he may have, but they will be personal converts, and their faith will stand in the preacher and not in Christ. There will be no assimilation of his joiners to the body, because they are not built on and grown in by the attractive assimilation of a vigorous life, but tacked on to be broken off by every wind of doctrine or by every change in the pastorate.

PASTORS MUST EDIFY THEIR CHURCHES

In a changing pastorate like that of the ministry, this is a vital question. He, who edifies an attractive and mature life into the church, makes it a vigorous vine, a stalwart and comely tree, a beautiful temple, a holy people, advancing in faith, growing in fruitfulness and zealous in good works. That pastor who edifies does far more for God and humanity than he who makes many converts, but leaves the life depleted, dissipated, feeble, and dependent in a large measure for its action and vitality on the stimulant of the pastor's hurrah, push or presence. The one puts an enduring and divine force, ever present and ever working, into the community. The other creates a sensation, a stir, which loses strength by its own exertion and is only agitated by the presence of him who must soon be away, and then the calm will be the return of death.

THE SUCCESSFUL PASTOR

The faithful and truly successful pastor spends his strength on his church, as the general spends his strength on his army. He fights through this trained and disciplined band. The general may be killed, but the army fights on and wins. The workman may be removed, but the direction of any spiritual and vigorous hand will continue. What we need all over this land is vigorous Christian churches which have the elements within them of edifying themselves in love, and these bodies will send out saving power like overflowing, perennial streams.

THE CHURCH PREPARED
Preparation for Revival
December 1, 1893

SPIRITUALLY UPLIFTING REVIVAL

There are revivals that count much for God and holiness. They are pitched battles where the foe has been swept from the field in ruinous route. There are revivals that create an era in the life of the church, the mighty spiritual uplifting of such a period may abate, but the great gain is permanent, the advance is marked by no return to the former state.

REVIVALS THAT PRODUCE SUPERFICIAL RESULTS

Many so-called revivals count nothing for God and holiness. The work done is superficial, imitative, and not original; emotion, sympathy, sensation, and sentiment are substituted for the presence and power of God; the show and shadow have been substituted for substance. An excitement, an interest, a wave of feeling sweeps over the church, but it is too ephemeral and thin to precipitate conviction; it leads to no turning from sin with the bitterness and loathing of a heartbroken sorrow. Such movements do not reach the church profoundly. They may enlist the interest of the church after a fashion, engage the members as spectators; but the great heart of the church is not broken into contrition and self-abasement for its sins, or into a tender, profound concern for sinners and sympathy for penitents.

A popular religious movement by which the feelings are wrought on, a religious stir excited, professions made, members secured, but by which the church has not been awakened to greater crying out for God, greater zeal for His glory, but left high on the dry docks of worldliness, merely sprinkled with the spray of a little religious sentiment or feeling, does much harm and no good.

We need revivals, but we want no dealing with untempered mortar. We need revivals that revive conviction for sin, and that will beget in the soul the conscious enormity, guilt, and shame of sin. We need revivals that will bring the power and consciousness of transforming grace to the soul. Revivals that will *"give beauty for ashes, the oil of joy for mourning, and the garment of praise for the spirit of heaviness"* (Isaiah 61:3). We need revivals that bring faith, holiness, and righteousness into being and make them abiding, conspicuous, and controlling factors. Ultimately, we need revivals that will convert men to God, put the Spirit of God in them so all the benign spiritual graces will grow in them, a revival that will put the hearts of men and women in Heaven. Many revivals fail to give birth to these cardinal principles; many sinners come in, but their entrance is not through the strait gate, if any sense of guilt is felt, it is feeble and flitting; no urgent, piercing prayers betoken the wrestling and sore conflicts within. The momentary impression exhausts itself on the surface, the sparkling wave passes, with no trace left on the hard and arid soil.

HINDRANCE TO REVIVAL

The serious defect in many of our revivals is mainly due to the condition and attitude of the church. The revival neither began nor ended with the church. The church really had but little connection with it. It seems never to have occurred to the church they ought to be one of the parties of the first part in the revival. The stewards were concerned to raise money to pay the brother who helped their pastor so it would not interfere with the regular assessments; further than this, they had but little concern. They gave casual attention and attendance to the meeting when other matters did not hinder, but neither the church nor its officials gave themselves to the meeting with hearty and prayerful interest. *The Independent*, [British newspaper] which cannot be charged with severity or pessimism in regard to the Church, has had its eyes opened by the inflow of worldliness, and the general drift of things. Sometime since, it delivered itself on this head. Its utterances indicate such a clear insight into the case that we copy:

It is our profound conviction the great revival needed is in the Church itself; bringing her back to a humble and lowly place with God. The wealth and luxury of modern times, the rush and drive of modern enterprise, the eager haste to get rich, the superfluity of ways and means for the gratification of the natural life, all tend to draw away God's people from a true spiritual ideal and experience. The affections are more set on things below than on things above. The result is, a large measure of spiritual power is lost; we are sure there is not that increase in the number of saved there ought to be in proportion to the means employed. Neither is there that high type of spiritual life the Scripture sets forth as being the distinguishing mark of the Christian. The energies used in the work of the Lord have a suspicious look of the merely human more than the subtle power of the spiritual. There is an absence of deep and thoroughgoing consecration to God and His service among the converts. There is not that whole-hearted devotion to the "Father's business" on the part of the Church at large which ought to characterize our work. On the other hand, sin and unbelief are rampant all about us. *"The faith once delivered to the saints"* [Jude 1:3] is in many quarters being openly questioned, or denied even by those set to defend it. The forces of infidelity arranged in many ranks and classes are pushing their attack against the right, left, and center of the Christian lines. Now and again we see a breach

118

made, and notice a painful tendency to waver and give ground to the enemy in places where we had hoped the army of faith was the strongest. This would not be, could not be, if God were in the midst of His people in power and might.

Little or no preparation on the part of the Church is the reason for the poor and superficial results of many a revival effort. The Church must, by confession of sin and repentance, abase herself before her Lord, and go with Him into the secret places and the sweatiness of a heartfelt, heavy agony. *"As soon as Zion travailed she brought forth her children"* [Isaiah 66:8]. Few churches are ready for a revival. The average church member, instead of being always ready to die, has to fix himself up by some Protestant hocus-pocus, like extreme unction, and secure dying grace before he is ready for his Lord, his crown and glory; so most of our churches instead of living in the spiritual altitude of revival, have to be put through some process of shriving [priestly absolution from sin] before they are ready for the revival. The preparation, though, for which we are pleading is not one of scolding, punishment, nor priestly absolution from sin, but the Church in her sackcloth garb lamenting the absence of her Lord, bemoaning her lukewarm, worldliness, and sin, and turning with a mighty turning and a broken heart to her Lord; this is the preparation demanded and which is the sign of the revival.

Many things fail from the lack of painstaking preparation, and the revival is one of these things. We begin at the wrong end. The first step usually is to engage some brother of reputation to help and the next step is to make sensation and capital for the revival of him, his coming, and his eminence. Faith is centered on him, and not on God. The preparation of the church is ignored. The church is treated as though its members were spectators and not heated and embattled participants. They are pressed to come and see what great things can be done for them. They are confirmed in their attitude as spectators. They are not made to feel this is their meeting; that only they are responsible for it, and that its measure of good depends on their personal attitude toward it.

They never have been burdened with its interests. They have never dreamed of crying out in agony of soul for its success. Sometimes the leading members will agree to be responsible for the financial outlay of the meeting. But most are unwilling to pay the price of spiritual or personal preparation for God to be their sovereign control, sovereign authority, and sovereign power.

THE REVIVAL
What Brings Revival?
December 14, 1893

REVIVAL IS THE SIGN OF SOUL-SAVING POWER

The revival is the sign of soul-saving power in the Church. The local church that has no revival has no soul-saving power. Such a church may add members to its roll, and have conversions from accidental causes, but as a soul-saving agency it has failed. The revival is the symbol of the presence and power of the Holy Ghost. The revival is to the Church what the rain is to the Earth; it is a refreshing and fructifying force.

Without the rain the Earth is barren. Without the revival, death reigns in the Church.

There is no conflict between the daily growth and edification of the Church and these seasons of great awakening and advance. They spring from the same source. The constant growth of the Church in spiritual graces is but the prelude and prophecy of the revival. The revival is not an abnormal condition, but normal. It does not find its only or chief end in recovering a backslidden Church. Its main end is to make the Church aggressive. Its greatest victories are not secured in calling into life the decayed spiritual forces, but in expending the full force of a thoroughly disciplined and embattled Church in an assault on the strongholds of sin and the world.

The bringing about of the revival is no holiday work. It will demand the expending of the mightiest energies. The average church life is so far beneath the Holy Ghost life, it will take serious heart-searching and heartbreaking work before the revival will come. It will come, however, when the Church is clothed with the garments of repentance, and when ardent prayer is the only language of its lips.

REVIVAL IS THE REVELATION OF GOD'S POWER AND GLORY

The revival is the coming of God, the revelation of His power and glory to the Church. The Church must be on her face and with her face in the ground, as Moses and Daniel were when the glory of God was revealed to them. The call to the Church today is in spirit the same which Jacob made to his family as preparatory to God's coming: *"Put away the strange gods that are among you, and be clean, and change your garments"* (Genesis 35:2), a call to the renunciation of all other gods and a call to purity. The Church is defiled. It must cleanse its hands and purify its heart. There must be a precedent to the revival—the thorough consciousness of sin, abasement for sin, and forsaking of sin.

A wave of genuine and thorough repentance rolling over the Church would bring revival in on its crest, the very revival of salvation and righteousness. We do not need a singing revival, the reign of sentiment and of surface work. Its results are blasting. We deplore a fleshly revival that simply arouses fleshly feelings and evaporates in feeling good. Its chief characteristics are shaking hands, exciting nerves, arousing sympathies, and feeling good. The Church does not need an amusement, a stir, a big hand-shaking, a few tears, and many songs. The Church needs a revival that will go down to the bottom of things. A revival that is projected on the line of salvation and righteousness, a revival that alarms consciences and purifies them, and implants righteousness and holiness as its fruits. A revival that brings new hearts and new lives to its people; which is neither a whitewashing, a veneering, or a reformation, but is a new creation by the power of God, felt by all and seen by all.

GOD SENT REVIVAL

God sent revival springs from the vital connection of preachers and people with God. These are revivals that are the birth throes of the Church in her agony of faith, repentance, and prayer.

Such a revival will not come by simply appointing a meeting and calling in the aid of a good brother who has skill in manipulating meetings and manufacturing success. A precedent work of great grace must be done in the heart of the Church and in the heart of its preachers. When this precedent work is done, and the Church and people are in the condition where the Holy Ghost can use them, the revival has come.

THE PRELIMINARY WORK
Revival: The Need and the Desire
December 28, 1893

The revival is the great need of the Church, and it must be a revival that will establish the reign of salvation and righteousness. This is no easy work. The revival will not come in a day. It will cost much more than a sigh. The revival that the Church needs cannot be imported. It must not be manufactured. The work that secures true revival will be costly and laborious work. This work must be done by the hearts and hands of God's people.

REVIVAL PREPARATION IS COSTLY AND LABORIOUS WORK

It is a flippant saying that we can have a revival if we please. Sentiments of this kind are not a good sign. They exhibit conditions of spirit and a want of apprehension of the profound work involved and of the divine elements which are necessary. Doctor Cuyler makes weighty statements in regard to a revival, which must commend themselves to everyone who has any true experience in this work. He says:

> After a long pastoral experience and frequent labors in revivals, I confess there is much that is utterly mysterious in regard to them. Our God is sovereign. He bestows spiritual blessings when He pleases, how He pleases and where He pleases. He often seems to withhold His converting power at the very time when, according to our fallible calculations, we ought to expect it. Never in my whole life have I arranged any peculiar measures to produce a revival which have been successful; nor have I ever made many such attempts.

123

Some such attempts ended in disappointment. On the other hand, several copious showers of heavenly blessings have descended when I was not expecting them.

PRELIMINARY WORK

A preliminary work is an absolute necessity for a genuine revival. To bring a kind of revival into a church over the heads and hearts of the church members by the generalship of some noted revivalist is a most damaging process. Such a meeting is a caricature on the true revival, and the debauchment of all the elements of spiritual piety.

The necessity of this preliminary work will be obvious if we remember many of our churches have a large majority of members in them who know nothing of regenerating grace. It is a rare exception to find a church member who has an experience of sanctifying grace. A church in full sympathy with the fundamental features of a spiritual movement would be an anomaly. We may not truly diagnose the case, but something is wrong, in fact very wrong, when a church with a membership of two or three hundred can no more have a revival springing from its vital relations to God than it could have an earthquake.

When we say the average church is in no condition to have a revival springing from its deep spirituality, we are declaring a fact, the proof of which we have in many cases. When we say to find a pastor who has power enough lodged in him by the Holy Ghost to bring his church to a spiritual travail for souls is the exception, we stand on the facts transpiring as evidence, cumulative and confirming. It is a rare thing among the churches of our chief towns and cities to find a preacher who would think of beginning an aggressive work without the importation of an evangelist with a large reputation and good singing. A church and pastor who would do this work themselves, by a confession of their own sins and an abased and conquering wrestling with God, would be deemed not only a folly, but an injury, if not an insult, when by the outlay of a good sum of money they could buy a first class religious movement.

DR. CUYLER'S COMMENT

Perhaps the preliminary work of the revival has rarely been stated more tersely and truly than by Dr. Cuyler. He says:

Lay hold of your heaven-appointed work of preaching the whole gospel, especially the cardinal truths of repentance, faith, the claims of Christ, and the Bible rules of godly living; soak your sermons in prayer; do your utmost to keep your people at work; and then leave the results with God. Do not worry; do not be discouraged because the seed does not sprout at once, do not scold your people, do not venture on rash or sensational devices, undertake nothing but the fearless and faithful discharge of your duty to your Master and to immortal souls. Keep your eye on Jesus only. Deal with sin boldly; press home upon the consciences of your hearers the tremendous claims of God and the necessity of immediate yielding to Christ. Watch with open eye and ear for the first tokens of an especial manifestation, follow it up promptly.

We add the unspiritual idea you can have a revival when you please. Do not stake the revival on any one meeting, or on any one effort, or the coming of any man. Wait on God with a resistless and unshaken faith, ceaseless, fervent prayer, and a quenchless zeal. Press the word of God with double edge on the consciences of the church, and press prayer with the irresistible vigor and ceaselessness of faith in God. Though it tarries, wait for it; because it will come and will not tarry.

A WORKING CHURCH
Spiritual Growth of the Church
January 1, 1894

EXAMPLE OF A WORKING CHURCH

The church at Sardis is the divine illustration that a church may have a reputation for piety and be almost destitute of it; very active and very dead at the same time. What is called a working church may be as far from the revival condition as a thoroughly backslidden church. Faith shows itself by works, but there may be much work without any true faith. There may be a busy activity which exhausts faith.

"Many will say to me in that day, have we not prophesied in thy name, in thy name cast out devils, and in thy name done many wonderful works; then will I profess unto them, I never knew you" (Matthew 7:22-23). This saying of Christ proves the truth of our proposition, there may be an immense amount of seemingly pious activity which is false, delusive, and damaging. Activity may spring from spiritual strength. It does spring from spiritual weakness. The mistake of working more than we pray is the mistake of being too busy to eat, a killing process. The more we have of this exciting and absorbing activity brings but an increase of spiritual feebleness.

The elements of a genuine revival are not found in obtrusive and bustling activities, but in the hidden and profounder graces that prostrate the soul before God. The church must come to the revival work with faces shining as Moses did from close and long communion with God. The church must continue the revival conflict and gain the revival victory supported by prayer, as Moses was supported by the hands of Aaron and Hur.

EVANGELIST CHARLES FINNEY

Evangelist Charles Finney, a man of unparalleled success in the revival work, and of great spiritual wisdom in these things, sets forth this danger and illustrates the remedy so well that we reproduce his experience and statements to give clearness and weight to the point we are making, He says:

You take what is called a "working church," where they have been in the habit of enjoying revivals and holding protracted meetings; you will find there is no difficulty in rousing up the church to act and bustle about and make a noise. But as a general rule, unless there is great wisdom and faithfulness in dealing with the church, every succeeding revival will make their religion more and more superficial; and their minds will be more hardened instead of being convicted by their efforts. Tell such a church they are self-righteous, and there's no Holy Ghost in their bustling, and they will be affronted and stare at you. "Why, don't you know the way to wake up is to go to work in religion?" Whereas, the very fact activity has become a habit with them shows they require a different course. They need first to be thoroughly probed and searched and made sensible of their deficiencies, and brought humble and believing to the foot of the Cross, for sanctification. When I was an evangelist, I labored in a church that had enjoyed many revivals, and it was an easy thing to get the church to go out and bring in sinners to the meetings, and the impenitent would come in and hear, but there was no deep feeling, and no faith in the church. The minister saw this way of proceeding was ruining the church, and each revival brought about in this manner made the converts more and more superficial, and unless we came to a stand and got more sanctification in the church, we would defeat our object. We began to preach with that view, and the church members writhed under it. The preaching ran so directly across all their former notions about the way to promote religion, some of them were quite angry. They would run about and talk, but would do nothing else. But after a terrible state of things many of them broke down, and became as humble and as teachable as little children.

CONCLUSION

The sum of it all is, true revival in all cases springs from the same elements, church and preacher prostrate before God, passing through the unutterable throes of a spiritual travail. A church reputed as a great working church may be as far removed from the spiritual birth throes as a church stark and frozen.

WORKED UP, PRAYED DOWN
Man-made or God Sent
January 4, 1894

MODERN POPULAR REVIVAL OR
WORKED UP REVIVAL

Worked up," or "prayed down" revivals separate at almost infinite distance two different phases of revival. The modern popular revival is almost wholly a thing of manipulation, the evident and controlling features are: committees, subcommittees, plans, advertising, generalship, and the reputation of the leader of the meeting.

The "Worked Up" revival may be a great religious movement, enthusiastic, full of religious activity and interest may be at high tide; but in the very nature of things the spiritual influence will be feeble. The emphasis placed on other things, and the prominence and display of the agencies do, by an irrevocable law of divine operations, retire and minify spiritual results. The "Worked Up" revival costs money and requires plans and work, but it is not a great spiritual outlay. It has cost no great heart-searching. It has cost no broken hearts. The expenditure of prayer has not been costly. Its repentance has not been a bitter, fearful, spiritual crying out for forgiveness. The whole movement, like David's first bringing up of the ark, has been projected on a low, unspiritual level.

WORKED UP REVIVAL ATTRACTS MANY, BUT NOT THE HOLY GHOST

The "Worked Up" revival attracts crowds. It moves with pleasing exterior and promptness. The contagion of enthusiasm and sympathy are felt, and everything works well except the Holy Ghost. His presence was expected as a matter of course, but He never comes by a mere matter of course, or on a general invitation. He must be invited specially. His attendance must be sought with an earnestness and singularity that discredits and ignores the presence of all other agencies. Can such things be, and can they overcome us like a summer's cloud without our special wonder? Yes, these great and enthusiastic religious movements without God in them, have been, and are, of regular occurrence.

THE PRAYED DOWN REVIVAL

The "Prayed Down" revival is the genuine one. The "Prayed Down" revival is the divine one. It is the one that gets to the root of things. It is radical, revolutionizing, and abiding.

Pentecost was a "Prayed Down" revival. It was a good one. Its converts could be numbered without mistake. Dr. Cuyler says:

> The late Dr. Thomas H. Skinner (a remarkably humble and holy man) told me two or three of his elders in Philadelphia met in his study to prostrate themselves before God and to ask for a baptism of the Spirit. They emptied themselves and prayed to be filled with Christ. He did fill them. They interceded most fervently for the awakening and conversion of sinners. Presently a most powerful revival shook the whole church like the mighty blast which filled the upper room at Pentecost.

Finney states, "For fourteen consecutive winters there was a rich spiritual blessing brought down upon a certain church just because it was the custom of the church officers to pray fervently for their minister far into the night before each Sabbath."

EFFECTUAL, FERVENT PRAYER

It is not an easy thing to pray down a revival. The effectual, fervent prayer is not an easy work at any time, much less is it an easy matter when interests so momentous and eternal are involved. The prevailing prayer has in it all the manifold principles of the revival. Ezra's prayer was the revival incarnated. The revival born in Ezra's heart flamed out in his prayer before it swept, regenerated, and revolutionized Jerusalem. God's house is the house of prayer. God's people are the people of prayer. God's revival is the revival of prayer. When God's people are in the throes of prayer, the revival is born. The revival is nothing more or less than God's coming, and God comes only in answer to prayer. The revival is surcharged, soaked, suffused, and impregnated with prayer. The revival begins, continues, and ends in prayer. The distinction between the genuine and counterfeit; between the "Worked Up" and "Prayed Down" revival is found in the spirit of prayer which prevails.

To have the church and the pastor as careless, or only interested spectators, to have the work done, and see it well done, and to take care that it never comes near them in any personal or radical way, is the attitude of the church and preacher toward the "Worked Up" revival.

To be first in the agony of conflict and of victory, to be the lowest in contrition and poverty of spirit, and to get the most of spiritual advance and sanctifying grace out of it, is the attitude the pastor and his church manifest for the "Prayed Down" revival.

A GREAT DANGER
Keeping the Fire in Evangelism
January 11, 1894

SEEING WITH SPIRITUAL EYES

The prophets were called seers and watchmen because vigilant seeing was one of their chief functions. An open and a far-seeing vision is an essential to protect religion from its innumerable foes. Religion is exposed to attacks from every hand. Some of the most fatal foes to religion seem innocent and natural, and seem not to be foes at all. One of the most seductive and common foes to vital religion is Churchism [Noun. Strict adherence to the forms or principles of some church organization; sectarianism], in the form of running church machinery. It has been the lament of holy men that a revival of religion bringing into full play all the powerful forces of a strong, fresh, spiritual movement, did not last more than half a century. After the lapse of this time the vigor, freshness, and purity of the movement lost itself in the routine of church machinery.

THE MACHINERY OF CHURCH ORGANIZATION

Searching for and saving souls, and perfecting these souls in holy graces, is a very different thing from running the machinery of a church organization. What relation can there possibly be between the Apostolic Church, with its simplicity, zeal, and singleness of aim, and that same church after organization upon organization had been piled on it, and ceremony after ceremony added to it? The Apostles spent their strenuous force to one point, making the individual holy. Now preachers and church leaders expend all of their effort in running the ponderous machinery of their denominationalism!

A CHURCH HELD BY THE STRONG ARM OF A HOLY PASTOR

An organization held strongly by the sinewy arm of some holy man seems to have in it the greatest aggressive force, like Paul with the early Church, or Luther, or Wesley in later times. The element of Militarism seems to secure for God's army the speediest and richest results. The Salvation Army owes its marvelous career in great part to this feature. But this feature is one easily depraved, and when the Military Church loses its animating principle of soul-saving, it hardens into the worst form of worldliness. When General Booth dies, and the Salvation Army begins a churchly career instead of a soul-saving one, it will be the dullest, deadest of all organizations.

Mr. Wesley had this nightmare to contend with during his life. The rocks and the rapids were on either side of him, but he steered clear. His personal evangelism kept the idea of soul-saving and soul-sanctifying fresh in the hearts of his people. Bishop Francis Asbury, Bishop William McKendree, and the earlier bishops did the same thing. Their overseership was evangelical, edifying, sanctifying, and not official, routine, or mechanical.

THE CHURCH AS A SOUL-SAVING INSTITUTION

To save the Church as a soul-saving institution is the imperative duty of the hour. We shall be blind if we do not recognize the natural tendency of a strong denominationalism.

We are doubly blind if we do not see how far we have gone in this ruinous way, and how the evangelical flame has been quenched!

How personal holiness has been retired!

How organization has been substituted for life!

How the running of church machinery has been hoisted into prominence!

How our conferences have become more like the meetings of bank directors than the gathering of God's men on God's business!

How our leaders have become great denominational statesmen, lawyers, diplomatists, noted for executive ability, experts in minute business, and great church mechanics, rather than mighty preachers of the fiery-tongue and holy and fiery life.

We must keep the evangelical fire glowing. We must have great preachers. A great church is a great curse if it is not given freely to the great and sole work of saving the individual from sin and perfecting him in holiness.

THE CHURCH PERPETUATED
Doctrinal Principles
January 18, 1894

THE CHURCH AS A SPIRITUAL FORCE

It never has been a difficult matter to perpetuate a church as an ecclesiastical organization. But to perpetuate the church as a spiritual force is altogether different. The machinery of the church at Sardis, was perhaps never in better running order than when Christ said of it, *"I know thy works, that thou hast a name that thou lives, and art dead"* (Revelation 3:1).

Commonplace principles, mechanical forces, or routine men, can work church machinery and keep it going with fair and deceptive results. It takes vigilance, and men of great spiritual force to keep the spiritual principles in a church in vigorous case. There are no powerful, secret, malignant foes to assault and undermine the churchly forces. These may be as harmless to Satan as "a painted ship upon a painted ocean" is innocent of motion. But Satan wars his mightiest and wiliest warfare against the spiritual forces. Churches that are eminent for their spiritual history are exposed to the greatest perils, and require the most wakeful and diligent fidelity and conflict to maintain their spiritual force. The successors of men who have made the church a great spiritual power must be men of superior spiritual power, and men of superior spiritual mold, for it requires more spiritual force if possible to maintain the spiritual vigor and elevation of a matured religious movement than to create that movement. The strong tendency is to relax the hold and to lose by conciliation and compromise those results that were won by conflict and which can only be maintained by a more strenuous conflict.

GREAT EVILS AGAINST THE CHURCH

Paul not only described the great evils that were arrayed against the Church in his day as an incentive to vigilant fidelity on the part of his successors, but he portrayed the perils of the future also to alarm and arouse. Wesley spent his last years in doing the same most important work.

The trend of all institutions committed to men is to degeneracy. This is doubly true of religious institutions. The primitive Church is a remarkable illustration of this fact; degeneracy set in before the apostles died. The gravest trust committed to the successors of the apostles was to maintain the Christian religion in its purity; ecclesiastical forms and polity were trifles to this.

MAINTAINING THE CHURCH AS A SOUL-SAVING, SOUL-SANCTIFYING FORCE

We are called to the grave trust of maintaining the Church as a soul-saving, soul-sanctifying force. The natural and inevitable tendency within us to decay is aided by the increase of members, the influx of unregenerate members, our material thrift, the attention and emphasis it demands, and our social position, culture, and wealth. These are the conditions that blind or bewilder the eyes of the Seer and relax vigilance and discipline. When these are relaxed, the gates are up and the desolating floods are on us.

We believe that primitive Christianity was the gospel as forceful and as unadulterated as the world has ever seen or will see. We believe the elements of its original strength and success are the elements of strength and success in all times and under all conditions. We maintain that the holier Christianity is, the more powerful it will be. We are sure its corruption and weakness will be in ratio to its departure from its original simplicity and purity. We have no fear it will cease as an ecclesiastical factor or force; its peril does not lie in that

135

direction; but our fear is it will lose its prestige and place as an institution to secure the holiness of the individual.

Reverend Freeborn Garrettson, [minister in the Methodist-Episcopal Church] in his semi-centennial sermon before the New York Conference in 1826, says:

> I fully believe the doctrine taught by Mr. John Wesley is scriptural and will stand the test; but what his people will be a hundred years hence we cannot say. They may be a numerous and learned people: but it is possible by slow degrees they may retrograde until they have very little of the spirit of Old Methodism. This certainly will be the case without a steady and conscientious perseverance in the good old paths. The letter is good in its place, but we shall be comparatively nothing without the life and power of godliness. We must look well to our doctrine and discipline, and guard the sacred ministry. Lay hands suddenly on no man, look more to genuine piety and to a real call from God than to any literary qualification without it. Keep a pure ministry and you will have a pure membership. The fall of the primitive Church began with the clergy and should we fall, it will begin here as well. It is better to have a pious, laborious, successful ministry, than to have wealth and ease without it.

WESLEY ON THE PERPETUATION OF METHODISM

Mr. Wesley was questioned as to how Methodism was to be perpetuated. He replied:

> The Methodists must take heed to their doctrine, to their experience, their practice, and to their discipline. For if they attend to doctrine only, they will make men antinomians, and if to their experience only, they will

make men enthusiasts, if to their practice only, they
will make men Pharisees, and if they do not execute
their discipline, they will be like men bestowing much
pains upon a beautiful garden, and putting no fence
around it, to save it from the wild boars of the forest.

This is perhaps the wisest advice he could have given.
This advice deserves to be written in gold upon every church
pulpit, and to be engraved on the hearts of all to whom the
church is committed.

Are we doing this?

Are we guarding with sleepless vigilance and passionate
jealousy this sacred treasure?

Are we keeping our doctrine pure?

Is our experience fresh and rich in our hearts?

Is our practice holy and perfect before God?

Is our discipline maintained with firmness and free from
worldly complicity or compromise?

These points are all vital, are all exposed, and are as
sensitive as the apple of the eye. They must be guarded by
Argus-eyed watchmen. [Argus: A 100-eyed giant in Greek
Mythology.] Vigilance and jealous suspicion of the least
encroachment or surrender are the sentinels to guard our
citadel and keep the Church as God intended it to be.

AFTER THE REVIVAL
Maintaining the Results
March 8, 1894

MAINTAINING THE SPIRITUAL ENERGIES

It requires far more effort to retain the grace of God than
to get it. It requires far more spiritual effort to conserve the

fruits of revival than to secure them. The revival in the full tide of spiritual flow will run itself, but to stay the waves of spiritual retrocession and keep the current full requires the full outlay of all spiritual energies. The world, the flesh, and the Devil will make their most insidious and powerful efforts as the spiritual tides begin to recede.

The true revival is not an episode, nor the flooding of a sudden summer shower to be followed by dryness and drought. The true revival is like the overflowing of the Nile which gives enduring life and fertility to the soil; the receding waters leave their rich deposits behind them. If the revival has been genuine, it has given new life to the church as well as to sinners. The revival that has not vitalized the church with a richer spiritual life and brought a great blessing to the preacher is not worth much.

STAYING ON THE HIGH SPIRITUAL PLANE

For the preacher and the church to move on a higher plane is one permanent end to be secured by the revival. To empower and sanctify the church, and to refocus and sanctify the preacher, are among the all-important ends of a revival. For the revival to be simply a strong wave of emotion starting good impulses, and creating good resolutions that end as soon as the wave passes, breeds barrenness and death. For the church and the preacher after the revival to return to their old self-indulgent, worldly ways with zeal abated, faith sluggish, lives low and questionable, can no more advance salvation and righteousness than can the slush of a January thaw produce the glow and fruitage of summer.

AFTER THE REVIVAL

The most important work of the church after the revival is to keep the church up to the spiritual condition that the revival induced, and to secure the permanent stay of the warm and rich spiritual principles to which the revival gave life. This is necessary to make the church affect the world, and impact every element of society in a powerful, spiritual way. This reveals God's presence and salvation for all through Jesus Christ, who will believe and call upon Him.

OUR SPIRITUAL WALK

CHRISTIANITY, CONSERVATIVE AND AGGRESSIVE
Christian Life
June 21, 1890

THE WORDS OF JESUS

The words of Jesus deserve to be carefully marked and pondered. He spoke nothing carelessly or casually. His whole life was a revelation, intended to teach neither more nor less than what is necessary for men to know of personal salvation. Where light was needed, He was sufficiently explicit in His utterances, where it was not needed He was cautious and economical of His words. Hence, we have reason to believe His illustrations of truth were not presented with a redundant profuseness. Take, for instance, His sayings as recorded by Matthew, *"Ye are the salt of the earth, ye are the light of the world"* (Matthew 5:13). Not only do these words have a deep meaning, but they must have been designed either to illustrate the same truth from different standpoints, or to teach different truths. The latter view is likely correct. These words were, no doubt, intended to set forth two distinct features of Christianity, the conservative and the aggressive.

SALT PRESERVES AND LIGHT EXPELS DARKNESS

Salt is eminently a conservative principle not intended to destroy that which is evil, or to restore life and purity to that which is corrupt and dead. Its office is to preserve that which is sound and pure. Hence it is an appropriate figure of the conservative element of the Christian religion. Light is aggressive, expelling darkness. In this statement we, of course, conform to the popular view, which looks upon darkness as an entity. Light is an emblem of truth, righteousness, and happiness. Darkness is an emblem of evil, whether in the form of ignorance, sin, or misery. As it is the province of light to drive away darkness, so it is the province of gospel truth to banish error, sin, and misery from the Earth.

CHRISTIANITY IS BOTH CONSERVATIVE AND AGGRESSIVE

It has not come to destroy everything in its path, but to destroy only what is evil and to preserve what is good. As a matter of fact there is a great deal of good in human nature, and for our present purpose we need not stop to consider whether it is so much of primeval purity as survived the fall, or the result of the saving grace of God that "hath appeared unto all men." We find, as a phenomenon, much goodness in human nature; valuable traits even in the most wicked men. These are worth preserving and fostering. They include natural affection, economy, industry, patriotism, humanity, courage, and fortitude. Upon these the Church should not make war, neither should she despise them, because they seem to be natural traits, but she should recognize, applaud, and encourage them. These traits of character, whether they spring from primitive nature or from gracious influence, are proper objects of sanctifying and fostering grace; they are gifts which God wisely stirs up and stimulates by the Holy Spirit. They are stamina upon which disordered and ruined human character is to be reconstructed; fulcra, upon which is poised the lever of gospel truth for the elevation of fallen man. They are tangential points of contact between the possibilities of the higher life and a fallen race.

The wise Christian will agree with the world as far as possible, without compromising truth or principle. Truthful maxims, harmless customs, and innocent pastimes are not to be repudiated, simply because they happen to be found among worldly people. Let the salt be applied to them to the end that they may not degenerate into things unlawful or morally hurtful.

But it is the duty of the Church not only to conserve the good, but to make war on the evil. She is the light of the world, the enemy of all darkness. She is an army of invasion as well as of occupation. She is the chosen instrument of God in banishing error from society, driving away all false doctrines, contending for the faith delivered to the saints, teaching, enlightening, and constantly contributing to that aggregation of Christian influences that is to cover the Earth with the knowledge of the glory of the Lord.

DECLARING WAR ON MORAL EVIL AND PRESUMPTUOUS SINS

It is the duty of the Church to make war on all moral evil, whether in the form of deadly and presumptuous sins, or of such pastimes and worldly amusements as have over them the trail of the serpent. It is the duty of the Church to be a comforter; to console and stimulate to high endeavor and lofty hopes the good and faithful, and to make all men happy as far as possible, by a war of extermination on sin, which is the root and source of all "the ills which flesh is heir to."

The several fights against error, iniquity, and misery, are distinct but not separate movements. Error is a source of sin, and error and sin are both sources of moral unrest. Light has different rays, but they blend in one life-giving force. So the gospel has its white light of truth, its electric, life-giving principle, and its warming, emotional power, but it is the one soul-saving energy.

The conservative and aggressive principles of the gospel are distinct, but they do not act separately. The power that destroys sin builds up the positive elements of Christian character, and the power that fosters the good found in man tends indirectly but powerfully to uproot all that antagonizes that which is pure, lovely, and of good report.

PRAISE GOD
Praise and Worship to His Glory
November 8, 1890

THE SPIRIT OF PRAISE

Praise means to set a high value on God, and to express this value in words. Praise is an essential as well as an initial element in religion. When God converts a soul He puts in it, as a germinal and organic principle, the spirit of praise. A true conversion is clothed in the garment of praise in exchange for the spirit of heaviness. The presence or absence of praise marks the depth and intensity, or the beggary of our spiritual life. Prayer and praise are joined as the sun and its light are joined, as the flower and its sweetness are joined. If prayer be the life of religion, praise is the wing by which that life soars to Heaven. Prayer brings God down to the soul and praise lifts the soul up to God. Prayer has much to do with our sins and ourselves and God; praise has much to do with grace, gratitude, and God.

THE FOUNTAIN OF PRAISE

The high esteem of God in the heart is the fountain and force of praise. To have this high esteem, luminous views of sin and salvation must be gained. A definite and powerful realization of sin and salvation is the prerequisite of praise. An Almighty rescue from an infinite and imminent peril lays the foundation of praise deep and broad.

SHOUTING GOD'S PRAISE

God was of such priceless value to many of the saints of old and His revelation of himself to them so glorious and transporting, that their consciousness of His being, His presence, and His power became so vivid and profound that they shouted out His praises. Our spiritual strength would scarcely bear the strain of such lofty and strenuous spiritual exercise, even if our low spiritual tastes were not offended by such exhibitions. In our estimate and action we must be careful to distinguish between Church music and praise. To confuse the two will be exceedingly damaging. In not a few congregations praise has been wholly substituted by Church-music. These two are distinct in their inspiration and aims. Praise knows the high price set on God by the grateful, adoring heart, and is expressed by holy, thankful lips.

THE SPIRIT OF PRAISE ABODE ON THE TABERNACLE

The spirit of praise abode on tabernacles as a cloud of glory out of which God shined and spoke. It filled our temples with the perfume of costly, flaming incense. It is evident to everyone that this spirit of praise is sadly deficient in our congregations now. The spirit of praise is a mighty force in projecting the gospel, and the decay of its vital forces must be equally evident. To restore the spirit of praise to our congregations should be one of urgent importance with every pastor.

SINGING

Singing is one method of praise; not the highest, but the ordinary and usual form. The apostle puts the whole matter in a small compass: "*Let the word of Christ,*" he says, "*dwell in you richly in all wisdom, teaching and admonishing one another in psalms and hymns and spiritual songs, singing with grace in your hearts to the Lord*" (Colossians 3:16). To do this the nature and quality of the preaching is important. The song of praise is the outflow of strong and spiritual principles. No songs exist where the Word of God does not dwell richly in the heart. The Word of God is the material out of which these songs are manufactured. The preacher lays the foundation on which the beautiful melody of a song is built. The Word of God implanted in the heart is the overflowing fountain from which this sparkling, musical, and refreshing stream flows. Praise is not the product of a song, not a forced or manufactured thing, or the result of outward or natural forces, but the spontaneous outgoing of mighty internal forces implanted by the ever potent and ever vitalizing Word of God. The earnest preaching of God's Word by a preacher filled with the Holy Ghost is the prerequisite to the existence of the spirit of praise in the hearts and lips of the hearers.

PRAISE PRODUCES MUTUAL EDIFICATION

One great object of praise is mutual edification, the telling of God and His wondrous works; exalting these with our hearts and lips is good to the use of edification. To this end the words that are sung are of prime importance. The benefit does not lie in the melody, this gives aroma, but the melody must have body. The tune and poetry may make it tasteful, but the nourishing qualities must come from God. These songs are to teach. They are to be the depositaries and channels of revealed truth. Poetry and music are used to give a high polish to the rich, hard dogmas of religion.

SONGS OF PRAISE ARE THE ILLUSTRATIONS OF EXPERIENCE AND DOCTRINE

Songs of praise are but experience set to tune, and experience is but the solid parts of the gospel reduced to liquid form. Songs are but experience and doctrine stereotyped and beautifully illustrated. We are more indebted to the songs of Charles Wesley for the dissemination and triumph of doctrines than to the Institutes of Richard Watson.

HYMNS OF CHARLES WESLEY

Charles Wesley's hymns are John Wesley's sermons in rhyme. We have lost immensely all the stable as well as the costlier and more beautiful parts by allowing the popular, inane melodies to substitute for our standard hymns. By this process the spiritual taste has been almost destroyed, the spiritual appetite and digestion impaired. It is a fatal mistake to aim at getting the people, old or young, to sing anything they can sing with a gush, or whatever strikes the popular ear, but better they sing something that invigorates and instructs.

ADMONISHMENT AND TEACHING OF GOSPEL TRUTH IS THE FOUNDATION OF HYMNOLOGY

The whole system of gospel truth is to flow along the current of song, and flood our souls, and deposit the rich sediment which will remain and fructify when the song wave has ebbed into silence. These songs are for admonition; they must be designed to prune. There is to be a touch of censure, an element of warning in them. Everybody, saint or sinner, is imperiled and weak; everybody, saint or sinner, needs to be admonished; and even our songs are to be charged with this necessary and saving element. They must admonish as well as teach and show us our danger as well as our duty. How deficient in this element are the popular songs which we have substituted for hymnology. Many of them are gotten up with the deliberate aim to eliminate these features we believe. It cannot be denied that they are almost wholly destitute of this scriptural, salutary element. It seems to us if preachers and people would relearn the lesson of the object of singing; nothing could induce them to allow this vicious, piety-destroying substitution. Our standard Hymn Book would be placed in every pew and in the hands of every worshiper and every one exhorted from the pulpit to sing; exhorted not once or twice in a decent, casual way, but strongly, sharply, and constantly, until they realized they had not only a glorious privilege to exercise, but a solemn duty to perform, and they dare not be silent. The heart must have grace in it to sing. It is not to be done by musical taste of talent, but by grace. Nothing helps the singing so mightily as a gracious revival. The presence of God inspires song.

GOD'S PRESENCE CREATES THE SONG

The angels and the glorified ones do not need presenters, choirs, or singing schools. God is present in their glorious assemblies, and His holy presence creates the song and teaches the singer. It is so on Earth. God's absence is the death of song. His presence, in power in our churches, would bring back the full chorus of song. Where grace abounds, song abounds. When God is in the heart Heaven and melody are there, and the lips overflow out of the abundance of the heart.

THE OBJECT OF PRAISE IS TO GLORIFY GOD

The aim of it all is for God, "to the Lord," for His glory, not for the pleasure of the music, not to glorify the choir, not to draw the people, but to the Lord. It is sacrilege for any but sanctified hearts and lips to direct this service. Praise is comely, it glorifies God.

As in the days of Luther music changed; also with the pen of Charles Wesley. The style may change but guard its purpose, to glorify God, and not entertain men. Does it draw people, saint and sinner to God? If not, resist such change.

HEAVEN
Our Home
December 23, 1890

MODERN PROGRESSIVE RELIGION

One of the efforts of modern progressive religion is to center Christian thought and hope mainly on this life, and to make as little as possible of the life to come. Heaven in the new creed is to have little or no place as an inspiration, a solace, or an end. It talks glibly with force and much truth of the necessity of work for humanity and Earth and of the Christian demands of this life. All this has a show of good, but the tendency, if not the aim, is to materialize religion, and so harden and deform it that it will be fit neither for Earth nor Heaven.

VISION FOR SERVICE ON EARTH

A vision of the spirit of Heaven, of the hopes of Heaven, its purity and inspiration, must permeate our service for Earth. The full force of this heavenly stimulant must replenish our souls and sublime them or our labors for Earth and men will exhaust and vitiate all solid principles.

The idea of Heaven and its prospect kept constantly before the mind are necessary to hold men to religion. God is in Heaven, Christ is there, enthroned and glorious, and our affections must be fixed on that center. He that has but little

149

of Heaven in his religion will have but little of God and Christ in it, for Christ and God and Heaven in this are one. Heaven has always been to the pious the most alluring and powerful motive. The earnest of Heaven, its foretaste and promise, are put into the heart by the Holy Ghost at conversion and its presence and realization grows stronger and more engaging as the years increase.

RESPONSIVE HARMONY IN THE CHRISTIAN LIFE

The Christian's life and effort should be in responsive harmony to the desire of Christ who said, and is ever saying to His Father, *"I will that they also whom thou hast given me be with me where I am that they may behold my glory which thou hast given me"* (John 17:24). The Christian heart ought to be a constant Amen to that prayer. This is not to deprave service in the interest of a sentiment, but it is the preparation for the highest service. No activity however important must be allowed as the substitute for love. Sinful is the churchly activity that alienates or enfeebles desire for Heaven. Worldly and idolatrous are those attachments that clip the wings for Heaven; earthly are those treasures that turn the soul's strong gaze from the City of our God. Feeble and cloudy is the faith that does not anticipate God's decree and goes to Heaven by love and not by law.

THE CITY WHOSE BUILDER AND MAKER IS GOD

This is not to surrender the practical to the sentimental. This is not substituting the poetry of Christian feeling for the prose of Christian work. God's most practical saints have the largest share of this heavenly flavor. Christ's most valiant soldiers and most laborious servants have luxuriated in the poetry of Heaven. It has relieved the tedium and heaviness of their daily crosses. It has given energy, courage, and endurance to their exhaustless efforts. Abraham, the father and the pioneer of us all, looked always for this city whose builder and maker is God. Jerusalem, the mother of us all, has caught her pattern, spirit, melody and name from Heaven. Christ endured the Cross, despised the shame under the full vision of these heavenly joys. Stephen, under the charms of its open vision, fell under the deadly stones of his murderers as to a gentle, prayerful sleep. Paul, the worker of all workers, the most practical of men, ever had Heaven in his eye and heart. His commission as an apostle was not more authoritative, nor more inspiring than his visions of Heaven.

MEDITATION ON HEAVEN BRINGS SOLACE AND STRENGTH

When Moses was balancing Egypt's crown with the reproach of Christ, his hope of Heaven relieved the present desperate conditions and nerved him for the sacrifice and its conflict. Paul labored under the constant inspiration of Heaven. The visions he had of it made him restless for its fruition and he died supported and enlivened by its crown. Christ braved the Cross and endured its shame with the prospect of Heaven in full view. Heaven has come into the faith and thought of God's people with increased force and brightness to soothe their sorrows or increase their fortitude. When sorrow and despair were oppressing the disciples, Christ pointed to His Father's house with its many mansions, and their entrance into it as a solace and strength for their trouble and fainting. It is said of the saints of old, *"They took joyfully the spoiling of their goods, knowing that in heaven they had a more enduring substance"* (Hebrews 10:34). What relief and ecstasy those words from Christ carried to the dying thief, *"Today thou shalt be with me in paradise"* (Luke 23:43). How the incorruptible crown and the house not made with hands, which the apostle brought before the gaze of the Corinthian saints, served to allure, to inspire, to strengthen for trial, for denial, and for the most strenuous efforts!

151

OUR CITIZENSHIP IS IN HEAVEN

Our hearts must be in Heaven, our eyes fixed there, our citizenship enrolled there; we must own its allegiance. Its language must be on our lips, its music on our ears, its purity in our hearts, our hands busy about its work, our feet ready and eager to enter its gate and press its soil. We cannot make too much of Heaven, cannot think too often of it, cannot long too greatly for it, cannot labor too hard for it. We must stay away from this songless, heartless materialism that makes sentiment earthly, blots out Heaven in the name of religion, seemingly in the interest of piety, but really stabbing piety to the heart.

The truth is, the Christian cannot do his full duty to man till Heaven is imaged in his heart; he is not ready to work well for Earth till his name is written on its jeweled columns and the visions of the third Heaven are in his heart and oppress his tongue. No man can work for God in true measure whose longings do not reach to Heaven. No man can be truly loyal to Christ on Earth till his desires are inflamed to depart and be with Christ in Heaven.

Instead of eliminating Heaven from our creed and work and life, we need a greater infusion of its power, a clearer experience of its reality, a more confident apprehension and a growing appreciation of our title to its incorruptible and fadeless inheritance. Instead of expunging it, we need a fuller inflow.

O would he more of heaven bestow, and let the
  vessels break,
And let our ransomed spirits go, to grasp the God
  we seek
In rapturous awe on Him to gaze who bought the
  sight for me,
And shout and wonder at His grace to all eternity.

Something similar to this heavenly experience would freshen us for work and strengthen us to bear and persevere. Instead of Heaven being an initial principle and motive only belonging to our childish spiritual state, it coexists with our whole Christian career, increases with our advance, and grows with our growth.

The fact of Heaven is an imperishable element in Christian character. The whole matter lies in the nutshell of common sense. The Bible being true, our religion real, Heaven is better, far better, than Earth; better people, a better country, better clime. Happy are they who have exchanged the pains, the sickness, the crying, the chill, and the graves of Earth for Heaven.

FASTING AND CHRIST
Benefits
January 3, 1891

In these latter days the very foundations of Christianity are being tried. The whole range of dogma and duty has been questioned. This is the day of spiritual censorship, and everything that does not suit the sentiment, taste, or reason of the self-established censors, comes under the ban. Fasting is to be stricken from the roll of duties as having neither form nor comeliness, fit only for Jews or monks.

FASTING

Fasting occupies a large space in the Jewish system, especially in the times when spiritual principles were made prominent. Moses put it into his system by his fast of forty days, and by the annual fast on the Great Day of Atonement. The prophets, in their severe struggles to stem the floods of idolatry, worldliness, and the formality of their day made this duty of fasting a powerful agent to save spirituality from shipwreck. Elijah, as the type and representative of them, fasted forty days.

The business of Christ was not to originate duties, campaigns, programs, and organizations; but to recover, to recast, to spiritualize, and to reinforce cardinal and original obligations. These three, involved in or antedating the law, prayer, almsgiving, and fasting, He found buried deep in the mire of Pharisaic formalism and hypocrisy. In the Sermon on the Mount He lays down the constitution of His system. He certainly would not put anything foreign or indifferent in that conspicuous and foundation place. The transference of fasting to that sermon makes it a duty of binding obligation. It is not in the company of conditional relations to be regulated, but in the company of personal and universally binding duties, side by side in verbiage and authority with secret prayer and almsgiving, as cardinal, as universal, and as binding as these. It is the same in regard to its privacy and spirituality, the same in its access to God, and the same in its rewards from Him. Surely such language used in such a place is not to polish a Pharisaic superstition, or regulate anything less than a duty. It is not a duty of such daily recurrence as secret prayer, but with almsgiving it is the duty of certain occasions and stages of the spiritual life through which God's favor flows.

RELATIONSHIP OF FASTING TO CHRIST'S TEACHINGS

The relation of fasting to Christ's system finds its full explanation and illustration in a conversation He had with some of the disciples of John the Baptist and of the Pharisees. The Baptist and the Pharisees taught their followers to fast and pray, but the Disciples of Christ did not observe either, it seems, with any regularity or distinction:

Then came to Him the disciples of John, saying, why do we and the Pharisees fast oft, but thy disciples fast not? And Jesus said unto them, Can the children of the bride-chamber mourn, as long as the bridegroom is with them? But the days will come when the bridegroom shall be taken from them, and then shall they fast. No man putteth a piece of new cloth unto an old garment: for that which is put in to fill it up taketh from the garment, and the rent is made worse. Neither do men put new wine into old bottles: else the bottles break and the wine runneth out, and the bottles perish: but they put new wine into new bottles, and both are preserved. (Luke 5:34-38)

There are three main points covered in the reply of Christ to these interrogators: His relation to His disciples at that time was of such a nature that the departure of its first missionaries was sanctified by fasting. But it said fasting is opposed to the system of Christ. It may be opposed to sentimental rationalizing or fleshly views of His system but not as revealed in the New Testament. He fasted forty days and forty nights as an introductory to His dispensation. Is not Christ's action based on those spiritual principles of which fasting is the exponent? Is not self-denial, of which fasting is the symbol and grace, and the cornerstone of Christianity? Is not the crucifixion of the flesh one of the aims and objects of a spiritual religion, and does not fasting mightily advance that painful but blessed end? Is not the flesh to be mortified under the reign of Christ, and is there a more efficient agent to secure that end than fasting? Paul beating his body black and blue, and keeping it in the chains of spiritual slavery is an illustration of the end to be secured by this duty. Of course all duties, prayer, fasting, and almsgiving have no virtue in themselves, and as legal performances are oppressive and vain; their efficiency is found in their uses as channels for the Holy Ghost. But why cannot fasting be this channel as well as prayer or almsgiving?

We are fully aware the average Christian in his fleshliness gets but little out of fasting save an empty stomach and a headache. But the men who have come to the highest forms of spiritual life, who have most thoroughly crucified the flesh, who are the purest examples of self-abnegation and of the Christ life; the robust, vigorous, self-denying New Testament patterns of piety, are the men to whom fasting is habitual and of great spiritual use.

SPIRITUAL VALUE OF FASTING

The most powerful spiritual movements have had fasting incorporated into their preparation. They began as the purest and highest form of spiritual operation, and the men who were its divinely chosen leaders were schooled in this self-denying ordinance.

MAKING OUT A CASE
Christian Piety
January 10, 1891

DEFECTIVE RELIGIOUS PIETY

Things are not going well when the preacher has to turn advocate and make out a case of defective religious piety for the individual or for the Church. This is often done at funerals or in memorial addresses. Hearers are sometimes surprised at the virtues of the eulogized persons, virtues of which their daily and intimate associates had no knowledge.

We have in mind a funeral address delivered by a very eloquent preacher over a distinguished man whose acquaintance he had made while in his home. The friends of the dead man would not have recognized the portraiture if his name had not been designated in the address. The preacher was simply making out a good case of virtue and religion for his friend who charmed him by his hospitality and misled him by a fair show of surface and virtues.

Cases of defective piety are often made by people standing around the coffin of a deceased person. The sympathies and solace of the hour seem to demand or excuse it. Grief may be assuaged, sometimes by a display of fancied good, but truth is always and greatly hurt by it. The dead may be praised, but religion and the living are damaged.

Religious men ought to be the author of their own cases. No preacher ought to assume the role of an attorney in the case of defective piety, even at the grave. The mantle of charity and silence may well be drawn over defects, but the parade of false grace is nowhere more offensive and out of place than in the solemnities of the coffin and at the mouth of the devouring and truth demanding grave. The life should be so full of heavenly aims, so strong in its piety, as to make its own case. It should speak with more than prophet's vision of the Heaven to which the pure, glad spirit has gone. It is a very questionable life that needs an attorney to make out its case.

PREACHERS ADVOCATING FOR A CHURCH

Frequently the preacher turns advocate for a church. True, its graces are dull and lusterless. True, the world holds most of its stock and has watered its original value; but a good lawyer can make a fair case out of a very bad one. It is surprising how much good a sharp church lawyer can find in a worldly or backslidden church, and how downright worldliness can be transmuted into rich Christian graces.

Many things are brought to light that never saw the light before.

Many things are counted pious that are not so written in the Bible.

Many virtues discovered, or reported as discovered, which were never seen in practical operation, a brilliant and saving faith without works!

And at last, as a general plea, charity, so often confused with spiritual blindness, is appealed to as a covering for the remnant of Church evil which cannot be made to play the part of or even look like religious virtue.

The truth is the church that needs to have a case of real piety made out for it ought to have a doctor, and not a lawyer. It demands physic, and not flattery. It needs new material and not paint, to cover its rottenness.

CHRISTIAN VIRTUE SHINES BRIGHTLY

There may be very fine virtues that demand the microscope to assure us of their being, but they cannot be of as much value as religious factors. Jewels may be in the rubbish, but if they always stay in the rubbish they are of no more value than the rubbish. The candle on the candle stand does not need witnesses to prove, nor a search warrant to find out its shining. The fool and the dim of vision can see and feel its light. The light whose existence requires so much effort to prove is not worth the name or the trouble of proof. A city set on a hill does not need a police force to find it. We do not have to go through a chemical process to prove the salt has savor. Open your eyes and you will see the city. Taste and you will find the saltiness.

HIDDEN FOUNTAINS OF PIETY

Many of the sources and springs of piety are hidden, but the results and streams that flow from these hidden fountains are seen and felt. We need not invade the privacy of the dining room to know the man eats, the vigor and force of these private feasts come out in the strength of his life forces. Prayer, almsgiving, and fasting ought to be shut in with God and ourselves, but the effects and rewards are open, and can be read of all men. Spiritual processes may, indeed, be hidden, but spiritual results must be open or they do not exist. The Church must so live that the office and duties of the Church attorney, like Othello's occupation, will be gone. We are not careful to dress the Church in the tawdry patchwork of a manufactured piety. We are laboring to make it a glorious Church, without spot or wrinkle, or any such thing, holy and without blemish, a golden city, a jeweled bride adorned for her husband.

We do not want funeral occasions to be commissions to search out and make decision on the piety of the coffined church member while kinsfolk and friends have to wait for a paid attorney to draw out the case by sharp examinations, and then by dint of argument and rhetoric, gain a decision. We want men and women to so live that all will know who knew them that they have gone to Heaven, as surely as the sun shines; that all tears may be turned to raptures and all the occasion is a glad stimulant.

> *Come; let us join our friends above, that have*
> *obtained the prize;*
> *And on the eagle wings of love to joys celestial rise.*
> *His militant embodied host, with wishful looks we*
> *stand,*
> *And long to see that happy coast, and reach the*
> *heavenly land.*

WORLDLY PRUDENCE
Conforming to the Ways of the World
January 17, 1891

DANGER OF ADULTERATED PRUDENCE

Prudence has been said to be a cowardly virtue, however, it is often the bravest of virtues, with much more strength and courage in it than rashness. Its chief danger lies in its exposure to adulteration. Its offensive protection is feeble. Selfishness very frequently debauches cowardice to compromise, and conservatism to surrender.

Christian prudence carries an exposed side without the porcupine quills to protect, and is in constant peril from worldliness. Mr. Wesley records this instance: "I was grieved to find prudence had made them leave off singing of psalms. I fear it will not stop here. God deliver me, and all that seek Him in sincerity, from what the world calls Christian prudence."

COUNTERFEIT CHRISTIAN PRUDENCE

The distinction between true Christian prudence and what the world calls Christian prudence was never more clearly set forth than by Mr. Wesley. Perhaps no distinctions are more necessary than this. It is at this point where the Church and the individual imperceptibly glide into worldliness and become thoroughly steeped in it, and yet all the while bearing the coloring of religion. He defines counterfeit Christian prudence "as pursuing Christian worldly maxims, or by worldly means." This is one of the insidious and general evils to which religion is ever exposed, and which most thoroughly eliminates its spiritual power and makes it the pleasing and happy ally of the world. By this method the antagonisms between religion and the world are avoided, and everything is toned down to amicable conservatism. Mr. Wesley sets forth these worldly maxims to which the Church has been seduced:

> The more power, the more money, the more learning and the more reputation a man has, the more good he will do. And whenever a Christian, pursuing the noblest ends, forms his behavior by these maxims he will infallibly (though perhaps by insensible degrees) decline into worldly prudence. He will use more or less conformity to the world, if not in sin, yet in doing some things that are good in themselves, yet, all things considered, are not good to him; and perhaps at length using guile or disguise, simulation or dissimulation; either seeming to be what he is not, or not seeming to be what he is. By any of these marks may worldly prudence be discerned from the wisdom which is from above.

This Christian prudence pursues Christian maxims and by Christian means. The end it pursues is holiness in every kind and in the highest degree, and usefulness in every kind and degree. And herein it proceeds on the following maxims: The help that is done upon the Earth God doeth it himself. It is He that worketh all in all, and that not by human power; generally He uses weak things to confound the strong; not by men of wealth as most of His choice instruments may say, "Silver and gold have I none," and not by learned or wise men after the flesh. No, the foolish things hath God chosen, not men of reputation, but men that were as the filth and off scouring of the world and all for this plain reason: "That no flesh may glory in His sight." Christian prudence pursues these ends upon these principles, and only by Christian means.

WORLDLY PRUDENCE VERSUS CHRISTIAN PRUDENCE

We emphasize the distinction: worldly prudence, when baptized for religious uses, is the pursuing of Christian ends by worldly standards and worldly means. It has the flavor of religion in it, but the covering and core are worldly. It has run up the flag of Christ, but it fights under the banner of the enemy. It does preach Christ, but leaves out the Cross. It professes to be sailing heavenward, but the vessel is entered for another port; and it is officered by strangers to the heavenly city, who have neither chart nor compass to direct them there. This kind of prudence goes hand in hand with the world; it makes no issues, smoothes off the sharp points of collision, pours oil on the places of friction, stirs no animosities, and sets the gospel in an attractive worldly frame.

True Christian prudence is aggressive; it may not make rash assaults, but its hostility is imperishable. It understands there is neither compromise nor peace in this war. The men who accomplish the most for God are aggressive at every point. They seek not the world, they do not use its methods, and they have no patience with its standards. But this quiet virtue finds the most virulent opposition. True Christian prudence is what the world hates. Christ, in His quiet gentleness, was its illustrious example, and yet who ever stirred the world as He stirs it? Who was ever opposed, hated, and hunted by the world as He? He says by way of encouragement, but in the declaration of the eternal principles are conflict and enmity. *"If the world hate you, ye know it hated me before it hated you. If ye were of the world, the world would love its own; but because ye are not of the world, but I have chosen you out of the world, therefore the world hateth you"* (John 15:18-19).

"Remember the word that I said unto you, The servant is not greater than his lord. If they have persecuted me, they will also persecute you; if they have kept my saying, they will

keep yours also" (John 15:20). So it was in the year 33 of our Lord. Times, principles, Christ, and the world do not change. These principles of hatred and conflict are eternal, and if there be peace it is because there has been surrender on the part of those who represent Christ.

ELEMENTARY PRINCIPLES
Foundation Principles
December 12, 1891

FOUNDATION PRINCIPLES

The whole Christian life takes its color and depth from the character of its primary elements. In religion the nature of the foundation is of first importance. If the foundation principles be impalpable or superficial, the Christian life is projected on a low plane and must be unsatisfactory in its process and results. We would discriminate between states and the expression of those states. There may be profound feelings with little expression. A great sorrow may not issue in tear. A fearful internal struggle may not agitate the surface. We are not so much concerned about the exhibition of states. The expression of the attitude of the soul toward God, though very important, is not prime. But the nature of these initial spiritual states, their depth and intensity, are all important.

DEPTH AND INTENSITY IN THE NATURE OF SPIRITUAL STATES

It is a matter of observation, of remark and of explanation, the states of conviction and repentance are not so pungent and profound as formerly; religion enters into the possession of the human heart in a more quiet and commonplace way than it used to; the sense of guilt is not so keen; the sense of sorrow not so painful; souls get rid of the thralldom of sin and of the power of Satan more easily, more naturally than they used to do. It is said the changed aspect of the spiritual condition is to be accounted for very rationally by the change in the times, the advance of intelligence, the dissemination of religious knowledge, and the increased aptitude of the soul and its surroundings for God. We are sure there is not a seeming difference between these times and the former, but a real difference. Conviction for sin is not as radical as it used to be. Sorrow for sin is neither so evident nor as powerfully existent as in former days. We do not believe this change is well accounted for on natural grounds. Whatever change of time or condition there may be, these cannot and do not in the least change spiritual operations. These cannot alter the eternal and immutable nature of sin, or of God. When the soul starts to God it enters into a realm upon which the passing current of the times has no effect, over which the fashion of the times has no sway. The same sense of guilt, the same distressing, and loathsome sorrow for sin are inexorably demanded of this age as of the former ages. There is no royal road to Heaven unmarked by the pain and struggle of repentance. A sense of guilt with its attendant sorrow is the heritage of every child of grace. It is not possible that the increased light and the increased opportunities of this day should lessen sin guiltiness, or the consciousness of it. Rather they increase our guilt, and should increase the sense of that guilt.

SIN CONVICTING POWER OF THE HOLY GHOST

There is but one true explanation to this whole matter, and that is the lack of the Holy Ghost in the full measure of grace bestowing His power and presence. The Holy Ghost is the sin convicting power of the Christian system. His office is to convict the world of sin. The Word preached without His presence only deadens a sense of sin. The Word is His sword. He handles it. The cutting that the Word does is done by the Spirit. His presence on the Day of Pentecost pierced the hardest hearts and made them cry out under the most painful and despairing sense of guilt. It is right at this point where we fail.

Whatever defects and disadvantages from many standpoints belonged to our fathers and to their times, they had two elements that invited the presence of the Holy Ghost in mighty grace; their times were simple times and their people were mighty in prayer. These fathers, many of them, had been mightily endued by the Spirit. They had an experience of His fullness and power and presence, which seems strange to us. Many of them could tell the hour when He came on them; not only in converting power, but as a distinctly increased and mighty witnessing aggressive force so elevating, enlarging, and empowering, that it seemed like a new factor in their lives, a new Heaven, a diviner and fuller force than they had felt.

REVEREND WILBUR FISK

As Wilbur Fisk, the great educator and powerful preacher said when he submitted to God in total availability, "I wept a few moments, I trembled, I fell, I sung, I shouted, and me thinks the spectators must have thought me filled with new wine." Ever after that he could say, "The Spirit of the Lord God is upon me," and his preaching was henceforth not with enticing words of man's wisdom, but in demonstration of the Spirit and power. It is the lack of this divine convicting power on the preacher and in the Church that has eased the sinner's conscience, and substituted so many other forces for the Holy Ghost. This lack has induced the change that is so evident and which has reduced spiritual operations to their minimum.

REVEREND JOHN WESLEY

Mr. Wesley records over and over again how the spirituality of the great Church movement was kept at flood tide. They did not leave the movement to its original spiritual momentum, but they met together and sought God in a concert of prayer and sought Him all night, till their own hearts were totally available to God and in submission to the Holy Ghost. As John Wesley, Charles Whitefield and others were seeking in prayer about 3 o'clock in the morning, the power of God came mightily on them so that many fell to the ground, and many cried out with exceeding joy, and the awe and solemnity of God's presence were answered by rapturous praises from their overflowing hearts. On another occasion Wesley records: "God was gloriously present. After midnight about a hundred of us walked home together, singing and rejoicing and praising God."

This is the way the leaders of the Church maintained the profundity and power of spiritual manifestations. And the same depth, intensity, and expression of desire after God would bring to us as full and rich spiritual manifestations, from the first sigh of penitence to the rapture of the new born soul. The entire process, its dependence and results, are portrayed by the prophet Isaiah in his delineation of Christ's mission. The statement is a descriptive and luminous expose of the truth we are emphasizing. The prophet declares:

> *The Spirit of the LORD God is upon me; because the LORD hath anointed me to preach good tidings unto the meek; He hath sent me to bind up the brokenhearted, to proclaim liberty to the captives, and the opening of the prison to them that are bound; to proclaim the acceptable year of the LORD, and the day of vengeance of our God; to comfort all that mourn; to appoint unto them that mourn in Zion, to give unto them beauty*

for ashes, the oil of joy for mourning, the garment of praise for the spirit of heaviness; that they might be called trees of righteousness, the planting of the LORD, that He be might be glorified. (Isaiah 61:1-3)

ANOINTING OF THE HOLY GHOST

If the anointing of the Holy Ghost is on the preacher and on his church, the mourners with their broken hearts, the rapture and praise of pardon with all the full vigor of expression of feeling and of life will be here with their marvelous results. All these opulent, heartbreaking, and joyous results flow from the basic statement, *"The Spirit of the Lord God is upon me."* Conviction for sin is a fundamental principle, and the bitterness and mourning which flow from it and by whose throes repentance is wrought, are not capricious effects dependent on the times, the calendar, or the thermometer, but are dependent solely upon the power of the Holy Ghost present on the preacher, on the church, in the word, and on the heart of the sinner. Christ put poverty of spirit and mourning as the first and second great principles wrought by the Spirit. He put the publican with his troubled and grief smitten heart, with his sharp and tearful prayer, as the impersonation of the true penitent for all times, for all conditions, and for all countries. The prayerlessness, the lightness, the frivolity of many so called revivals, are the very elements that quench the fire of God's Spirit and retire His presence, so keenly sensitive to conditions.

DRAWING NIGH TO GOD

The Church should make serious business of seeking God in the fullness of His Spirit, as the Apostle James charges us with startling, earnest emphasis:

Draw nigh to God, and He will draw nigh to you. Cleanse your hands, ye sinners; and purify your hearts,

167

ye double minded. Be afflicted, and mourn, and weep;
let your laughter be turned to mourning, and your joy
to heaviness. Humble yourselves in the sight of the
Lord, and He shall lift you up. (James 4:8-10)

If we will humble ourselves thus, we will see troubled
consciences, broken hearts, and all the sorrowful adjuncts of
confession and prayer crowding to and filling our altars. If
the ministry and Church will seek God till a new outpouring
is with us, then the unconverted will be smitten as of old, and
fall down and confess truthfully that God is with us. Then we
will not have to resort to the arguments of unbelief to satisfy
our consciences and justify our conduct and failure, but will
see the pulpit empowered, the Church drawing sinners to God,
all filled with power and praise.

DECAY OF REVERENCE
Hindrances to Reverence
January 2, 1692

LACK OF REVERENCE

The Reverend Price Hughes wrote an article on "Reverence
in Public Worship." He gave two reasons for the lack of
reverence. The first is revulsion from the grossly superstitious
formalism of the medieval ages. This is going too far in all
kinds of distances to find a solution for an evil that lies close
at hand. Recoil against an evil must take place in times and
conditions that one is familiar with. The knowledge we have
of those times is too bookish and too strange to us to affect
this present age so seriously. "Our Democratic era with its
detestation of shams and wind bags" is the second reason Mr.
Hughes gave for the flippancy of our worship. He said:

Our danger is not superstition, but flippancy; and there is very little fear indeed of our attaching undue importance to the outward forms of reverence. How shocking it is to loll about in our pews when we profess to be praying to God and when, no doubt in many instances, we are praying! How desirable it is that everyone should be punctually in his place at the commencement of public worship, and the singing, the reading of the Word of God, the announcing of the notices, the making of the collections, and everything else should be done decently and in order.

As the remedy for the evil he suggests "the use of a liturgy at the Sunday morning service."

We are assured by indisputable accounts of observation and experience that this is an age of irreverence. We are in danger of losing all the sacred and profound elements of a divine worship. But we cannot lay the charge of our sins in this respect to those who were struggling amid the errors and darkness of centuries ago. We do not believe either the solution of this condition of things lies in the advancing purity of our politics. Pure democracy is a ruinous thing if in trying to destroy shams and humbugs it tears down in its lack of discrimination and reverence everything sacred. We do not believe a better era in politics has conditioned this state. It is a religious decay, and that cannot be called a political advance which works a religious decay.

CAUSES FOR THE DECAY OF REVERENCE

There are many causes for the decay of reverence. Among the most prominent is the method which prevails in many pulpits and with many gifted preachers of mixing politics, social and religious questions, and treating them with equal importance. That is elevating political and social questions to the sanctity and authority of the things of revelation and bringing down the things of revelation to the level of political and social questions. We do not detract from the importance of social and political questions. We would not arrest their fullest discussion. Some of them are burning questions, which appeal to the patriot, the philanthropist, and the man. But reverence is an attitude of the soul toward God. It pertains to thought, to faith, to meditation on the character and nature of the unseen and eternal things. Reverence cannot be secured by political or social questions, however important, however interesting, however profoundly they may agitate or arouse, vital as they may be to good government, to all worldly economics, they concern the present state only, and can be engaged in by Jew or infidel, Mohammedan or Christian, with the same zest.

PANTHEISM

We think this the serious mistake made by the gifted editor regarding the "Forward Movement." His sermons are mixtures of social questions, politics, and religion, and this mixture wherever found will vitiate reverence. It will not do to say these are religious questions; they are not religious, and to make them so is to confuse all distinctions and create a spiritual pantheism that subverts and destroys religion. That religion when vigorous and properly asserted will affect all questions social and political is true, but that is quite a different thing from making all these questions religious ones. Pantheism does not deny the existence of God, but makes Him the inspirer of all things, and elevates these things that God inspires, and thereby destroys His personality and being. To make all these social and political questions religious ones is to break down all distinctions and destroy religion and its effects. One of the inevitable effects of religion is to beget worship of which the component parts are adoration, reverence, humility, and awe; and this worship never can be secured but by the deliverance of the weighty and solemn truths of God's word, by a man filled with the Holy Ghost, and to a congregation filled with the same thoughtful, serious and prayerful spirit.

The discussion by a talented man of social and political questions appealing to the people, their interest, to their prejudice or party, will beget an enthusiasm and awaken responses. But these are essentially different and belong to departments which are separated as distinctly and widely as the things of Heaven and the things of God are separated from the things of Earth and the things of self. Mr. Hughes assisted at the opening of the New City Road Chapel in London, famous as Wesley's Foundation Church. "The report of that occasion," says Mr. Hughes, "was received with long continued outbursts of applause." A paper commenting on the occasion, says:

> But a more uncomfortable feeling has been excited by the fact at various points of the opening sermon there was applause, excited by the telling passages of the discourse. The old time "amen's" and "glory's" which were formerly heard in the Church sanctuaries were sometimes boisterous, but they were appropriate as outbursts of quickened feeling and were spontaneous responses to the tremendous earnestness of the men in the pulpit. But it is a token of degeneracy, clear and unmistakable, from religious feeling, though somewhat noisily expressed, when for such manifestations the applauses of political meetings, and of dashing lectures is substituted.

THE UNMIXED GOSPEL VERSUS THE HIGHLY SEASONED MIXED GOSPEL

Give us the unmixed gospel and all the prayerful, reverential elements of worship; and they will be secured and manifested with solid spiritual gravity. Give us a highly seasoned mixture of the questions of the times and we will have the cheers and applause of the pleased and prayerless excited partisan. We have suffered much in this country from mixing questions so essentially different. The pulpit, consecrated to the great revealed principles of religion, has dealt with the popular themes until many good people cannot tell the difference between social, political and religious questions, but all are of equal authority to them, and they will after awhile be equally indifferent to all. Our "Ecclesiastical Politics" and "Irreverence in Public Worship" are the legitimate outcome of this popular but unwise and impious blending of things heavenly and earthly.

We do not have space to refer to other causes. Immature and flippant leaders, novices in piety and age, have been thrust forward to lead and train in spiritual matters. The gospel of fun has filled the pulpit with witty, smart sayings and filled the pew with frivolity and prayerlessness. The Church organization and the Church house have been used to get up all kinds of entertainments, the very things that destroy reverence, especially when they come in the guise of churchly affairs, under the direction of the Church and in the place set apart for holy uses. The pulpit, giving out politics and social questions, the Church audience responding by rounds of applause, the Church organization devoting itself to Church theatricals and things for the flesh, the Church house profaned by these entertainments, and the spiritual life trained by flippant novitiates.

THE SOLUTION: RESURRECTION POWER

These are some of the essential causes of the decay of reverence in worship. A liturgy, as suggested by Mr. Hughes, will only embalm and proudly coffin us. We hope and pray the Church is not hunting for an undertaker and providing for a costly funeral. We need resurrection power, and this a liturgy can never give us.

A LESSON FROM ELI
Family and Personal Christian Growth
January 14, 1892

TWO GREAT FUNDAMENTAL PRINCIPLES

The Bible makes prominent the fact God and men are partners in working out the spiritual good of men. It brings out most distinctly the failures that have brought disaster and sorrow on individuals or on nations that have been caused by the lack of fidelity on man's part in discharging the duties imposed by this partnership. These two great fundamental principles find their illustration more fully perhaps in the history of the Hebrew people than elsewhere. The Old Testament Scriptures are written for our instruction in this regard, and this history, instead of being obsolete, is receiving constant attestations of its truth and being daily reproduced in its facts. Never will the race of man get away from the principles taught and exemplified by Jewish patriarch and prophet.

ELI

One of these lessons for all times is found in the life of Eli, one of the priestly judges of Israel. Eli seems to have met his public trust with fidelity. We find no charges against his official integrity. His judgeship was pure, if a man is to be accounted pure who executes public trust with honesty, and yet fails to meet important and sacred private trusts. No fault is alleged in his sacred functions as priest; he devoted himself to the temple duties. His solicitude for the Ark of God and his sorrow at its capture cost him his life. God marked his early career, his purity, and consecration with approval, with a promise of honor to him and his posterity.

ELI'S FAMILY

Eli had a family. He was a father as well as a priest and a judge. In the narrower but not less responsible or sacred sphere of his family Eli failed. Govern the State he did, govern the Church he could, but govern his family he did not. The causes of this failure, the home secrets, are not given, but the fact he was responsible for the government of his sons and did not govern them is stated as his crime. Some of the milder functions of family government he exercised; easy tempered opposition, and weakly passionate reproofs. But these mild tempered or hasty reproofs were not enough. His duty was to apply the severest penalties until his sons yielded to the restraints of rightness of the law or suffered the rigor of its penalties. The charge that God brings against him is *"his sons made themselves vile and he restrained them not"* (1 Samuel 3:13). He failed at the very point of vital importance, the home life; and failure there debauched the Church and State. Politics and piety share in the laxness of the home rule. His strength and fidelity as judge and priest cannot save either Church or State from the disaster of the failure to govern in his home. In a most important manner Israel's home life made Israel's Church and State life. It is always so; neither politics nor religion can be pure or flourish when the family government is loose.

ELI'S LIFE WAS FAULTLESS BEFORE HIS SONS, BUT...

Eli did not teach his sons vice. His example was faultless, his precepts pure; but precept and example are not enough to restrain and cure the depraved impulses of the young. Children must be brought up in the nurture and admonition of the Lord, and in these terms are included all the salutary training and penalties which are absolutely necessary to order and government. Eli by parental weakness changed the good purposes of God toward his family, affected to a ruinous extent the interests of religion, and enslaved and desolated his country. The original purpose of God toward Eli and the reason of God's change are stated thus:

Wherefore the LORD *God of Israel saith, I said, indeed thy house and the house of thy father should walk before me forever, but now the* LORD *saith, Be it far from me, for them that honor me I will honor, and they that despise me shall be lightly esteemed.* (1 Samuel 2:30)

FAILURE TO GOVERN THE FAMILY DISHONORS GOD

God was dishonored because Eli did not govern his boys; religion was corrupted because Eli did not correct his sons. Sin was greatly strengthened and Eli's closing days covered with sorrow and shame from the same prolific source of evil. Eli lived the life of a faithful priest, and died a martyr to his fidelity to his priestly office, but these did not atone for his guilt in neglecting to govern his family. Neither official integrity nor personal piety could prevent the dire results of the failure to rule his house for God. The luster of official purity was stained in the neglect of the duties which the cradle and the fireside demanded of him.

The pretentious learning and lack of faith of this and other times may sneer at the divinity of these Hebrew books that record these lessons, but the wisdom of any age holy enough to accept the lessons will prove their divinity by the practical test. On the other hand, the spiritual weakness and sin prevailing in the times which did regard these lessons are the best arguments for their divinity.

APPLICATION FOR TODAY

This age needs the lesson taught in the life of this Hebrew priest and judge. Spiritual officialty and the intensive importance of social and political questions are so absorbing as to lead to the neglect of the less obtrusive but not less important interests that gather about our firesides.

A false democracy and a false spirituality have loosened our hold on the family. In the richness and parade of our church altars we have neglected the home altars. In this looseness, piety, order, and politics, all suffer. Even our wives and mothers have caught the vicious contagion, and are rushing away from the cradle and the home to curb the unbridled waves of social and political evil; forgetting that at home they have these lawless floods as little ills to be shaped by the hands that have the patience and wisdom to do it. In our restless eagerness and pride we forget the hands that rock the cradle rule the world. We are very anxious to rule the world, but are too proud to do it by rocking the cradle. Eli would have done better for religion and the state by training his boys with a firm, and wise hand, and punishing them as they had need, than he accomplished by his long priesthood and judgeship. The benefits of his official integrity were swallowed up even before his death by his lack of restraining and ruling force at home.

LESSON FOR THIS AGE AND ALL AGES

The lesson for this age and all ages to learn is that to rear a righteous family of children is the best thing a man can do for himself, for his country, and for the Church. No good he can possibly do can atone for or avert the evil that he does to himself, to the State, and to religion, by rearing an unrighteous family.

THE SOCIAL VERSUS THE SPIRITUAL
Spiritual Decline
November 10, 1892

ONE CAUSE OF THE SPIRITUAL DECLINE
IN THE CHURCH

One great cause of spiritual decline in the Church is the substitution of natural forces for spiritual ones. The Spirit of God creates and quickens the forces that impel the Church of God. It is not some conspicuous, natural force combined with the Spirit, but solely the Spirit. We begin with the Spirit, continue in the Spirit and end with the Spirit. At no point, either beginning, continuing, or ending, do we call in the aid of the flesh. It is not because natural forces are sinful, but because they cannot secure spiritual ends.

We might spend our mealtimes in the innocent pastime of whistling instead of eating. The diversion might be entertaining, but the body would soon perish because of the pleasant but vicious substitution. The Church of God must have unity, but this unity does not spring from the coherence of natural forces. Many natural and even unholy forces may give unity to a church, and this unity will answer many ends and have the semblance at many points of the unity of the Spirit. But it will be as different as can be explained with light and darkness, as far removed from it as Heaven is from hell. The Spirit of God, when filling the hearts of God's people, creates a oneness, a tender, unselfish, loving brotherhood, which knits them together more strongly than blood or kinship. This unity breaks down every wall of separation and makes them *"of one heart and of one soul"* (Acts 4:32).

SUBSTITUTION OF SOCIAL FORCES
FOR SPIRITUAL ONES

One of the evils now imperiling the spiritual strength and life of the Church is the substitution of social forces for spiritual ones. These social forces are very popular; they accord with unregenerate tastes, they have to the world none of the odium of a self-denying piety. They beget an interest in church matters, an acquaintance with church folks, and an introduction into fashionable church life. They attract the young to the entertainments of the church and put them in the circle of churchly influence and into connection with church organizations; but all these things can be done without a touch of God's spirit. These social forces, while bearing to the unspiritual eye some resemblance to the spiritual have no affinities for the spiritual, only antagonisms. Spiritual forces are the product of the Holy Ghost in a regenerate heart, binding in a holy brotherhood against sin and for Heaven and issue in all holy and reverent graces.

The social forces are pleasure giving, often light and dissipating. There is nothing distinctly religious about them. Faith is in no way necessary to them; prayer does not burden their thoughts. The sinner enjoys them with a richer relish than the saint. The east wind with its noxious vapors will spread health with a rosier tint than will the social forces spread holiness. They are training schools of the non-devout, for self-indulgence and not for religion. True church agencies are channels for grace, conduits for faith, holiness, prayer, praise and heavenly mindedness. The Holy Ghost does not honor these social methods as conductors for eternal life. We never seek His aid to get up a lawn party or for success at an ice cream festival, nor do these things fail for the lack of faith; they have no connection with it. Faith and entertainment are at opposites.

SOCIAL LIFE CANNOT BE A TRUE BASIS
OF CHURCH UNITY

The social life, which is natural or worldly, is not the true basis of Church unity. Its bond of agreeableness does not enter into the domains of the Spirit. Lively talk, social chat, the pleasant intermingling of the sexes, the relish for ice cream, or tableaux, are not in the line of the spiritual, their natural, and when these enter largely into the life of the Church the distinctly spiritual forces are disrelished and retired. These things attract the unregenerate or half-hearted Christian, but they can never be means of grace. They displace God's established means of grace, and the church that adopts this sacrilegious usurpation is entirely cut off from the golden pipes through which the golden oil flows to the soul.

To such a church, without a thorough turning away, a thorough work of God is an impossibility. Its life is far below the regions of divine operations. Its hands are preoccupied, and its spirit possessed by a whole range of work and activities outside the province of the Spirit. The hearts of the members are not in tune for spiritual harmonies. A burning desire for the increased revelation of God, which must be the absorbing idea of God's Church, has for these socially-immersed church people no attraction but is a stupid indifference or an absolute distaste. A revival would run counter to their habitudes, destroy their occupations, and interfere with their indulgence and tastes. They could no more join themselves to the joyous work for God than they could join themselves on to Mars. A deep work of God would be as much out of place in such a church as it would be in a clubroom.

Churches in which the social prevails can never be centers of spiritual power. They may increase the number of showy organizations. They may make their churches the centers of churchly activities, they may stir young blood and flush it by vivacity or vanity; such churches may be of pleasant entertainments, imposing exhibitions, elegant luncheons, and feature programs of fashion or finance. But they can never be centers of spiritual power where holiness and the fear of Heaven is cherished in a real exultant way, or where self is denied and the world crucified, nor headquarters for great spiritual movements. The social, the light, the enjoyable, have been emphasized and cultivated till the spiritual is swamped.

SOCIETIES IN THE SOCIAL CHURCH

The societies based on social principles in many a church are far more numerous and popular than the spiritual ones. The church parlor and the kitchen, the symbols of self-indulgence and social cheer, have displaced or overshadowed the class and prayer meetings or reduced them to their own level. The love feast is a thing of the past, and fasting is voted to be pagan. The very atmosphere of such a church is repressive of holiness; the air is more congenial to flippancy and devoted to materialism and carnality than to the serious interests of eternity. The surroundings are as unfriendly to the sigh of penitence or the throes and triumphs of faith as Polar Regions are to tropical fruits and flowers. If the preacher is not tainted, or if his spiritual nerves are not softened, the air chills his utterances and they are stillborn, fall into vacancy or hit against adamant minds. The preacher is powerless. The church is disarmed, her militant attitude destroyed; an enforced, unholy truce is declared, and a weak, timid, conservatism cuts her sinews and binds her arms. She has declined from her elevated position. Her light becomes darkness, which bewilders and betrays. She has neither face nor heart to fight the world, whose principles she has espoused, whose dress she has adopted, and whose spirit she has imbibed.

THE WORLD'S ALTAR IN THE TEMPLE OF GOD

The world has erected its altar in the Temple of God. Defend or apologize for the social church as we may, it has entered into the Church of God. It did enter at the instance of deep piety, not by inspired prayer. It did not enter as the fruit of the Spirit, but as a cloak and substitute for spiritual failure, worldly compromise, governed by worldly principles, and directed in the main by prayerless hands, nourished by worldly tastes. Social churches debauch worship to entertainment, destroy reverence, banish prayer, and fill the house of God with the buzz and frivolity of gossip. They make devoutness impossible, turn the church into a theater, opera, or picnic, and efface every reverent and devout grace.

FAIRS, FESTIVALS, AND PARTIES

The fair and festival, parties for pleasure, for eating, for courting, must be eliminated from the church. The church kitchen and the church parlor must go, or the revival goes. We cannot regain our spiritual altitude and energy while we are flooded by the social. Young people are the ones who are damaged and deluded by this imposition. They need neither training in social cheer nor schooling in pleasurable indulgences. They need restraint rather than laxness and help in that line. Sobriety and not indulgence is the virtue they are to learn by many a hard lesson and under many a severe teacher. The young trained into church habits by social methods will not only be lacking in spiritual knowledge of the conflicts, victories, and conscious experience of God's power, which is the glory of Christianity, but we will rear a generation to whose tastes such an experience will be exceedingly offensive. We are told the young people cannot be attracted and held without this worldly alliance. This only shows our ignorance and unbelief.

181

A CHURCH FOUNDED ON FAITH

Spiritual affinities are the mightiest, sweetest, and most powerfully attractive of all affinities. Gravitation scarcely draws and holds in sphere and harmony the worlds than do genuine spiritual forces chain and hold the young soul intent on immortality and eternal life. A church founded on faith, lustrous with holiness, glowing with love, cemented and ribbed with divine fellowship, filling the air with the fragrance of its gentle and flowering graces, draws young hearts as the pole draws the needle, and allures and holds them like the city walled with jewels. The young are embosomed and cherished by its influence; they cry for and cling to it as the babe to its mother's breast. Primitive Christianity held its young people without these worldly devices, despite the dungeon, the stake, and the wild beasts. The Primitive Church relied wholly on spiritual ties, and it bound its young people to it with cords of steel in the face of sneers, ostracism, persecutions, and the seductions and bribes of the world.

ARRESTED DEVELOPMENT
Personal Christian Growth
February 2, 1893

PERSONAL PIETY

Personal piety must grow. It must grow more and more. It must grow exceedingly. Its stages of advance must be marked, transitional, and transforming. There is much controversy about the manner of growing. We spend all our time in disputing as to which fork of the road we must take, and fail to take either. The getting there is the thing. It is better to get there by a wrong road than not to get there at all.

When Paul sounded his clarion call, *"Let us go on unto perfection"* (Hebrews 6:1), he was seeking to arouse a Church that had lost immensely the vigor and manliness of Christian character by feeding on milk and indulging in the lazy luxury of being children. He raises a standard, and marks a point for them to gain. The point is far ahead, but a real point, as real as the point at which their steps had been stayed by a ruinous stay. Paul calls them out of the cradle and away from the nursery to the strength, conflicts, and perfection of a royal manhood. The eulogy on Wesley by a great writer of being "the first of theological statesmen," pays him no high compliment; but his spiritual perception, the man of open, divine vision is his highest eulogy. This is evidenced by the fact he reechoed the trumpet call of Paul and sought to stir a forward movement into the Church, and quicken its members to seek an advanced position, which had not only dropped out of their experience, but out of their hopes and creeds.

BEGINNINGS ARE BEGINNINGS ONLY

God gives religion in its beginnings and these beginnings are glorious; but to be content with the beginnings of religion is to forfeit not only its possibilities, but its beginnings. Additions to our spiritual capital are the conditions of solvency, and of the retaining the capital as well. To stand still in religion is to lose it. To enter into camp at regeneration is to forfeit regenerating grace. To stop at any other transitional advance station is to go backward. The weakness of men is inconstancy to a great aim. The drafts of a long and exhaustive spiritual strain are intolerable. We are willing to pay the cost of nerves for a great temporal success, but the price is too dear for religious success. The tendency in religion is to be satisfied with rudiments and to die in infancy. Teething time is a perilous time for spiritual babes. The great sin of the Israelites was hugging the shores and not going up to possess the land. The marvelous glory of their entrance into Canaan paled in the lethargy and timidity of their after advance.

SPIRITUAL ARREST

Spiritual arrest is not confined, though, to the initial steps. Life-blood may chill and its step halt at the point of highest advance. Many Christians are so enthusiastic over some marked advance, some higher elevation gained, they become enchanted with the beautiful and lofty regions and are lulled to sleep, and like Bunyan's Pilgrim, suffer their loss. Instead of pressing on with tireless steps, they but cover the future with their imaginations, and while their fancies are filled with the rich colorings of their advanced position, their feet have declined and are in the vale again. They are so happy it is almost impossible to bring them to their senses and make them understand there is many a weary and toilsome step between their Red Sea deliverance and the Promised Land. Even after the desert is crossed and the Jordan divided, and the sanctified soil of Canaan pressed by sanctified feet, there is many a battle to be fought and many an enemy to be destroyed before the goodly land is all possessed. A singing and shouting sanctification is good, but if it is not joined with a marching and fighting sanctification it will sing and shout itself as thin as a ghost and as dry as a shuck. *"Forgetting those things which are behind and reaching forth to those that are before"* (Philippians 3:13) is the divine process to hold what we have by getting more. Paul's marvelous career was simple, not complex. He sums it up: fighting, running, and watching, are the three elements of continuous advance. Many a great battle has been lost by the demoralizing effects of the halt caused by a partial victory in the earlier part of the conflict. It is no easy matter to keep place and march in rank when the spoils of a half-gained victory cover the ground. There is no position this side of Heaven free from the dangers of spiritual arrest.

CONFLICT AND VIGILANCE

The conflict and vigilance of advance must mark every step till our feet are within the pearly gates. It would be well for us if spiritual arrest belonged only to the higher regions of spiritual advance. While not a few, doubtless, of those who have received a great spiritual baptism after the grace of conversion, have crystallized around this point of advance; yet the far greater number of our people and preachers have crystallized around the initials of grace. We may have some specimens of Christian mummies who in size approach to maturity, but the number of the dwarfed and cradled ones are legion.

There are doubtless cases of spiritual arrest resulting from magnifying the gifts and grace of sanctification in a way which magnifies the work of regeneration. This is what the Apostle terms spiritual pride, independence and schism, the head saying to the foot, "I have no need of thee;" but within our observation, in the trend of Church thought, deliverance and experience, the popular if not the main cause of spiritual arrest is found in magnifying regeneration, enlarging it beyond the teachings of Scripture and experience until its distorted enlargement does away with the necessities of any further advance. From many sources the erroneous declaration or the most damaging impression is made as gospel truth that the advanced stages to which our fathers arrived only by toilsome and struggling approaches, fighting and praying and reaching out under the mastery of a mighty faith. To belittle the grace of regeneration in the interests of any advanced stage of the Christian life is a dangerous and reprehensible error. No folly is more fatal than this save the folly which magnifies regeneration until it covers the whole realm; this is to stretch regeneration until it is thin as water and tasteless as a wafer.

SANCTIFICATION

To magnify sanctification to the detriment of regeneration is the folly of the scholar who in the pride of his advance defames the alphabet, which has been the foundation and ladder to every step of that advance. To discount or destroy sanctification by exaggerating regeneration is the scholar who to his folly and pride adds stupidity and ignorance by declaring that the alphabet is the sum and perfection of all learning. It is true Paul calls the Corinthian saints baby saints, but this was the point where their sainthood turned back to carnality and lost its fragrance, sanctity, and strength. Their great sin and backsliding were found in their babyhood, not that they began as babes, but that they stayed babes. Baby sainthood is the popular sainthood of these days. To begin as babes is well, but to remain babes for forty years is a fearful deformity.

CAUSES OF SPIRITUAL ARREST

One cause of spiritual arrest is ignorance of the nature of love. Love has in it the possibilities of a present perfection and of an endless increase in capacity and volume. The baby's love may be perfect in baby sweetness and baby strength, but perfect baby love is not to be compared in volume, ardor, or strength, to the love of mature years which has "grown with the growth and strengthened with the strength."

Another cause of spiritual arrest is the losing sight of the exhaustless riches which are in Christ Jesus for us. To think we have received all of His fullness at conversion is the mistake of one who fancies one drink has emptied the ocean, and the mistake of the Pilgrim Fathers that they had pierced and possessed the continent. Our people must be taught the nature of love, not that strange and erroneous hyper-Calvinistic idea God is at work trying to perfect His love toward us, and then we will by some kind of mystery count it for perfection to us, but that our love to Him is to be made perfect, and to be kept perfect as our strength increases and vision enlarges. We are to love God with all the heart and with all the understanding and with all the soul and with all the strength and love our neighbor as ourselves; and this is to be done when our spiritual capacities are small and the volume feeble, and it is to be done with exhausted comprehension at every step of advance and enlargement.

THE PROGRESS OF PERFECTION

Our people must be taught and urged explicitly to this perfection in all the stages of its progress. We must call them to perfection like that to which Paul and John Wesley called their followers: a perfection in holiness, the perfection of love; a perfection not ideal nor visionary, but real, practical, possible, absolutely necessary. A perfection of love expelling fear and sin, filling the heart and governing the life, its motto, "hard after God; filled with all the fullness of God." The spiritual life will be arrested, the world will riot, stagnation and death will ensue if our Church people are not strongly and explicitly exhorted to go on to perfection by leaders who have gained this blessed point or who are on the stretch for and groaning after it.

THE PRESENT EVIL WORLD
Worldliness
March 9, 1893

There is in the very nature of things an antagonism between the world and the religion of Christ. Few things are as sadly suggestive and impressive as the way the world treated Christ, the world in the Church at that. An eminent man remarked: "If virtue were to appear to the world in human form, all men would fall down and worship it." His companion answered: "Virtue did come into the world, and men crucified Him."

Christ declares to His disciples in the world they "shall have tribulation." He forewarns them of their relation to the world: *"If the world hate you, ye know that it hated me before it hated you. If ye were of the world, the world would love his own; but because ye are not of the world, but I have chosen you out of the world, therefore the world hateth you"* (John 15:18-19).

In His prayer, His statement to the Father sets forth the relation of hatred between the world and His disciples, a statement which is for all time and for all disciples: *"I have given them thy word; and the world hath hated them, because they are not of the world, even as I am not of the world"* (John 17:14).

APOSTASY OF THE CHURCH

The apostasy of the Church always begins when it fails to recognize and act on the eternal war between it and the world. Under the alluring dazzle of the world's seductions the Church has ever been trying to escape the sharp conflict by toning down the words of the Lord.

When times of secular prosperity, wealth, culture, taste, and social position flow into the Church, these are the times of her greatest peril from the world. When the Church ceases to offend the world she ceases to please Christ. Loyalty to Christ secures by an inviolate spiritual law, the hatred of the world. The trueness of the Church to Christ may be readily understood by the attitude of the world to her.

The late Dr. Mendenhall, editor of the *Methodist Review*, commented on this subject before his death. He said:

Worldliness has ever been one of the great banes of piety since the fall of man; but the growth of the race and the closer contact of mankind in the rapid communication among civilized and particularly Christian countries have intensified greed and ambition until selfishness prevails to an extent that threatens to extinguish the of principles of scriptural religion.

These are true words. *The New York Observer* says of the world:

We believe it must be regarded as the prominent hindrance to the work of Christ on Earth. The world was never more alluring than now; but with all its comforts and luxuries, with all its attractions and allurements, it is still to be described as "this present evil world," present in the sense of transitory, not eternal or enduring, and evil in its tendencies, its downward course and its final doom. The world of inspiration says in tones of deepest solemnity: *Love not the world, neither the things that are in the world. If any man love the world, the love of the Father is not in him. For all that is in the world, the lust of the flesh, and the lust of the eyes and the pride of life, is not of the Father, but is of the world; and the world passeth away, and the lust thereof* (1 John 2:15-17). The spirit of the world is the same as it was when these inspired words were penned. The gilded outside may gleam more brightly than ever, but the principles within are as bitterly opposed to Christ as ever. The call to the people of God is more emphatic than ever to come out and be separate.

This sterling Presbyterian paper is being cured of its delusive and unsoldierly optimism, and had put on its armor and unsheathed its sword. Its eyes being wide open its calls for self-examination into heart and life against this all-powerful and all seducing foe, the world in us, and in the Church through us.

THE MODEL STEWARD
Growth in Stewardship
April 6, 1893

COMPARISON OF THE GOOD AND BAD STEWARD

The steward is an important member of the Church economy. The well-being and harmonious movement of the system is to some extent dependent on his fidelity. The condition of his church, its unity, efficiency and liberality, results from his example and efforts. The preacher comes and goes, but the steward never itinerates; he is fixed and around him the center of the itinerancy revolves. He welcomes the new preacher, holds up his hands during his pastorate, and sends him to other fields free from financial stress and strengthened in heart and hands. A good steward is without price. A bad one is a nuisance and a sin. The model steward is to be met with much appreciation and their model work is their highest praise. The signs of spiritual thrift are seen on every hand. An inefficient steward is worse than an incubus; he not only hinders the good, but educates in evil. By his neglect the preacher suffers in purse and honor and the church suffers with him; the grace of giving and with it all other graces, are arrested and church affairs have the air of looseness. The steward gives character to his church, the grace of giving being a chief one; the church which habitually falls behind in that will be behind in other things.

THE MODEL STEWARD

The model steward must be a Christian in deed and in truth, inside and out. One who loves the Church; is jealous for its honor; most sensitive to everything that concerns its welfare; one who is devoted to its economy, familiar with its doctrines, careful of its discipline. A Christian by conviction and if to conviction there are added education, heredity and tradition, it will be well. Men listless in their devotion to Christianity, ignorant of its doctrines, history and essential features, untrue to its discipline, should not be put into the office of steward. Their relations and functions are not wholly financial, and if they were there is much in thorough loyalty in strong convictions, in ardent devotion to secure success in church finances as in other departments of church effort.

While devotion to Christ is first, and must always be so much so as to have no other first, but devotion to Christ works through the agency of devotion to a particular denomination. It is an orbit limited to and shining in its fixed sphere. A churchman may be a poor Christian, but it would be an anomaly to find a Christian in the Church in official relation who was not devoted. The model steward, a Christian in warp and woof, must add to this deep spirituality, that is, his piety must be "solid" as the discipline enjoins. Religion in the steward must take no second place. To estimate financial ability as the first, and religion as a secondary matter, is to degrade the office.

When the apostles saw the necessity of separating the secular from the higher spiritual work of the Church they did not propose to relegate the matter to secular or indifferent men, to men of finance or influence merely; but they weighed the matter and the men they sought out were men of high character, *"of honest report, full of the Holy Ghost and wisdom"* (Acts 6:5). Stephen, the first martyr, is an illustration of how deeply spiritual the men consecrated to the temporal affairs ought to

191

be. The more truly spiritual a steward, the better suited he is to his work. The tendency is to allow these offices to be lowered by the spiritual degeneracy of the men who fill them. Devoted as the steward's office is at many points to the secular, his spirituality is the more important, that by his spirituality he may spiritualize the secular, thereby not allowing the secular its full sway in the perfection of church effort.

THE MODEL STEWARD KNOWS THE PEOPLE

The model steward knows his people and their two main points, financial ability and willingness. By all legitimate methods he seeks to enlarge their willingness until it becomes cheerful, liberal, generous giving that keeps pace with increased ability. The model steward keeps his church fully informed as to the demands on them, and the receipts and disbursements. Ignorance is the parent of many things besides superstition. Hosea 4:6, *"God's people perish for lack of knowledge,"* is a truth as applicable to finance as anywhere else. Information often surprises as to the situation the church was not aware of. Information quickens conscience, awakens sympathy, and arouses to prompt and liberal response.

PUNCTUAL AND CONSCIENTIOUS

The model steward is always conscientious and punctual in attendance at the official meetings. With the model steward church duties are first, private interests subordinate. He has a zeal for duty that leads to sacrifice. His office, its duties, and the honor of his church engage him. He is concerned his church should pay its debts and meet to the full its obligations as honestly as he meets his personal obligations. He has conscience about paying what they have agreed to pay, while on the part of his self-denying pastor there is no suspicion that with him it is hire and salary. Yet, this is even more reason why the church should respond faithfully to the last cent of its promise and even beyond the mere letter. As nature is said to abhor a vacuum so the model steward abhors a deficiency. He will not allow it, if in the range of possibilities. He will pay and plead and work until the foul blot is erased.

GIVES LIBERALLY

The model steward is a liberal man. He will set his people an example of large and unselfish giving, as well as of fidelity in office and holiness in life. He will have an eye, a heart, a hand, not only to keep his pastor from actual need, but from any concern as to the generosity of his support; not only supplying his present wants, but anticipating the future. He will not only labor to pay up the last cent of the outgoing pastor's claim, but will so manage the church finances as to have a surplus in hand to greet the incoming pastor. The steward who allows his pastor to wait among strangers till the first quarterly meeting for financial help is far from being a model. The model steward labors as hard to bring up in full the first quarter as the last; for he knows his pastor needs it at the first as badly and perhaps more so than at the last.

SEEKS OUT THE NEEDY AND DISTRESSED

The model steward looks to his functions outside of the finances. He will not allow his office to be narrowed and hardened by being the more financial agent of the church. The steward not only disburses the alms of the church, but it is his duty to seek out the needy and distressed, not only to give financial aid, but to comfort them. This will enlarge his sympathies; keep his heart mellow, his solicitudes vigilant. The steward dishonors God and prostitutes and enslaves his church by looking at every member from a moneyed standpoint and measuring the new convert by the dollar and cents value.

193

DISCIPLINARY OVERSIGHT OF THE CHURCH

The discipline, among other duties of the steward, declares "he is to seek the needy and distressed in order to relieve and comfort them; to inform the preachers of any sick or disorderly persons; to tell the preachers what they think wrong in them." We see from these duties how large and important, how tender and delicate, his functions outside of the finances are. The steward is a helper by virtue of his office, to discipline the church people, to keep them in line and in battle trim, by a watchful oversight. The model steward is the preacher's wise and faithful counselor; the friend of the poor, the useful and honored servant of the church, whose name is written on the hearts of the church and in the Book of Life, and whose value is priceless.

HOME KEEPER
The Christian Home
April 20, 1893

ATMOSPHERE OF THE CHRISTIAN HOME

The welfare of the country and of the Church is bound up in the home. Piety and character have their birth and nurture there. The home shapes the men and women who are to shape the world. The mother shapes the home; she forms the home atmosphere which molds the life. The father is rarely felt in the home in such a molding form as the mother. Man's unquestioned power and preeminence cannot shape the home and give character to it like the woman. Strong the father may be in all the elements of manly strength, yet he cannot set afloat the thousand unseen forces that flow from the mother's heart, the mother's voice, the mother's contact, and the mother's influence. The oak cannot touch the springs of affection nor laden the air with aroma like the rose.

The duties of home keepers cannot be met by men. God made a more patient, enduring, gentler creation than man to fill this most important station. If the men were put in our homes to nurse and rear the children, and bear the innumerable challenges that fill a mother's daily life, the mania for suicide would be increased and our insane asylums would overflow with inmates. There are no trials so heavy, no challenges so wearing, no responsibilities greater, and no rewards more glorious than those of the true mother.

WOMEN ARE TO GUIDE AND RULE THE HOME LIFE

God made woman and put her in our homes to make and rule the home life which makes and rules all lives. Though in it she is subordinate to her husband, the chain is golden and bright when worn well, and the subordination is a note of the heavenly harmony. The transforming power of grace works out for her a far more exceeding and eternal weight of glory.

THE HIGH CALLING OF THE HOME KEEPER

For this high calling of keeping our homes our women are to be trained. Paul, by inspiration, directs the older women to teach the younger ones to be keepers at home. The word means watchers at home, as well as stayers and workers. The injunction demands the higher virtues of vigilance and protection be combined with domesticity and location. There must be, as some of the old translators have it, care for the home, the concentration of thought, heart, and labor. While the rearing of a family for God requires the outlay of the costliest graces, it is the best and greatest work that can be done in this world. The gracious, ever-growing and ever-widening results of such a work cannot be summed by any arithmetic save that of eternity. "These are my jewels," said Cornelia, the mother of the Gracchi, as she introduced her two noble boys into the presence of a Roman woman who was displaying her costly jewels. Cornelia and Rome lived in the person of her sons. The richest jewels though, but poorly type the value of a family raised in all the virtues of our religion, and who go out from under the training of a mother's hand and tears and prayers to adorn the doctrines of Christ, and to bless the world and send down to the latest generation the product of the mother's skill.

These faithful sentinels of our homes can do more for the Church than the greatest ecclesiastical dignitary, for they make the preachers who mold the Church. Ten thousand mothers and grandmothers like Eunice and Lois transmitting the purity and strength of their faith to thousands of Timothies would bless the world more than all other institutions.

The ambition, insubordination, and impatience of a proud, selfish and materialistic age are ever ready to discount and despise the unshowy works of these home keepers whose all important vocation is shielded from the glare of the world's eye, but their record is on high, and though their toil is in secret, God will reward them openly. Whatever the reckless age, the abnormal times, or vaulting ambition may say as to woman's sphere; wherever hard necessity or restless insubordination, or a pseudo-advance may put our women, God has put them in our homes to keep them for Him. No angel in Heaven guarding God's new creation from the invasion of Satan has heavier responsibilities, a weightier account, or a more glorious reward than the true mother in our homes. They are guarding a young world, more than that they are fashioning a world, and employing great vigilance in their calling.

THE CHURCH IS INDEBTED TO WOMEN

The Church under God is indebted to the mothers for the sons who have shaped its history, won its victories, and filled its Heaven. "What wonderful women those Christians have," was the pagan exclamation in the early days of the Church. And from the homes where these wondrous women presided came the saintly soldiers who conquered the world's conquerors. Well does the Bible charge the men to cherish these wifely women as Christ cherished the Church, embracing them and engulfing them in a love that has no limit in its wealth of tenderness, appreciation and comfort, and that is dearer than life. For our women are the keepers of our foundations, the cherishers of our hopes, the nourishers of our life, and the bride of our homes and of our souls.

CHRIST AND THE OLD TESTAMENT
Christ's Connection to the Old Testament
May 4, 1893

WAR AGAINST THE TRUTH

The war which error wages against truth is always on hand. The attack is generally hidden; but whether hidden or open it never abates. The methods of attack are changed, but the intensity and bitterness never change. The fiercest war used to be waged against the divinity and sacrifice of Christ; but the Scriptures being the court of appeal, truth prevailed. The whole ground of attack is changed now; there are no violent assaults on the person or the relation of Christ, but the most studied eulogies of His character and mission. The assault is more insidious. The Old Testament Scriptures are attacked in the most defaming manner, their authority impugned, their authorship disputed, their antiquity denied. While destroying the foundations of faith in Christ, the person of Christ is being extolled with the highest praise, killing the prophets while garnishing their sepulchers.

WHAT DID CHRIST THINK OF THE
OLD TESTAMENT SCRIPTURES?

The personal character of Christ being so stainless, His honesty and truthfulness without question, the purposes of His mission being generally recognized, and the question presses itself with force, what did Christ say and think of the Old Testament Scriptures? If the view of His mission accepted on all hands be true, and if He were in any measure calculated to fulfill that mission, one item of knowledge He must possess, He must have a thorough understanding of God's Word. If He was deceived about its nature or misunderstood it at any point, He was eminently disqualified for His mission. Did He pass it by as an indifferent thing? Did He center faith and thought on himself so as to be independent of the old Bible? He did none of these. He removed the wrong interpretations and glosses induced on it, and endorsed it to the fullest extent. Not only did He accept and make His own the popular ideas of its being God's Word, but He gave the whole weight of His authority in character and mission to its most miraculous parts, those which are most offensive to the critical and rationalistic tastes of this age.

CHRIST IS CONNECTED TO THE
OLD TESTAMENT SCRIPTURES

The most eventful points in His life are connected in a conspicuous way with His endorsement and estimate of the Jewish Scriptures. The temptation is a striking and familiar illustration. This was a crucial and most notable era. The Jewish Scriptures are the conspicuous factor in that conflict, every attack by Satan is foiled by a quotation from them. On the Mount of Transfiguration Moses and Elijah, the representatives of the old Jewish scriptures are with Him. When He cleansed the temple with a scourge of cords He justified the act by quoting the Old Testament. In His controversy with the

Sadducees about the resurrection He silences them by an appeal to Moses; and when the Pharisees deem themselves wiser and wittier than the Sadducees, and attack Him, He doubly defeats them by an appeal to Moses and to David. He begins His ministry by reading from Isaiah and applying it to himself.

CHRIST QUOTES FROM THE SCRIPTURES

In a notable controversy with the Jews He defended himself by quoting from their Scriptures, and declaring its inviolability by saying, *"The scripture cannot be broken"* (John 10:35). He charged them *"to search the scriptures"* (John 5:39). He restrained asking for twelve legions of angels to defend Him because such a course would nullify the Scriptures. He quotes these Scriptures during the last night with sad and pitying emphasis; declares their truth in His expressions on the Cross and dies uttering the very words these Scriptures ages before by prophecy had put into His mouth. His life and death were fashioned by the strictest loyalty to these Scriptures. Not only did He make conspicuous His adherence on many vital occasions and in many approving ways, but He seemingly goes out of the way to give His credence to their most marvelous features such as the creation of man, the death of Abel, the deluge and Noah, the destruction of Sodom, of Lot and his wife, of Moses and the burning bush, Moses lifting up the serpent, the manna in the wilderness, Elijah and the widow, the healing of Naaman, and Jonah and the whale. His belief in the existence and personality of its chief characters as Abel, Noah, Abraham, Lot, Moses, David, Solomon, Elijah, Isaiah, Daniel, and Jonah is notable.

If these Scriptures be the defective, ill-sorted and misleading documents which these modern critics make them, the endorsement that Christ gave them complicates Him in a most serious and fatal manner. If He did not know these facts that are so easily known and confidently declared by these modern critics, then He was clearly was not what He professed to be, and was wholly unfitted for His mission. If He did not know these destructive facts, then His truthfulness and integrity are most seriously and most damagingly implicated. But the stainless character of Christ and His superhuman knowledge, coupled with His involvement in the truth of these Scriptures, stamp them as divine and refute "stronger than proofs of holy writ" all the literary and scholarly criticisms of this or of any other age.

TOTAL DEPRAVITY
Sin
May 18, 1893

We do not seek to contend about words. But we must have settled doctrines, and doctrines can only be stated in words. The corruption of man's nature by the fall has been termed "total depravity." This term is not in our creed. It is the popular summary of the doctrine of original sin, or rather the summary of the effects of Adam's fall. Modern technology takes large exception to the term, and presses it out of its declared meaning so as to make the doctrine offensive. This term is a rock of offense, and stands in the way of many of the opinions that are popular in this day. It confronts the system of evolution with an unabridged and fathomless abyss, and all phases of rationalizing misbelief that would educate and unfold men into faith without the basis of the great change in regenerating grace. We would not tie faith to any given form of words. We would not make a Chinese wall of words and make heretic and false all the regions outside the wall. Neither would we make men offenders for using words that differ from our words; but we are not to surrender great truths at the demand of every spiritual marauder, though he flies the banner of progress. Neither are we to tone down our statements of these truths at the instance of the same imperious demand. To change the words of a truth is often to surrender the truth that it embodies.

TOTAL

The term total refers to the extent of the depravity and not to the degrees of it. A tract of land may be totally covered by water either in a shallow or deep way. The land being wholly covered with not an inch of dry soil is one thing, the depth of that covering is another thing. One drop of poison will totally poison a glass of water; every drop of the water is impregnated by the poison. The poison may be mild or deadly, but in either case the water is totally poisoned. Total depravity means the poison of sin affects the whole man, his principles, habits, and inclinations, in spite of how they may be modified or restrained by outward conditions the evil is through the man in a mild form or severe, restrained or lawless.

We must not be jealous for words only, as they are the key to the citadel which holds the city and its treasures. We are sure in this case the attack is in the doctrine. The words are only assaulted because an effort against the verbiage opens the way for an assault on the doctrine. When this is the case to surrender the statement is to surrender the truth it holds in its keeping.

DOCTRINES ARE THE JEWELS OF OUR FAITH

These statements of great truths as formulated by the wisdom and piety of the past are not dead accumulations, but are instinct with spiritual life and wisdom, and are the fittest cases to enshrine the jewels of our faith. This generation demands these gold deposits of the faith of the past be softened and debased by the alloy of the present. We yield to no such demands. These rugged and rich truths need circulation as the genuine currency, and they must not be depreciated in value or limited in circulation.

THE TERM "TOTAL DEPRAVITY"

The term "total depravity" declares in a direct and strong way that "man is very far gone from original righteousness. His nature is corrupt, and of himself only inclined to evil and that continually." It does not mean man is a graduate in the school of hell.

It does mean the inner man as originally organized on the principles of holiness and perfect obedience has been broken up. The harmony and integrity are lost.

It does mean the vital principle of love to God, which moved and conserved the whole machinery of man's moral nature, is destroyed.

It does mean the whole combination of high and holy purposes, divine communion and heavenly aspirations are gone: Earth draws man and not Heaven. The flesh pleases him and not the spirit.

That which is left of the fair original is but the corpse; corruption, earth, and worms prey on it, and if it comes out of the ruin and shame of its grave, *only* the voice of the Son of God can breathe on it the life giving dews of a glorious resurrection. Depravity means crooked; total depravity means crooked at every point. An old report says of the river Jordan, "It is the crookedest river what is." So we may say of man's nature, it is the crookedest thing that is. If man is not crooked, there is nothing that is crooked. Heaven's plummet declares every inch of him out of plumb. God's straight edge touches him at but few points. Total depravity does not mean men are as bad as they can be, and there is neither conscience, grace, nor good about them or in them, but it does mean this conscience, grace, and good come from God, and are not the fruit of man's inner spirit as alien from God.

DEATHBLOW TO SELF-RIGHTEOUS PRIDE

The doctrine of "total depravity" deals a deathblow to the self-righteous pride of man and is exceedingly offensive, but it is the very lesson the pride of man needs. He will never become a saint until he sees the fearful state of his heart, and cries out in an agony of despair at the appalling revelation: *"Behold, I was shapen in iniquity; and in sin did my mother conceive me"* (Psalm 51:5).

HOW THEY CAME INTO IT
Saintly Character
May 25, 1893

The Church on Earth has never been destitute of saints of a heavenly type, saints who have been put on the saintly calendar by men of all phases of belief. God does not leave himself without witnesses; He always has on hand some models of His best work, models, which illustrate His skill in making a saint.

FORMATION OF SAINTLY CHARACTER

Character is formed by example to a great extent. Holiness of character is not an exception to this. We need saints to make saints. The ordinary modern saint has so much of the earthly and so little of the heavenly in composition, that in imitating them, we unconsciously follow the main elements, not noted for saintliness. Saints have been put in calendars and in cloisters in the past until we look on them as an abnormal fanaticism, wholly unfitted for a working the utilitarian condition of things. This divorcement of sainthood from practical piety was a great evil, and continues to be a continuing evil with us. There is no conflict between the highest form of saintliness and the greatest effort and energy in doing. Of Archbishop Leighton, Pastor Burnett said, "In a free and frequent conversation for above two and twenty years, I never knew him to say an idle word that was not a direct tendency to edification; and I never once saw him in any other temper but that which I wished to be in the last moments of my life." His biographer says, "It may be doubted whether Christianity in the days of its youthful vigor gave birth to a more finished pattern than Leighton on the love of holiness. It was truly his reigning passion, and his longings to depart hence grew out of an intense desire to be transformed into the Divine likeness. Often would he bewail the proneness of Christians to stop short of that perfection. It was his grief that good men are content to be low and stunted." And yet the annals of the Church may be challenged to find one more zealous in work, more tireless in efforts for the peace and welfare of the Church. Fletcher of Madeley, of whom Isaac Taylor said, "In a genuine sense he was a saint such as the Church in every age has produced a few examples. The character of Fletcher was Christianity as little lowered by a mixture of human infirmity as we may hope to find it anywhere on Earth." "A seraph he is," says Robert Hall, "who burns with the ardors of divine love." And yet the influence and results of his practical efforts, his more abundant labors survive after he has been in his grave over a hundred years. Who was greater in labors than Henry Martyn? Of him it has been truly said "If ever there was a saint on Earth he is one."

SAINTS INFLUENCE SAINTS

We refer to these men not to beget saint worship, not even to eulogize the saints, but to make saints. We abate nothing in the demands for efficient work, a holy activity is imperative at the back of the working, as the spring of a strong and impressive activity we need saintly characters. The necessities of holy living were never more urgent, and yet there can be no holy lives without saintly character from which these holy lives are to flow.

We do greatly need some Church saints, not to be embalmed for future use, and as a satisfaction to the antiquarian or to the curiosity of the future; not to put in the calendar, but for practical, everyday uses. Saints, the purity and elevation of whose lives will give satisfaction to God and of whom it may be said, as it was said of some of old, that "God was not ashamed to be called their God."

EVERY AGE OF CHRISTIANITY SHOULD PRODUCE SAINTS

Every age ought to produce these saints. This age, prolific in almost everything else, has no special facility in saint-producing qualities; yet it does produce them, good types too, but rare. A judge of note, a member of another church, said to us of one of these, "She is a universal saint." She was fashioned after the old Church type. She came into this enlarged spiritual sphere along distinctive Church lines of sanctifying grace, but she came into it all the same. These holy ones have adorned the Church in all ages, in all climes, and in all creeds. We confess to a liking for the Methodist ones, but we are happy to find them in any church. We need them now in the Church.

Do these saints illustrate New Testament Christianity? Who doubts Leighton, Fletcher, and Martyn illustrate New Testament piety? Who dares say they have gone beyond the limits of Bible privileges and demands? How did they come to these saintly elevations? Not by nature, for they were dug from the hole of the pit where we were dug. They were made of the rock where we were hewn. Why the difference? Of grace we say, and truly it was of grace, but the same stores of grace are open to us. The one thing that lies open to each of us is to be great in holiness. While making all due allowances for the

205

divine sovereignty in classifying and qualifying the members of His spiritual body, we believe their condition of saintly eminence was secured by their personal efforts after God, by their relinquishment and renunciation of the world, and their striving after God and Heaven.

That which was said of Leighton may be said of them all, and explains the mystery of their spiritual advance, "The wish nearest his heart was to attain to the measure of the stature of the fullness of Christ; and all His singularities, and such arose from this desire being in him so much more ardent than it is in ordinary Christians." And as said of Fletcher, "His whole conversation was in Heaven, and his life from day to day was hid with Christ in God." They sought and found the royal road to Heaven. They were saints by the grace of God, but their personal efforts responded to every call and allurement of grace. They drank often and long of the fountain of life from which we occasionally sip. They were insatiable with their deep and long draughts; we are satisfied with our sips. They drank of the ocean and longed for more; we drink of the rills and are content with a taste. They renounced the world, crucified self in their pressure after God; we hold to the world and pamper self. They launched out on the great deep of His failures caring only for the fathomless blue sky of His grace above them, only for the fathomless ocean of His power and love beneath them. We linger near the shore chained to it by a timid faith and by a worldly cable.

CHRISTIANS JUST LIKE US

These were not cloistered saints denuded of human sympathies, divorced from the practical and real; saints among men they were with all human sympathies and passions tempered by grace, and full of labor and success. Thomas Walsh, chief among Methodist saints, was the instrument of converting more souls in comparison to his years than any man Mr. Wesley ever knew. They worked for men, lived and meditated on God and His word. They fasted and prayed; they availed themselves of all means through which grace flows, and used them to their utmost capacity. Their hours of devotion told on their lives. They really communed with God. They plunged into the solitude's of devotion and knew how and when to find God. Everything gave way to their hungering after God. Wesley was at it by four o'clock every morning. Simeon invariably rose at four. Alleine spent from four to eight in holy meditations and praise. Fletcher, like Christ, spent many a whole night in prayer.

THE SECRET: INTENSE FELLOWSHIP AND PRAYER

Rutherford rose at three to meet God and so runs the roll of saintly ones longing for God, like David in his eagerness after God, getting up before the day dawning to find Him. Herein is their secret, their hearts were after God, their desires on Him. They communed with Him, sought nothing of the world but sought great things of God, wrestled with Him, conquered all opposing forces, opened up the channels of faith deep and broad between them and Heaven. Holy meditations, holy desires, and heavenly draining swayed their intellects, enriched their emotions, filled and enlarged their hearts. The men who have thus communed with God, and sought after Him with their whole hearts have always risen to eminence in holiness, and no man has ever risen to this eminence whose flames have not been all dead to the world and all aglow for God and Heaven.

CHRIST'S DYING TESTIMONY
Fulfills Scripture
June 1, 1893

VITAL CONNECTION OF THE
OLD TESTAMENT AND NEW TESTAMENT

The superior light of the New Testament tends to shade that of the old. Some good people are indifferent to assaults or discredits of the Old Testament, deeming themselves secure in having Christ and the New Testament. The inseparable and interdependent nature of the two is not sufficiently considered by this class. The relation of the two Testaments is not one merely of resemblance, not one of contrast and displacement as between the Old and the New, but one of vital connection. They are one as the foundation and building are one. It takes the two to complete God's revelation to man. The Old is as much a comment on and illustration of the New as the New is the complement of the Old. The New Testament no more sets aside the Old than do the laws and decisions which explain and execute the constitution set aside that constitution.

What Christ thought of the Old Testament Scriptures must, with every pious, sincere inquirer after the truth as it is in Jesus, be conclusive as to its worth and will fix its estimate with all His loyal followers. We desire to ascertain Christ's estimate by His utterances at the hour of His death. That sacred, severely truthful hour will show us how the principles, prophecies, and words of the Old Testament were treasured up and poured the light of their utterances giving the strength of their divine and supporting arm to the darkness and weakness of that terrible ordeal. It also shows us how these scriptures were appealed to and how their directions shaped that event.

CHRIST VIEWS HIS REJECTION BY THE JEWS

As Christ approached His death and viewed His rejection by the Jewish church builders as at hand, He questions, *"What is this then that is written, the stone which the builders rejected, the same is become the head of the corner?"* (Luke 20:17). Looking with divine eye to the terrible results, to the Jews, of this rejection, He declares, *"For these be the days of vengeance, that all things which are written may be fulfilled"* (Luke 21:22). Immediately preceding His death, in full sight of the shame and agony of that death, His mind is full of the Old Testament Scriptures in regard to it, and He is jealously careful that the smallest minutia of the transaction be in the strictest accord with those divine prophetic Scriptures. When Peter would fight with a sword for His rescue, He orders him to put up his sword and declares, *"Thinkest thou that I cannot now pray to my Father, and He shall presently give me more than twelve legions of angels? But how then shall the scriptures be fulfilled, that thus it must be?"* The moment of His arrest He inquires why they did not take Him while He daily taught them in the temple. *"All this was done that the scriptures of the prophets might be fulfilled"* (Matthew 26:53-56).

JUDAS

The case of Judas goes with distressing keenness, like a sharp knife, to the heart of Christ. He can scarcely dismiss it, but strengthen and consoles His heart by constant reference to the Scriptures. He appeals to them, *"The Son of Man goeth as it is written of Him, but woe unto that man by whom the Son of Man is betrayed! It had been good for that man if he had not been born"* (Matthew 26:24). Again He refers to the traitor and the tragedy of his treason and appeals to the Scriptures for relief from the painful sight and attests His divinity as well as the truth of the Jewish Scriptures by the foretelling as He declares, *"I know whom I have chosen: but that the scripture*

209

may be fulfilled. He that eateth bread with Me has lifted up his heel against Me. Now I tell you before it come, that when it is come to pass ye may believe that I am He" (John 13:17-19). In His prayer, Judas and his infamy are before Him, and to him He refers in a terrific statement backed by Scripture: *"Those that thou gavest me I have kept and none of them is lost, but the son of perdition; that the scripture might be fulfilled"* (John 17:12). He declares to His disciples their cowardly desertion. The Scriptures are appealed to as the basis of this true, yet seemingly unkind, charge: *"All ye shall be offended because of me in this night; for it is written, I will smite the Shepherd and the sheep of the flock shall be scattered abroad"* (Matthew 26:31). Christ viewed His own death from the standpoint of Scripture and in its very words, *"For I say unto you, this that is written must yet be accomplished in me, and He was reckoned among the transgressors"* (Luke 22:37).

CHRIST'S DEATH

All the incidents of His death were but the fulfillment of these same Jewish Scriptures. The 30 pieces of silver, the price of Judas' betrayal, the buying of the potter's field with them were as the Scriptures had foretold; the soldiers dividing His clothing and casting lots had been in prophetic eye and was done, *"That the scripture might be fulfilled which saith, They parted my raiment among them and for my vesture they did cast lots. These things therefore the soldiers did"* (John 19:24). By His death between two thieves *"the scripture was fulfilled which saith, And He was numbered with the transgressors"* (Mark 15:27-28). When on the Cross it is said of Him: *"Jesus knowing that all things were now accomplished, that the scripture might be fulfilled saith I thirst"* (John 19:28). The cry of agony when dying, *"My God, my God, why hast thou forsaken me?"* (Mark 15:34). His shout of triumph and prayer of calm confidence in Luke 23:46, *"Father, into thy hands*

I commend my spirit: and having said thus he gave up the ghost." The words He spoke were the very words from the Old Testament Scriptures. The failure of the soldiers to break His bones and their wanton cruelty in piercing His side were done *"that the scripture should be fulfilled; a bone of Him shall not be broken, And again another scripture saith, they shall look on him whom they pierced"* (John 19:36-37).

CHRIST, THE ROAD TO EMMAUS, AND THE TWO DISCIPLES

In His appearance to the two disciples on their way to Emmaus after His resurrection, He upbraided them for not believing the prophets. *"And beginning at Moses and all the prophets, He expounded unto them in all the scriptures the things concerning himself"* (Luke 24:27). When He appeared to all His disciples after His resurrection glory, the Scriptures are the burden of His theme, the foundation and sum of His message to them.

> *"These are the words which I spake unto you, while I was yet with you, that all things must be fulfilled which were written in the law of Moses and in the prophets, and in the psalms concerning me. Then opened he their understanding that they might understand the scriptures. And said unto them, Thus it is written, and thus it behooved Christ to suffer and to rise from the dead the third day."* (Luke 24:44-46)

From these passages we see how thoroughly the death of Christ was saturated with the Old Testament Scriptures and how wholly He was committed to them and His death is the strongest and most undeniable proof of their truth and sacredness. It comes to this and nothing short of it, if He was what He professed to be, the Son of God, these Scriptures are what they profess to be, the Word of God, true as He is true, infallible as He is infallible. The truth of the death and resurrection of Christ is bound up with the inerrancy of the Old Testament Scriptures; Paul sums it up, *"He died for our sins according to the scriptures, He rose again the third day according to the scriptures"* (1 Corinthians 15:3-4).

THE MAN
Personal Purity
June 15, 1893

MAN COUNTS FOR EVERYTHING WITH GOD

With God, the man counts for everything. Rites, forms, and organizations are of small value. Unless they are backed by the holiness of the man, they are offensive in His sight. *"Incense is an abomination unto me; the new moons and Sabbaths, the calling of assemblies I cannot away with; it is iniquity, even the solemn meeting"* (Isaiah 1:13). Why does God speak so strongly against His own ordinances? Personal purity had failed. The impure man tainted all the sacred institutions of God and defiled them. God regards the man in so important a way that He places a discount value on all else. Men have built Him glorious temples and have striven and exhausted themselves to please God by all manner of gifts; but in lofty strains He has rebuked these proud worshipers and rejected their princely gifts.

"Heaven is my throne and the earth is my footstool, where is the house that ye build unto me and where is the place of my rest? For all those things hath mine hand made, and all those things hath been said, saith the LORD. *He that killeth an ox is as if he slew a man; he that sacrificeth a lamb, as if*

he cut off a dog's neck; he that offereth an oblation, as if he offered swine's blood; he that burneth incense, as if he blessed an idol." Turning away in disgust from these costly and profane offerings He declares, *"But to this man will I look, even to him that is poor and of a contrite spirit, and trembleth at my word"* (Isaiah 66:1-3).

GOD REGARDS PERSONAL PURITY IN MAN

This truth that God regards the personal purity of the man if fundamental and eternal, a truth that must not be taken for granted, but must be stressed and kept to the front by reiteration. This truth suffers when ordinances are made much of and forms of worship multiply. The man and his spiritual character depreciate as Church ceremonials appreciate. The simplicity of worship is lost in religious aesthetics or in the gaudiness of religious forms.

PERSONAL PURITY VERSUS MATERIALISM

This truth that the personal purity of the individual is the only thing God cares for is lost sight of when the Church begins to estimate men for what they have. When the Church eyes a man's money, social standing, or his belongings in any way, then spiritual values are at a fearful low level, and the tear of penitence and the heaviness of guilt are never seen at her portals. Worldly bribes have opened and stained its pearly gates by the entrance of the impure.

PERSONAL PURITY VERSUS GREED FOR LARGE NUMBERS OF CONGREGANTS

This truth that God is looking after personal purity is swallowed up when the church has greed for numbers. "Not numbers, but personal purity is our aim," said the Church fathers. The parading of Church statistics is mightily against the grain of spiritual religion. Eyeing numbers greatly hinders the looking after personal purity. The increase of quantity is generally at a loss of quality. Bulk abates preciousness.

CHURCH ORGANIZATION AND MACHINERY

The age of Church organization and Church machinery is not an age noted for elevated and strong personal piety. Machinery looks for engineers, and organizations for generals, and not for saints to run them. The simplest organization may aid purity as well as strength; but beyond that narrow limit organization swallows up the individual, and is careless of personal purity. Organization puts a high value on adult, young people, and children's groups and activities but they come in as the vicious substitutes for spiritual character. Holiness and all the spiritual graces of hardy culture and slow growth are discarded as too slow and too costly for the progress and rush of the age. By dint of machinery, new organizations and spiritual weakness, results are vainly expected to be secured by faith, prayer and waiting on God.

GOD IS SEEKING TO BUILD
SPIRITUAL CHARACTER IN MAN

The man and his spiritual character is what God is looking after. If men, holy men, can be turned out by the easy processes of Church machinery readier and better than by the old-time processes, we would gladly invest in every new and improved patent; but we do not believe it. We adhere to the old way, the way the holy prophets went, the King's highway of holiness.

DISCIPLINE OF EXAMPLE
Setting Examples
August 10, 1893

W e cannot be too often reminded that discipline does not simply mean the application of penalties, nor does it mean turning people out of the Church. Discipline means so training them that penalties will never be necessary; so training them that they will always stay in the Church, obedient to all its rules and fit for something. An army is not disciplined to be discarded, but to fight battles, gain victories, endure hardness, and to be subject to authority. It is not so difficult in the impulse of patriotism and the pressure of a popular call to get volunteers, but to train these raw recruits into veterans is serious work. Members of the Church are made mature by training. If we had skilled drill masters for our young Christians, court-martials would become unknown. Many influences must press on the character before the training is complete. The Word of God preached plainly, simply, personally, and the private admonition, along with the vigilant pastorate, all conspire to meet the ends of discipline.

THE PASTOR SETS THE EXAMPLE

The example of the preacher stands foremost as an efficient and authoritative agent in securing a disciplined Christian soldierhood. The preacher's life is the gospel cut out and held before the eyes in the glowing colors of a life. It makes the gospel more real, less difficult to live. The preacher's holy life diverts his ministry from the mere professional, intangible and impersonal. His life makes it real and clothes it with flesh and blood. Without his example to give point and backing to his preaching the whole transaction is hazy and nebulous. His example is a simple and beautiful model of the working of the system and trains like a well-ordered school. He preaches with authority because he preaches by his life.

THE HOLY PASTOR DOESN'T FIT THE WORLDLY CHURCH

The present trend of the Church is to overlook or discount the life. A halfhearted or worldly church does not want a holy ministry. It is too strait-laced and legal for them. Such churches clamor for men of talent, of gifts; men who can draw the crowds, help the finances without offending or disturbing consciences. They do not want holiness, but license. Preaching in the pulpit they may stand, but preaching by the life is too severe. The Church must have holy lives to train it. The Church needs holy living by the pulpit more than beautiful sermons. The gospel must be lived powerfully as well as preached powerfully. Heterodox living is worse than heterodox preaching. The preacher will never burn his message into the consciences of his hearers if he does not burn it in by his life as well as by his words. Nothing lives so long, affects so strongly, molds so effectually as a holy person. Paul's sermons are gone in the main, but Paul's life lives a matchless heritage, a matchless force, and is a training school for Christian soldiers.

MAN'S ACTIONS SPEAK LOUDER THAN WORDS

The voice is silent, the words have been spoken and are gone, but the life is always speaking, always warning, molding, suppressing, inspiring; always in the eye, always in the ear; like a lighthouse on a treacherous cliff or a beacon on a friendly shore, it draws or repulses, it wins or warns. The preacher's example must be an illustration of the entire gospel, not simply of its decencies and moralities. The positive graces, the sterner features, the uncommon and ostracized principles must shine luminous and stand out knotty. His decent, common life will show the virtues that the gospel holds in common with a virtuous public opinion, but his example must go far beyond these if there is any training force in it. The whole list of unworldly and neglected spiritual graces must be embodied in his life, so it will come on the Church in a commanding way.

FRAMES
Christlike Thinking
November 2, 1893

DISPOSITIONS OR FRAMES OF MIND

A frame is a particular disposition or frame of mind. Religious frames or dispositions are not the basis of salvation, and not always the tests of salvation. Every Christian must accept fully the truth of the hymn, "My hope is built on nothing less than Jesus' blood and righteousness; I dare not trust the sweetest frame, but wholly lean on Jesus' name."

COMMON SENSE REGARDING THIS POINT

While all this is true, it is still unwise and unscriptural to disregard frames which are simply the effects, the purifying, quietly, elevating, stimulating effects of a genuine faith in Christ's blood and righteousness. Frames, the powerful and conscious influence of God's power on the inner man, are decried or ignored; it will do well to pause a moment and question about these matters. If a present, full, conscious, and mighty salvation does not bring good dispositions and states to the soul, what does it bring? Mr. Wesley speaks with his usual sanctified common sense on this point. In answer to the question, what is the difference between the frame of my mind and the state of my soul? He replied:

217

If there be any at all, it is perhaps this: the frame may mean a single, transient sensation; the state a more complicated and lasting sensation; something which we habitually feel. By frame, some may mean fleeting passions; by state, rooted tempers. But I do not know that we have any authority to use the terms thus or distinguish the one from the other. He, whose mind is in a good frame, is certainly a good man as long as it continues. I would therefore no more require you to cease from judging of your state by your frame of mind, than I would require you to cease breathing.

Lady Maxwell, an old Methodist of rare intelligence and piety, in her statement of the case discriminates clearly in saying:

They err greatly who make either duties or frames the foundation of their acceptance with God. Yet the former is indispensably necessary, and the latter very desirable is our privilege and is also evidential of a thriving soul. Many of the children of God sink into a careless and supine spirit by paying too little regard to their frames, when perhaps, they only desire to be preserved from building on them; hereby Satan lays a snare for them, which they fall into unawares.

WAKING UP
A Call to the Church
November 2, 1893

CHRISTIAN PRESS

No more serious responsibility exists anywhere than that which rests on the Christian press of this country. The membership of the Church is so numerous and widespread its press wields a mighty influence, and in the very nature of things is largely responsible for the public sentiment which prevails, as well as for the morals and religion of the country. The pulpit and press of these United States fired with the zeal and courage which exist in apostles and saints, would mold public sentiment, preserve the purity and power of the Church, and inspire and elevate the national life. To secure these salutary ends there must be an ever open and vigilant eye, positive convictions, fearless outspokenness, and a constant war against all evils. The salvation of ancient Israel was to come out of Zion. The spiritual vigor of the Church secures the welfare of the nation.

The Church seems to be awaking to the conditions, responsibilities and demands of the hour. They recognize the strength and malignity of the evils that threaten the purity of the Church and the integrity of the nation, and the urgent need of a more powerfully vitalizing pulpit, and a more powerfully aggressive Church life. A pastor writes to one of their papers as follows:

> Pardon the suggestion, but allow me to plead you urge all our people and preachers to commence revival efforts, and not delay until the so called week of prayer. I believe the only salvation from the awful drift of sin that confronts our nation is in a mighty reformation.

219

Their press is striking loudly in harmony with this keynote. *The Michigan Advocate* puts it strongly:

The crying need among us is for rousing pulpit work. The condition of our social life demands it. The apathy of our denominational life demands it. Ten thousand Whitfields' ought to be turned loose in America today. The masses do not come to our churches; hence our pulpit should go to the masses. Ringing truth on fire with the Holy Ghost should flame out in city and country, denouncing sin in high and low places, proclaiming perdition for gamblers, drunkards, robbers, thieves and rascals generally. Never was there a time when wise and stirring pulpit work would have better effect or be appreciated more. For a dozen years, Ingersolism, rationalism, and liberalism have been doing deadly work in our American society. No great pulpit reformer has arisen to counteract their influence. Excepting here and there an evangelist, no man has come to the front preaching pure and undefiled religion in a manner to awaken the attention of the continent and push Christianity to the front.

The New York Advocate outlines the fearful condition of things as a plea for an earnest and most exhaustive effort by the pastors. It says:

A wave of demoralization sweeps over the nation. Sunday traveling was never so common. Devotion to amusements was never so intense; absorption of the people in general questions never more complete. Political activity was never greater in a non-presidential election. Gambling pervades the land. Pool selling is common throughout the country. Horse-racing gains in popularity and strength; its promoters are more arrogant, and traps for the young in every direction are set with unusual skill and openness. In various states, legislatures are corrupt, pandering to the liquor and other base interests. The fibers that bind the Church together are relaxed, and its energies, such as are available, absorbed in "enterprises" and "causes," while growth in grace and the conversion of souls receive only the remnants of attention. The general report is prayer meetings are dull and slimly attended, and signs of spirituality few and occasional.

It declares, "If the *financial stringency* passes without a general revival, the drift of Christianity toward the abyss of utter worldliness will be frightfully rapid." This apprehension of our condition is a most hopeful sign. A clear view of the evils which are rampant and threatening is absolutely necessary to arouse to immediate and energetic action. A complacent, congratulating view of conditions paralyzes all vigilant and zealous effort, destroys all reformatory and revival agencies, turns the nation over as an easy prey to all phases of corruption and decay, and rivets anew the chains of Satan and the world on the Church.

TESTIMONY VERSUS BOASTING
How to Testify
December 14, 1893

There is such a dearth of Christian testimony one scarcely feels like laying down rules for direction in this imperative religious duty. Much less ought the spirit of criticism to be exercised toward those who honestly attempt to exercise it. But the sincere ones accept in all meekness every attempt to instruct them in regard to duty and are kindly open to criticism.

WITNESSING FOR GOD

Extremes beget extremes. The fact so many tongues are dumb in witnessing for God may cause those who are ready to perform the sacred work to do it in an excessive way or in an improper spirit.

That the Christian is to bear testimony for God is a truth fundamental to the gospel. That this testimony is to be performed by the tongue, and by fiery tongues at that, is a truth equally authoritative.

There is always danger in verbal statements of high advance in times of great religious feelings and movements. The times of great floods are not the times to take the depth of the river. High water mark is a high and dry mark to the ordinary stage of the water.

TOTAL DEPENDENCE ON THE HOLY SPIRIT

In one sense there is only a step between a Christian testimony and boasting. In another sense the distance is like opposite poles. There may be but the space of one step between the highway and the precipice, but that step makes the infinite distance between safety and death. The Corinthian Church is a warning of how the richest spiritual gifts may be perverted by the poison of boasting, and breeds all kinds of spiritual evils. The difference between the proper edifying use of spiritual gifts and their boastful display lies in total dependence upon the Holy Spirit for how, when, where, who, and in what manner they are presented.

SPIRITUAL WISDOM

We can scarcely admire enough the spiritual wisdom which was given Mr. Wesley, that he might direct primitive Methodism safely through the dangers which threatened to swamp it. We have a direction given by early Methodism on this very point. Hasty and ill-guarded professions had brought offense and the following advice, which can never be out of date, was given "What has given," they say, "most offense hitherto is what perhaps may be best spared as some people's confident and hasty triumphs in the grace of God. Not by way of humble thankfulness to Him for looking upon them, or acknowledgment of some peace and strength unknown before which they hope will be increased in them; but insisting on the completeness of their deliverance already from all sin, and taking to them every apostolic boast in the strongest terms." "Let us speak," they say, "of everything in such a manner as may convey glory to Christ without letting it glance on ourselves by the way. Let us profess, when we can with truth, how *really* the Christian salvation if fulfilled in us rather than how *sublimely.*" This is the most important advice, and a clear and wise distinction between the real salvation and its sublime succeedants, which if observed, will rid Christian testimony of all semblance of boasting and relieve our profession of an offense which is not really the offense of the Cross. We will have enough of offense inevitably attaching to those who bear the Cross truly; but we must not, at the peril of souls, add offenses of our own manufacture.

CHRIST AND DISCIPLING: PART ONE
Making Disciples
January 25, 1894

The system of Christ is a training school. It has for its object the prevention of sin and the perfection of character. Christ's organized Church is a brotherhood. This Christian brotherhood was to be maintained inviolate by correction and disciplinary measures. Offenders against this brotherhood who would not repent and amend were to be excluded from its circle of immunities. No vicious sentiment against excluding violators existed in Christ's mind. In Matthew 18:15-17, Christ lays down His method of classification for wrongdoers step by step. Offence, process, and penalty are all stated. The offences which are amenable to this process are not crimes which by their publicity or guiltiness would bring scandal on the Church. They are wrongs which affect the relationship, the rights, and the person of a member of the brotherhood. This wrong is to be righted, be it great or small or the wrongdoer is to be excluded from the Society. Church discipline, as Christ enacted it, was to be maintained on the strict, high, and sensitive plane of a brotherhood.

THE CHURCH MUST REQUIRE STRICT ADHERENCE TO FOUNDATIONAL PRINCIPLES

Christ put it as a foundation principle that His Church could not fulfill its mission of saving the world unless its organization was that of a simple brotherhood, loving and compact. Everything which marred or broke that brotherhood was to be removed at once by private explanation, brotherly reproof, or by Church action. Violation of the brotherhood brought weakness and anarchy into the Church, and the damage could only be repaired by the repentance or exclusion of the wrongdoer. Christ's Church has no tolerance for old scores, old feuds, alienations, chronic wrongdoing, or chronic wrongdoers.

It seems not to have occurred to Christ that nothing but scandalous sins were to be the Church discipline. Offence against brotherliness is as foreign to His system as the wrongdoing that defames in public esteem. The Church that disciplines only scandalous wrongs will soon be unable to discipline them. There is no method by which the purity and power of the Church can be maintained except by maintaining its brotherhood inviolate. The Church that does not protect and intensify its brotherhood will lose its ability to protect its morals. The brotherhoods which have sprung up in the Roman Catholic Church, by their strict discipline, have been the only savor in that corrupt and powerful ecclesiasticism.

THE WESLEYAN MOVEMENT PROMOTED HOLY BROTHERHOOD

The discipline in the English Church in the days of Mr. Wesley is described as a rope of sand. Fellowship was unknown. There was no power to cut off its dead and putrid members. All were jumbled together in one mass, without unity, sympathy or fellowship. The Wesleyan movement at once formed a striking contrast to this spiritual jumble and anarchy. They were united together in a holy brotherhood. Unity, fellowship, and all brotherly ties were the result of its animating principle and strict discipline. The dead members were cut off as soon as hopes of recovery were gone. The General Rules of Methodism were adopted to maintain these potent and happy ends. We will inevitably fall to the position of spiritual decadence and putridity which existed in the Church of England before the rise of Methodism if we do not enforce the Christly and vital discipline of our General Rules.

The Church owes as much to its discipline for its marvelous success as to anything else. The decay of that is the decay of our right arm. A Church which was brought into being by Churchly legislators, and maintains itself by ceremonials or by the decencies of moral training, may keep up some kind of decent reputation, but the Church will fall low in proportion, as her privileges and spiritual immunities have been great. Methodism must be an army or a mob, subject to spiritual discipline or become demoralized. Christ could not be guilty of the folly and weakness of having a procedure corrective and disciplinary in its nature without any penalty. *"If he neglects to hear the Church, let him be unto you as a heathen man and as a publican"* (Matthew 18:17). Excommunication is Christ's penalty. "We will admonish him of the error of his ways: we will bear with him for a season; but then if he repent not, he hath no more place among us."

CHRIST AND DISCIPLING: PART TWO
Making Disciples
February 8, 1894

PURITY OF THE CHURCH

The purity of the Church is the great end to be secured. The value of the Church as a divine institution and its ability to secure the ends of its establishment depend on its purity. Without this purity the increase of its members, enlargement of its plans and activities, and the addition of machinery will profit nothing. It will be as impotent for the advance of holiness as the flowers which cover the coffin are impotent to bring our dead to life or assuage the bitterness of our grief. The enforcement of discipline is one of the potent agencies to secure that purity. It secures purity by correcting and training the individual member or by expelling him if he will not yield to the training and correction.

CHRIST CLEANSING THE TEMPLE IS AN EXAMPLE

In the cleansing of the temple by Christ we have an illustration of His zeal for the purity of His Church and the strong and severe measures He used to secure that end. By this act Christ was not making a passionate appeal for the purity of the Jewish temple and its service. He knew that service was decayed and obsolete. The temple itself was soon to be destroyed and never to be rebuilt. He was in this remarkable action asserting and vindicating the elementary and eternal principles of God that His Church is to be kept pure and also declaring the fiery indignation of God against those who desecrate its service by worldly and selfish adulterations. The commercial spirit had touched its ministers and polluted its altars. The spirit and ring of money were there, and not the spirit of prayer. The spirit of gain, and not the spirit of holiness, was on its sacred men and in its sacred places.

His action in this case is in marked contrast with the rule He laid down in Matthew 18:17-19, because the conditions and the aims were different. There the process was one of recovery, and readjusting relations, the method progressive and brotherly until the final issue. In the cleansing of the temple, the world had entrenched itself in many forms in God's house. The vitals of piety were involved, the whole service debauched and all those who were responsible for its purity were parties to the great wrong. The conditions had passed beyond the mediation of brotherly ties. In fact, there was no brotherhood as the basis of mediation. Matters had gone so far these sacrilegious wrongdoers must feel the whip of divine authority and indignation. An example must be made of the chief offenders and they were expelled from the temple which they had defiled, and others taught the lessons of reverence and fear. The conditions were so malignant nothing but a heroic remedy could cure.

PURITY OF THE CHURCH DEMANDED EXTREME MEASURES

The purity of the Church demanded the course Christ took in this case. The purity of the Church often demands the resort to the extreme measure of authority and law. A Church trial and an expulsion are not unmixed evils, but often salutary measures, establishing Church authority, saving to the member dealt with, and saving to others who see it and fear. By this act, Christ asserted His authority and used His key of discipline to shut out these sacrilegious offenders. The world is always crying out against authority in the Church as narrow, arbitrary, unloving, and the Church grows afraid and becomes timid and sometimes timeserving in her policy and puts authority over against love and loses both; by throwing away one key the others become useless. When the Church grows too timid to exercise her right to bind spiritual matters in an authoritative way, then spiritual interests go loose and die.

DECAY OF DISCIPLINE RESULTS IN DECAY OF AUTHORITY AND HOLINESS

Christ was actuated by zeal for God's authority and for God's holiness. The decay of discipline is the decay of authority, and irreverence and universal unfaith follow. The decay of discipline is the decay of holiness and the decay of holiness dries up all the springs of righteousness.

Christ, by this act, met the divine requirement, *"The zeal of thine house hath eaten me up"* (John 2:17). At any cost and in the face of all difficult and delicate conditions Christ was bound to maintain the purity of the Church. Christ's zeal is the only principle which can understand the relation of purity to discipline, and combine with this perception the courage and nerve to maintain discipline. Gentleness and moderation without zeal degenerate into weakness and acquiescence. Prudence divorced from zeal weighs the difficulties, hesitates in decision, and lapses into cowardly complicity. Lukewarmness never makes a fight for discipline. Policy never risks its interest in a conflict to maintain discipline. Christly zeal only has the insight, earnestness, energy, courage, and faith to see the interests involved and lay itself out to secure them.

This action on the part of Christ exposed Him to the charge of severity and rashness. The administration of discipline for the purity of the Church in extreme or complicated cases exposes the administrator almost inevitably to these charges. Discipline is law enforced and law is always severe on its violators. It takes seeming severity to vindicate law and any efficient legal action will be charged to rash action. Opposition will be aroused, criticism provoked, and authority questioned. Discipline enforced will be sure to offend someone, and they will be heard from. Discipline strikes the seat of worldliness in the Church, the place where the devil has his headquarters and, of course, there will be fire and friction.

Christ created a sensation. The taking hold of money and the world in the Church will always create a sensation. The devil was never exorcised without a scene.

THE STRANGER
Following Christ
February 15, 1894

In the tenth chapter of John we have a graphic picture of the shepherd and the sheep drawn by Christ's own hand. The sheep are in the keeping of three different characters; the stranger, the hireling and the good shepherd.

THE STRANGER SHEPHERD'S HEART IS NOT WITH THE SHEEP

The term *stranger* means belonging to another, not the sheep's own. The stranger shepherd does not belong to the sheep by tender, deathless ties. His heart is not with the sheep. The stranger shepherd is no enemy to the sheep; he does not come to devour them. He may be well skilled in the shepherd's art. Professionally and theoretically he may be adept in the shepherd's trade. His heart may be in his trade, but it is not with the sheep.

The shepherd's work is heart work. It is the shepherd's heart that keeps his eyes open day and night. The heart gives him the shepherd's courage. It is the heart of the shepherd which binds the sheep to him. The winning, warning tones of the shepherd comes from his heart. It is the shepherd's heart that gives the shepherd life for the sheep. The stranger shepherd lacks heart. To lack heart is to lack everything; love is wanting, along with sympathy and tenderness. To lack heart is to lack everything which wins and holds sheep or men.

THE STRANGER SHEPHERD'S HEART IS COLD

The stranger's heart is a cold heart, and a cold heart cannot move or govern men. The stranger shepherd may be held to his trade by custom, by salary, or even by higher considerations, but his interest centers somewhere else than in the sheep. He goes through his duties mechanically and with routine haste and regularity; but the stranger shepherd does things coldly, he does them hurried because he does them without heart. Order, law, and duty may be in his work, but love and heart are not always their companions. The stranger shepherd does the shepherd's work awkwardly because he does it without love. The spiritual shepherd above all things must have a heart for his sheep, a heart full of sympathy; without this, a head full of knowledge is worse than nothing. If God's shepherd is not warm and heartfelt with men, he is nothing.

THE STRANGER SHEPHERD IS NOT ACQUAINTED WITH THE SHEEP

The stranger shepherd is not acquainted with the sheep. He lives and sets on the surface because he has no thorough knowledge of the sheep. Men, not simply man, are the great study for God's spiritual shepherds. The stranger shepherd has studied books and not men. The stranger shepherd may know science, theology, and learning but he does not know God's sheep. He has not made himself acquainted with their habits, wants, or sorrows. He has not made himself one with them, laid himself open to them, willing to give his life for them, borne their grief, and carried their sins.

The stranger shepherd may come in contact with the sheep, but he does not know them. He has not made them his own by a thorough, minute and individual knowledge of them. He may know a few of the leading rams and ewes, but he does not know the sheep. The spiritual shepherd must have the names and the peculiar characteristics of each of his flock engraved on his heart.

THE SHEEP WILL NOT FOLLOW THE STRANGER SHEPHERD

The stranger shepherd cannot govern the flock. He cannot feed or fatten the flock. The sheep will not follow a stranger; they know not his voice and will flee from his presence.

THE MODERN IDEA
Rationalism versus Revelation
March 15, 1894

RATIONALISM

The modern idea is essentially rational. It has no special regard for revelation, no great reverence for authority. The modern idea takes its cue from the Bible, but makes havoc of Bible facts and principles. It may range itself under the name of some great Bible doctrine, but it disembowels the doctrine, and leaves us nothing but an empty, delusive name. No one conversant with the trend of things can be ignorant of the fact that rationalism, under the cover of modern ideas or thought, is affecting the granite foundations of God's truth.

Doctrines which the wisdom and faith of the Church have reduced to axiomatic dogmas are so changed by the transforming process of modern thought that no essential part of the original doctrine remains. The new dress has altered not only the outward appearance, but the heart of the precious old truths is entirely changed. It is marvelously strange how widespread the false views of Christ are, His atonement, the resurrection of the dead, and eternal judgment. These pernicious views are found in literature, commentary, and exposition; they are clothed in such attractive garb, and found in so many places they fix themselves in thought before we are aware of it. Moreover, we have so little knowledge of the Bible we cannot detect the counterfeit. It comes to pass views always rejected by the great body of believers as unscriptural, are deferred to without scrutiny or protest.

Dr. Lyman Abbott, editor of *The Outlook* and pastor of Plymouth Church in Brooklyn says:

> I accept the Apostles' Creed, though I give to the phrase "resurrection of the body" the modern interpretation. In explanation of the modern idea of the resurrection he says: The modern doctrine repudiates this idea of a literal resurrection of the flesh. Yet it holds that the spirit has in another world some sort of organism through which it acts and by which it has its connection with the material universe. What that organism is and how it operates, no one pretends to know. Swedenborg held there is in the human body a spiritual body and this spiritual organism rises at death, so the soul is not yet clothed with an immortal tabernacle. This is one form of the modern doctrine of the resurrection of

the body. In sentence then, the modern doctrine of the resurrection of the body, so far as that doctrine is in any form intelligently held, in that the spirit has in the other life a spiritual organism, and this spiritual organism has some sort of connection, not by us understood, with the material organism which it possessed upon the Earth.

It is one of the problems of this age to find out the process of how the current of orthodoxy, purified, deepened, and made strong by the confluent piety of ages, finds itself almost lost in the shallows and sands of the ancient and worst forms of heterodoxy.

HETERODOX IDEAS

These modern ideas are not modern though they may bear its imprint. They are almost as old as Christianity and are as heterodox as they are old. We would not oppose them because they are new, nor reject them because they are hoary reprobates. We put no store by the modern idea. No special store do we put by the ancient idea. We do, though, put store, all the store we can muster, by the Bible idea. We measure all that is old and all that is new by that infallible standard, and whatever is new or whatever is old which does not agree with that, we say let it be accursed, and he who bids it God speed is partaker in the sin.

DOCTRINE OF BODILY RESURRECTION

This doctrine of the resurrection of the body is not a mere inference from Bible statement. It is the statement itself, the key of its arch, the corner stone of its foundation. It is not a rich afterthought of the gospel, but coordinates; "Jesus and the resurrection" are the gospel. Is this modern idea the Bible idea? Is it worthy of being put to the front of gospel statements? How vague and intangible this modern idea of the resurrection! How strange that reason should reject as unworthy of credence the Bible statement of the resurrection, and yet gulp down with greediness the dreamy vagaries contained in the modern idea. The Bible idea of the resurrection of the body is the fact of a literal resurrection of the body. The Bible declares our bodies are parts of us, they are included in the recovering scheme of grace, they are partners with the spirit in its earthly course of faith or disobedience, and they are to share in the honors or shame of the eternal future.

CORRUPTION IS TO PUT ON INCORRUPTION

The resurrection of the same bodies that we put in the grave is the doctrine that pervades the Bible through and through. All its truths are soaked in this great doctrine. The same body put in the grave is to come forth. Its weakness is to put on immortal energy. Its corruption is to put on incorruption. This comforting doctrine:
- is full of enrapturing, deathless hope
- supports martyrs and saints
- has quenched for them the violence of the fiery stakes
- has quickened their faith
- has wiped away their tears
- has relieved the bitterness of death
- and has enabled them to triumph over the grave.

This doctrine which commends itself to reason as well as to faith, is to be relinquished for this modern idea, which for practical Christian uses is as profitless as *Aesop's Fables* or *Arabian Nights*.

SELF-DENIAL
Death to the Self-Life
April 26, 1894

THE TAPROOT OF CHRISTIANITY

Self-denial is the taproot of Christianity. It is the last as well as the first rule of discipleship. Self-denial is not confined to any special or sacred season. It belongs to all times and makes all seasons sacred. It is not expressed by a week of self-denial, but covers every minute of the whole life. It is not the abstaining from this luxury or even that necessity for a given length of time. Though the act of abstaining may be the expression of self-denial, it may be but a vicious substitute for it.

A week of self-denial may be the illustration of this rich grace. But to mistake a week's abstinence from some favorite indulgence for the principle of self-denial is a fatal delusion. This is like fulfilling the self-denying ordinance "of plucking out the right eye," by paring the fingernails. Self-denial can no more be confined to one week than the ocean can be confined to a rill. Abstinence for a few days from one or all indulgences is no nearer to self-denial than the cutting off of the tiniest bough is the felling of the tree.

THE HINDRANCE OF SELF

The great hindrance to religion is self. It carries off by a thousand pipes and appropriates to its own uses the streams which might water and bless with good a hundred fields. Self-denial is the stopping of a great leakage. Self-denial is a safety bank that saves the income from waste. It hoards like a miser the great and small amounts for every good investment. Self-denial stops outlays and leaks with economy and frugality and gives the savings to God.

Self-denial is not simply the economic or financial principle of the gospel. It is the principle which radiates Heaven in the Christian. It is the loss of this life, and by this loss the gain of the life to come. It is the lack of this principle that runs the pulse of religion. Spiritual famine marks its decay. Spiritual death always attends on the absence of self-denial.

LACK OF SELF-DENIAL LEADS TO SPIRITUAL DEATH

Look at this picture! A woman in Lowell (Sarah Hosener, she deserves to be named) learned that $50 would educate a young man in the Nestorian Seminary. This woman, more than sixty years of age, living in an attic, and by working in a factory and taking in sewing, sent out six missionaries. This illustrates the marvelous results of self-denial in one phase of its expression. Self-denial with this woman was an ingrained principle; lifelong, ever flowing, and powerful. What miracles would follow if this principle was active in every professing Christian!

FAITH
Viewing Faith
May 3, 1894

There is an emasculated idea of faith which will scarcely allow a man to pray or fast or weep or be troubled in any way about his sins, for fear it will impair the power of faith, infringe on its prerogatives, or detract from its authority. This is a bastard faith, born of a vicious sentiment, the offspring of healing the hurt of sin easily. This view, while professing to honor faith, robs it of its fair possessions.

Mr. Wesley had to deal with it. He says: "I began examining the Society, not before it was wanted, for the plague was begun.

I found many crying out, 'Faith, faith! Believe, believe!' but making little account of the fruits of faith, either of holiness or good works." Mr. Wesley met one of these converts. He says of him: "A new creature indeed! (though not in the gospel sense), so extremely happy, easy, and unconcerned, one of the primitive Christians instead of supposing him to be at rest as he termed it, in the wounds of Jesus, would have judged he had never heard His name, much less of taking up His cross daily."

The Earl of Shaftesbury got religion from an old pious nurse, and kept it unspotted from the world. He was stanch in his orthodoxy because it was grounded on his personal and experimental relation to Christ. He watched with a jealous eye all the inflow of vicious views. He saw with pain the tendency of the times toward this sickly view of faith. In his diary he notes and comments:

...is falling rapidly into the errors of the day. He preaches very smooth things. In a long sermon about forgiveness and God's mercy, he mentioned sin only once. Then at the close of the sermon, in order to magnify the mercy of God, he exclaimed: "There is no one in this congregation who, having come to the service an unbeliever may not leave justified before God." That is true, no doubt, but is it truly stated? What is belief? What does it contain? What does it demand? Does it demand conviction of sin, confession of sin, repentance, and faith? All these things except faith are dropped nowadays, and people are led to believe, to accept Christ as a Savior, and to wish for His salvation is the sum and substance of a heart turned to God. It requires no self-abasement, no confession of the justice of the divine wrath, no acknowledgment of inherited corruption; and disguise it as the preacher may, no sense of demerit, and no sense of deserved condemnation. It is in fact reduced to an easy, agreeable acceptance of a pleasant invitation to be had at any time that is convenient to you. Herein lays the seed of an incipient Antinomianism.

This is a discriminating and Scriptural distinction and deserves to be pondered well in these times of religion made easy. This misleading view of faith, and this wrong way of putting it, have in them the destruction of regeneration, the death of holiness, and the seeds of Antinomianism, and are the prolific source of a worldly and rationalistic religion.

VOLUME III

LEADERSHIP GOD'S WAY

THE LEADERSHIP OF FAITH
Leaders and Faith
October 18, 1890

FAITH IN GOD'S LEADERS

God must have leaders in His Church, Christians whose distinguished spiritual ability move them to the front as an inspiration and example in the work of God. The distinguishing and elect factor in these leaders is faith. Other elements may be material or immaterial; in other matters these leaders may be deficient, or in contrast, but in this one of faith they are a unit. It is faith that placed them on God's roll of position. Aspiring men and women, destitute of faith, may hoist themselves into Church leadership, but God has no hand in their elevation. For them He has no vote and He had no voice in their election

TRUE FAITH IN LEADERS

The only true leaders are those whose faith in God has placed them at the head. These are the only ones who can do God's bidding and be led by God's hand. Faith is the imperial grace of Christ's system; a simple but very rare grace. Much of that which circulates as faith has but little if any of the elements in it. If we subtract from this current article education, sentiment, prejudice, enthusiasm, and habit, we have but little left.

Faith is the stuff out of which God makes His saints, martyrs and apostles.

239

Faith is a divine energy implanted in the heart by God. By it we have the foundation, the sight and the vital force of the unseen and eternal.

Faith is an energy that masters everything for God; an eye that sees God in His nearness, majesty, and supremacy.

Faith is not a subordinate principle, but supreme. It is not to be hid under a liberal education, not to play second-hand to a large brain, or much or little of anything else.

Faith makes brain, educates God's leaders, and gives them courage, conviction, bone, and muscle.

Faith must be stronger than brain; it must curb and direct the mind.

Faith must rise above education, talent, taste, genius, and be more evident, more controlling than any of these.

Only men of commanding faith can project God's cause, grasp God's plans, and lead God's people.

Without faith, intellect will fail; its wisest wisdom will be but blunders, its keenest vision but blindness.

God's leaders cultivate their faith above all things. Students they may be, but their studies are turned this way; they study God, and faith is the only school in which He can be studied. Gifted they may be, but all their gifts wait in lowly docility on the guidance of faith.

Faith is cultured by the Bible. God's leaders are too often ignorant of God's word. They may know it as the Commentaries know it; they may know it as the lawyer knows his text book; know it as the scholar knows his classics; but they must know it in the heart, feed on it in the inner spirit, water the roots and invigorate the life of faith by meditation on its essential truths. This is the way to pour the ocean streams of revealed truth into faith till it expands and grows to marvelous dimensions.

PRAYING AND FAITH

Praying aids much in bringing faith to its throne. Faith will never be authoritative or supreme where praying has not fastened itself on the spiritual habits. Faith is founded or perfected by self-denial, and praying is not only the symbol, but a cardinal grace in self-denial. It mortifies the flesh, lays it low, breaks the force of appetite and passion, and fits the soil to grow faith.

SECRET PRAYER

Faith is brought into leadership by secret prayer. Long, habitual, closeted interviews with God are the sunny seasons for the growth of faith; interviews in which God's searching eye and light discover all the hidden hindrances to faith; interviews in which God reveals himself so faith is mightily strengthened. God's true leadership does more to strengthen its faith than to do anything else. It seeks this one element of power, this secret of spiritual success, at the sacrifice of other things. It keeps its eye fixed not on place or plans, but on God. The leadership of faith has no alliance with ambition, they are eternal foes. Ambition may give leadership in the Church, has done it, does do it, but faith has no part in this leadership. Faith is debauched by its touch; God is not in the leadership of ambition.

THE LEADERSHIP OF FAITH

The leadership of faith is the leadership of humility and meekness is bloom. Faith leads because it is lowlier than all. It is master of all because it is servant of all. The leadership of faith is the leadership of convictions that reach into the unseen and eternal with such a real and absorbing hold as to lose sight of the visible and temporal. These convictions only grow and feed on the decay of the things that are seen and felt. The man who has a strong grasp on the visible and earthly has but a feeble hold on the unseen and heavenly. It is the province of faith to discover and bring near these unseen things, and fill itself with them, their grandeur and stability.

LEADERSHIP OF FAITH IS SPIRITUAL LEADERSHIP

The leadership of faith is the leadership of the spiritual as distinguished from the material, the visible, and the secular. Churches are focusing on getting the most money and building more churches. This material leadership is doing great damage to the vital interests of spiritual life. It puts a low grade on ministerial character. In so doing, spiritual estimates of the ministry are discounted and spiritual impulses hardened. We need men of mighty faith as officers, non-commissioned, in all the rank and file of God's army. The men of faith are the men of God's renown. The men of faith make God's history, work God's miracles, fight God's battles, and gain God's victories.

AN OLD REMEDY
Discipline
December 27, 1890

An old remedy is sometimes best for an old disease. This is especially true of spiritual maladies. *The Methodist Discipline of 1798*, with explanatory notes by Thomas Coke and Francis Asbury, calls attention to many evils, and applies remedies. The evil of talking so much before and after service is dealt with. In the notes these general regulating principles are stated: "Holiness becomes the house of the Lord. We go there to speak to God and hear His Word and not to converse with each other."

This old *Discipline* takes the matter in hand and calls attention to the evil. "Is there not," it asks, "a great indecency sometimes practiced among us, talking in the congregations before and after service?" The old *Discipline* calls this an impropriety, a great indecency, and a vile practice. Are these words too strong? Not if we remember how unsightly this practice is and how improper for this occasion.

- It destroys the foundations of a solid and reverent worship.
- It dissipates the spirit of prayer that must fill God's house and solemnize every worshiper.
- It comes into the spiritual air so that faith languishes.
- It distracts and enfeebles the spiritual concentration and grasp of the hour.
- It possesses the thoughts with worldly and foreign interests at the very time when God and Heaven should fill, inflame, and absorb.

THE REMEDY

The remedy for the evil is laid down: "Let all the ministers and preachers," says this old *Discipline*, "join as one man, and enlarge on the impropriety of talking before and after service; and strongly exhort those that are concerned to do so. In three months, if we are in earnest, this vile practice will be banished out of every church congregation. Let none stop till he has carried his point."

The *Discipline* puts the remedy in the hands of the preacher. He is the doctor for the disease. He must administer a strong dose of exhortation and reproof; direct, plain, but kindly. It would be a remarkable case and a remarkable cure if one dose sufficed. The dose must be repeated with regularity and earnestness and continued with great patience and pertinacity till the cure is wrought, which will be soon. These old practitioners thought three months would bring the cure. It

243

may be sooner, may be not so soon; but whether three months or three years, or whether the perfect cure is ever effected, the remedy must be applied. The remedy will certainly check the disease and prevent its fatal results, if it does not remove all traces of it. But the cure will come, partly orin whole, if the remedy be administered faithfully, persistently, and patiently.

FOCUS ON REVERENCE

This discipline provides a focus on reverence in silence before the service, to prepare the heart to receive God's word. Following the service, the worshiper needs to personally reflect on God and time to adequately absorb what he has heard. Fellowship among Christians is helpful and needed, but it does not replace worship.

THE LEADERSHIP OF HOLINESS
Holiness in Leaders
January 3, 1891

A CHURCH CANNOT RISE ABOVE THE CONTROL OF ITS LEADERSHIP

An eminent historian has said "the accidents of personal character have more to do with the revolution of nations than either philosophic historians or democratic politicians like to admit." This is eminently true of the Church; its periods of high ecclesiasticism are marked by the hand of strong Church men. Times of great spiritual vigor have occurred when men of spiritual might have been at the helm. The Church, divine as it is, is subject to the mold of the human; its principles and its men will fashion it. These two factors form leadership. Principles cannot enforce themselves. Men must incarnate and execute them. If the principles are pure and the men strong, zealous, and faithful, the Church will be patterned after the heavenly; its light crystal, its walls jewel, and its streets golden. But if its principles be adulterate or its executors be weak or worldly, the Church will be marred in its foundations, its light unsteady and treacherous. It is impossible for a Church to give conspicuous and controlling influence to a policy or a principle without being affected in its essential being. It is impossible for a Church to rise above or diverge from the control of the men who lead it. The Church must banish and murder its prophets, or obey them. The false prophets must be silenced or followed.

HOLINESS THE PRINCIPLE OF PURITY

Holiness, the principle of purity, must be incarnated and give headship to the Church. This is the principle to be advocated, enforced, and perfected. The Church has a history, a theology, a terminology, a hymnology, a literature on the able means of "Holiness Associations;" not relegated to the keeping of an elect few, nor to be programmed through and narrowed by specialists and evangelists; but every preacher and every member is charged to possess it, enjoy it, live it, and have continuous accessions of its peace, power, and perfection, and to be constant witnesses of its ability to emancipate the soul in full from the guilt, power and pollution of sin.

HOLINESS IS THE A GREAT NEED
IN THE CHURCH TODAY

Our great need in the Church today is for men to execute this principle of holiness in a way that will make it commanding and exacting; men who are noted for its possession, men who are struggling, fighting, and praying to give it dominancy in their own hearts and lives and in the Church. That our men and Church be thoroughly saturated with this idea of holiness; that it be with us no side issue, not subordinate nor even coordinate with other things but first, conspicuous and authoritative.

Holiness is not enthroned into leadership as a matter of course. Official position, organization, churchly aims, and ecclesiastical thrift will not put this crown of holiness on us; brains cannot do it, neither education, nor genius. Men of the single eye, of the snow white heart, men who prosecute their personal holiness with as much courage and self-surrender as the soldier who seeks reputation at the cannon's mouth; they only under God can coronate this principle. I will emphasize that to give leadership to this holiness is our duty and safety. To do this will supply the men and money to sustain our work at every point and occupy other fields. The money would come or the men would go without it under the propulsive power of this divine and all-commanding principle.

TENDENCY TOWARD ECCLESIASTICISM OR MATERIALISM

The tendency of all spiritual movements is to harden into the rigor and deadness of ecclesiasticism or be debauched by material prosperity. The Church's policy is the best to serve the purposes of a strong, aggressive holiness. Depraved from its holy ends it can be made the readiest slave of High Churchism or the fittest engine for bigotry and party passion. Nothing but a full head of scriptural holiness will save it from being thus debauched.

A Church cannot rival other great religious bodies in material advance, in ecclesiastical power, in the pomp and parade of religious movements, in worldly, national, or political influence. We must have some peculiar feature we eminently embody to distinguish us from others, to justify our existence and secure our prosperity. To relinquish all other claims to recognition and center our aim in a pure and powerful spiritual Church is the highest wisdom and truest loyalty to God. To be the depositories, the conservers, the advocates of this prime gospel principle of holiness, for this, reduced to its last true analysis is truly but the highest form of spiritual life, the Heaven of heavens, and perfect love. This is the only thing that can break down the prejudice and geography that wall us in. A provincial church must perish in contact with powerful and ecumenical bodies. Our churches featured and projected by the principle of holiness, as our spiritual leaders and their co-laborers stressed it, would distinguish and widen us from other strong churches more than slavery or any other question, and give us the world for our parish.

WORLDLINESS

The giant evil in the Church of this day is worldliness. The two specific and aggravated forms of it from which we are suffering most severely are covetousness, the desire of money in the pew, ambition, and the desire for place and position in the pulpit. If the Church can be saved from worldliness, so these two forms of it will have no more place among us, then these are reasons that will give us a marvelous future. The one great specific cure for worldliness in general and these forms in particular, is a stronger type of holiness, differing in intensity, degree, and perfection from that which we have; a holiness that will impregnate the pulpit and the pew and go to the root of the matter in saving power.

THE CHURCH FILLED WITH HOLINESS

The Church filled with holiness from center to circumference, from head to foot, with ecclesiasticism, Church pride and power, and material resources with a consuming zeal for God's glory could carry the gospel to the world in a few decades. Such a quickening along all spiritual lines would take place as was never seen this side of Heaven. A contagion among us for Heaven would break loose, a consuming need to spread the gospel would prevail; such a cleaning out of hearts; such a regenerating of lives and business; such selling out of real estate; such an opening of purse strings; such a checking out of bank accounts for God's uses would take place as has not been known in our history. What powerful preaching, what mighty praying, what profound convictions, what sound conversions, what sanctifying grace would then be seen and felt and Heaven would have impulses of joy and accessions to its company as was never known before.

PAUL'S GLORYING
Tribulation
January 10, 1891

THE APOSTLE PAUL GLORIED IN TRIBULATION

Paul approached nothing on a low level. Neither secondary motives nor quiescent virtues were in great demand by him; with him their value was nominal. The term resignation scarcely belongs to his vocabulary. His virtues were active, not passive; they had hands and feet and tongues; they talked and walked and worked. He did not resign himself with folded arms, a placid countenance and a pulseless breast to tribulation, but he gloried in tribulation. He made his spiritual fortunes where others are shipwrecked. He grew rich by the disastrous graces. Out of tribulation the strong, shining chain of graces were to be wrought. Infirmities with him were not the sources of complaint but the theme of glorying, because through his weaknesses the power of Christ rested on him. Christ and not sin got in at his weak points. If sin had come in through his infirmities, it would have been cause of shame and not of glorying. His weaknesses were not held as apologies for sin, or offered as the cause or excuse of a defective piety. Nor were they points to invite the attacks of the enemy, but to be doubly fortified against the enemy and so he rejoiced that Christ got in to his weak places with greater power.

HANNAH MORE
(ENGLISH RELIGIOUS WRITER BORN IN 1745)

The sister of Hannah More said when dying: "I love whatever comes from God; I love my sufferings." Paul's piety was made after this high pattern. He took pleasure in his trials; *"Sorrowful, yet always rejoicing; poor, yet making many rich; as having nothing, and yet possessing all things"* (2 Corinthians 6:10). The Cross was the theme of glorying, not because of its philosophy or poetry, not from its sentiments of the grand or sublime, but because of its painful experimental process. He puts it strongly: *"God forbid that I should glory, save in the cross of our Lord Jesus Christ, by whom the world is crucified unto me and I unto the world"* (Galatians 6:14).

Paul gloried in the things that killed him because by Paul's death to the "self-life," Christ lived. In very few persons does the gospel reach this climax of its power, this double crucifixion; but short of this the gospel has nothing worth our glorying.

DRIVING OUT EVIL THOUGHTS
Renewing the Mind
January 31, 1891

ALL CHRISTIANS TROUBLED AT TIMES
BY EVIL THOUGHTS

There are good reasons for supposing even the holiest men are troubled at times by the presence of evil thoughts. The revelations of biography teach us the highest saintliness is no absolute bar to the entrance of these intrusive and unwelcome messengers of Satan, these foul and hateful vultures of the spiritual world. It is not uncommon for Christian people to suffer greatly from them from time to time. Most of us need travel no farther than our own experience for the full confirmation of this statement. How we may therefore guard ourselves against the perils involved in such a fact becomes a matter of no small consequence. It is not enough that we be aware of the fact itself. The highest wisdom requires us to form an intelligent scheme of self-defense and to consistently adhere to it for it does little good to follow our mere random fighting against the suggestions of the devil. We must study all his methods of approach and assault and learn how to anticipate and neutralize them.

A COMMON MISTAKE CHRISTIANS MAKE

It is the common mistake of young Christians and of some older ones, to suppose evil thoughts can be driven out of the mind by a mere naked fist of the will. Such a view betrays great ignorance of the elementary laws of our spiritual being. Our control over the processes that are all the while going on within us is for the most part only indirect and mediate. By no single act of mere self-assertion is it possible for us to stop the current of these processes or to turn it in another direction. Our present states are bound by the law of association to those that went before them. A little introspection will serve to convince even the most skeptical of the truth of this assertion. One state calls up another with undeviating regularity and uniformity. To initiate a new line of thinking, we must manage somehow or other to introduce a new set of associations. We cannot pick up our wicked thoughts by the neck and ears and toss them out of our minds by mere main strength, any more than we can lift ourselves over a fence by our bootstraps; but we can accomplish this great result by calling to our aid, in ways to be presently noted, the beneficent influence of purer and better thoughts. The meaning of the phrase "expulsive power of a new affection" is when an enthusiastic love for the best things is stirred in the heart; it easily drives out with little effort everything that is in collision with it. We may get rid of any unwholesome spiritual conditions by bringing in better ones in their place.

GOOD COMPANIONS, NEW THOUGHT LIFE

To be more specific, let us indicate these ways in which a new train of associations may be started: First, we may seek for it in good companionships. This is often a very effective method. If you feel you are being overmastered, go and talk to some wise and true friend. It is not always necessary you should mention to him your difficulty. In fact, it is often better you should not do so. Let the subject of the conversation, as far as you can control it; be of such a character as shall naturally divert you from the matters that have before occupied your attention. This suggestion, if faithfully heeded, will bring you material help.

GOOD BOOKS

Second, if no friend is near, get hold of a good and stimulating book. By a good book, we do not intend to designate exclusively a treatise of devotion; it may be a book of theology, philosophy, history, or poetry; no matter, as long as it calls you off from the wrong direction and sets you going on the right one.

PRAYING IN SPIRIT AND TRUTH

Third, let it not be forgotten in genuine and fervent prayer there is such an excitement of the nobler faculties of our rational and emotional nature and suppresses and puts down, as by a miracle, all base and unholy imagination and desires. Of course, there is no such power in the merely lifeless repetition of a set form of words. Real prayer is alive; it is aflame with passionate eagerness and earnestness; it is penetrated with the spirit of faith; and it asks for great things and gets them. He who has learned to pray in spirit and in truth has learned the final secret of victory over all that is bad and vicious in his own soul, and over all that is alluring and dangerous in the snares of the devil.

CHRISTIAN PERFECTION
A Command
January 31, 1891

Mr. Wesley affirmed Christian perfection is the grand depositor of the Church; Christians were raised up for this special purpose, and they had the distinctive mission to spread this scriptural holiness over these lands.

The clearest expression and enforcement of this doctrine was put into the Church discipline; the doctrine being incorporated in the very life of the Church. Let us strongly and explicitly exhort all believers to go on to perfection. That we all may speak the same thing, we ask once for all, shall we defend this perfection or give it up? We all agree to defend it, by the love of God and man filling our heart.

HOLINESS LEADING TO PERFECTION

Some say this cannot be attained until we have been refined by the fire of purgatory. Others: "Nay, it will be attained as soon as the soul and body part." But others say it may be attained before we die; a moment after will be too late. Is it so or not? We all agree we may be saved from all sin before death, and from all sinful tempers and desires. The substance, then, is settled. But as to the circumstances, is the change gradual or instantaneous? It is both the one and the other. But should we in preaching insist both on one and the other? Certainly we should insist on the gradual change and that earnestly and continually. And are there not reasons why we should insist on the instantaneous change? If there be such a blessed change before death, should we not encourage all believers to expect it? Because constant experience shows the more earnestly they expect this, the more swiftly and steadily the gradual work of God go on in their souls, the more careful they are to grow in grace, the more zealous they are of good works and the more punctual in their attendance on all the ordinances of God. Whereas, just the contrary effects are observed whenever this expectation ceases. They are saved by hope, by this hope of a total change, with a gradual increasing salvation. Destroy this hope and that salvation stands still, or rather decreases daily. Therefore, whoever would advance the gradual change in believers should strongly insist on the instantaneous.

This covers the whole doctrine in a practical way, and is of the utmost importance to every believer who is in earnest about securing the highest eminence of Christian experience, the fullest blessedness and usefulness on Earth and in Heaven.

CHRISTIAN PERFECTION DEFINED

This doctrine defines Christian perfection as taught by the Church to mean salvation from all sin, without and within; salvation from all sinful tempers and desires as well as from all outward sin; so that these tempers and desires are molded into the most stringent demands of God's law. Love—perfect love—fills, inflames, and purifies the soul and reigns supreme; long-suffering, harmony, sweetness, temperance, gentleness, and goodness are its obedient and ever-attendant handmaids. This doctrine shows the distinction between Christianity and other systems on this point. The Roman Catholic Church holds to perfection, but they say it can only be secured by the fires of purgatory which will purge away our dross and fit us for Heaven. Others say this perfection will be obtained by death. We say it can be and must be obtained before we die; that neither purgatory nor death has any purging flames or power. This perfection is not designed simply to fit the Christian for Heaven, but it is the preparation for the fittest and most useful service we can render God, either on Earth or in Heaven. That while it is the necessary condition of entering Heaven and for performing its high and holy service, yet without it the service of Earth is lame, and but half a service. But the most vital point to us as Christians is the last one stressed, which declares this perfection is both a gradual and an instantaneous process. It is both a growth and a transition. It is an advance and a climax. It is development and perfection. It is a running and a getting there, a groaning after and an obtaining. It is generally neither the whole of the one nor the other. God's power is unlimited; the work may be cut short in righteousness, in a moment, in the twinkling of an eye, but while the climax may be reached in a mighty effort and exaltation of faith, we are always to be in the school of perfection, always learning its difficult lessons, always in His highway marking an advance by eager steps.

BOTH GRADUAL AND INSTANTANEOUS CHANGE

We must insist on the gradual change, in this we are all agree; but we must also insist on the instantaneous work, that the two are interdependent and must coexist. To ignore the one or to discount it is to ignore the other and disregard it. These Church leaders, who were very wise in the things of God, stress with great force the fact that the gradual work depends for its being and growth on the constant urgency and expectation of the instantaneous work. They say constant experience shows the more earnestly they expect the instantaneous work, the more swiftly and steadily does the gradual work of God go on in the soul. And they also say those who are anxiously looking for the instantaneous work, are the more careful to grow in grace and the more zealous of good works and in their attendance on the ordinances of God. They further state the contrary is true; where the instantaneous work is neither urged nor expected, the gradual work stands still or decreases daily. Therefore, whoever would advance the gradual change in believers must strongly insist on the instantaneous.

WEIGHTY WORDS FROM MASTER BUILDERS

These are weighty words from men who were master builders for God and laid these foundations of the Church with adamant fervor. We do not hesitate to declare our belief in the truth and wisdom of these statements. Our observation extending over many years and embracing many localities, and every variety of spiritual manifestations; an observation actuated by the most tender solicitude for the spiritual prosperity of the people under our charge, substantiates these views. Our experience is corroborative of our observation and also of these vital words of the Church fathers. We have fully realized this gradual work of perfecting holiness only advances with vigor as we are looking for and groaning after the instantaneous and complete work. We do believe the absence of that deep groaning after this perfection in its mightiness and completeness is the never-failing sign of a feeble or decayed experience among our Christian people.

DUTY
Christian Duty
March 7, 1891

The present generation is impatient with obligation. Duty is a discredited word and obligation has the odium of compulsion. We do not wish to feel bound to do anything. We desire to be a law unto ourselves and are resentful of outside pressure.

FREEDOM AND LOVE ARE EXALTED ABOVE DUTY

Two things are degenerate by modern definitions; freedom and love. The first has fallen into license and means to do as we please without consent or hindrance; and love has become a sickly sentiment without strength to stand alone, a flavor, without body or parts. These two things with their perverted meanings are exalted above duty. We heard a world-renowned evangelist say he was sorry the word duty was in the Bible. It is in only a few places; but if the word duty were not in it at all, what does that signify? Those preachers who would discard the term duty are as foolish as those who leave the term obey out of the ceremony which binds woman to man as wife. What if we do strike the terms duty and obey; this would affect all the verbiage which implies the pressure of obligation from our Bibles, our vocabularies, and from our church ceremonies. But we get rid of nothing but the shadow; the thing remains, and we will have to rescind revelation, revoke all relations, and subvert the foundations of the Church before we are rid of the principles and obligations of which the word duty serves.

DUTY MEANS WHAT IS DUE

Duty means what is due; it owes its existence to our relationships; it belongs to our being. We come into duty by being born. We cannot live without being subject to its demands. It is a part of our life. Law, conscience, and revelation are based on duty and impel to it obedience to God in its fullest and highest expression. Duty is a thoughtful and grave principle; it belongs to serious persons and serious affairs; it fills life with soberness, stability, and earnestness. Duty holds like an anchor in stormy times and speeds us with delight and song in placid times. Gratitude, the noblest of principles, is the fair child of duty. Love, the most divine of graces, results from duty. We love God because He first loved us. The will of God creates duty; love is the law that fulfills it. Duty is the cross, the yoke of this life; and duty will crown the heavenly life.

O that each in the day of His coming may say: "I have fought my way through; I have finished the work He gave me to do." O that each from his Lord may receive the glad word: "Well and faithfully done; enter into my joy and sit down on my throne."

THE TRUE RELATION
Heaven
February 4, 1892

WHAT DOES HEAVEN MEAN TO THE CHRISTIAN?

What is the true relation of the Christian to Heaven? Is it an asylum to which he is carried by death; a place of flowers, of taste, magnificent, yet an asylum?

Does it require the heroic submission of a martyr to reconcile him to the going, or does he go to it as the conqueror goes to his triumph, as the supreme day of life?

Does he go to it as an exile hastens to home and native land? Does he go to it by means of God's decree, or does he go by an impassioned desire?

Does he go drawn by a supreme love with rapid wing and fixed eye, or does he go reluctantly "casting many a longing, lingering look behind?"

What is Heaven? Is it the place for death's bankrupts? Is it God's home for the elderly or infirm? Does it suffer by comparison with Earth? Are we the losers or gainers by going there? Is the blessed company of Heaven a lot of shivering, beggarly, shipwrecked ones?

These are not questions of sentiment, but they relate to the practical things of religion. They strike at the root of things. They concern our loyalty and our love to Christ. We submit that these questions are justified by the condition of things and by the public and Christian sentiment. They are justified by the value we put on Earth and by our reluctance or sadness at leaving it. These questions are justified by the way a majority of Christians live and by the way a majority of Christians die. If Heaven is a far off land with only a remote bearing on us and the things of this life, if it is only an unseen reward that we are to receive at some future time, the nature of which we have scarcely any information and the value of which we can make no estimate, then the less we think about it the better it will be for us.

HEAVEN: THE PLACE WHERE OUR TREASURES ARE LAID UP

But if Heaven is:
- the place where the treasures we can gather in these earthly lives are to be laid up and enjoyed,
- if it is the country to which our Lord, whom we love above all earthly things has gone,
- if it is, indeed our home country,
- if here we are but pilgrims and strangers;

- if Heaven be the country to whose soil, language, clime and occupation we are to school ourselves in then it must come to us as a most engaging attraction.

Heaven becomes a present, pressing, interest; a study that demands our richest thought; a struggle that commands our fullest energy, and a pursuit that inflames our purest and most intense ardor.

THE CHRISTIAN THOUGHTS ON HEAVEN AND . . .

Our attitude toward Heaven then becomes not only the source of inspiration and happiness, but also the test of our loyalty to Christ and the gauge of our faith. We may be well assured that they who have little of Heaven in their thoughts will have little of Christ in their hearts.

UNWILLINGNESS TO DIE

It is very common for us to regard an unwillingness to die as not only natural, but in keeping with a high order of faith, and it is the evidence of a singular and sublime faith to indicate on one's deathbed a calm acquiescence in the will of God and yet expressing at the same time a preference to stay. Such a taste is natural and may be saving, but it is indicative of a feeble love, a near-sighted faith, and does not measure up at any point to the standard of a triumphant New Testament faith. The normal relation of the Christian to Heaven is a desire to depart and be with Christ, and to stay here is to sacrifice desire in obedience to God's will; the staying is to be the reluctant part, if reluctance there be, and the desire to go is the native product of a vigorous working, clear-sighted faith.

THE APOSTLE PAUL

Paul's declaration was the calm, judicial statement of his personal attitude to Heaven. He says, *"I am in a strait betwixt two, having a desire to depart and to be with Christ; which is far better"* (Philippians 1:23). His statement in view of death speaks the same language of inspired desire and joy. His language is that of the uncrowned king, whose throne has been tossed on the issues of many a hard fought field, but coming at last to the day of his victory and coronation.

> *For I am now ready to be offered, and the time of my departure is at hand. I have fought a good fight, I have finished my course, I have kept the faith. Henceforth there is laid up for me a crown of righteousness, which the Lord, the righteous judge, shall give me at that day.* (2 Timothy 4:6-8)

In Colossians, Christians are called to the divine business of fixing their desire on heaven.

> *If ye then be risen with Christ, seek those things which are above, where Christ sitteth on the right hand of God. Set your affection on things above, not on things on the earth. For ye are dead, and your life is hid with Christ in God.* (Colossians 3:1-3)

The demand is a strong one. It calls for divorce from Earth and earthly things; they are all about us, and if they must touch us it is to be only a touch. We must not set our efforts, our hopes, or our hearts on them; to do this is to lose sight of Heaven, to lose sight of Christ and to perish.

The charge is twofold; it divides us from Earth and it marries us to Heaven. We are to seek the things which are in Heaven where Christ is; not only to seek by strained tension of effort, but with all the violent sweetness of a love-fired soul. We are to be drawn to Heaven as the gold draws the miser, as the pole draws the needle or as home draws the heart. Christ is there; is that not enough for us? Our lives are there also;

we are to set our love on Heaven and heavenly things. Our heart's dearest treasures are to be laid up in this golden city.

We are to be citizens of heaven, speak its language, breathe its spirit, enjoy its fellowship and be thrilled by its fadeless beauties. All these mean anticipation and longing.

PILGRIMS AND STRANGERS

The old saints confessed that on Earth they were pilgrims and strangers, and they desired a better country, a fatherland; that in Heaven they had a better portion. In Second Corinthians the relation is set forth in strong terms, the Christian is represented not as reluctant to go, not as simply submissive to an inexorable decree, but as choosing to go with an ardent desire.

> *For in this we groan, earnestly desiring to be clothed upon with our house which is from heaven. If so be that being clothed we shall not be found naked. For we that are in this tabernacle do groan, being burdened, not for that we would be unclothed, but clothed upon, that mortality might be swallowed up of life.* (2 Corinthians 5:2-4)

This statement of the attitude of the Christian to Heaven is seemingly as strong as it could be made, but receives additional strength from the other verses:

> *Therefore we are always confident, knowing that whilst we are at home in the body, we are absent from the Lord. We are confident, I say, and willing rather to be absent from the body and to be present with the Lord.* (2 Corinthians 5:6-8)

This position is no tame attitude, no senseless concern, but it is the whole nature intensified on the stretch for a known and seen good that lies beyond the realms of the flesh and the present. Its unspeakable good has struck its value deep in the soul and made it restless under its present poverty and eager to leave the fleeting, earthly, dying, and to inherit the heavenly, enduring and the immortal.

SELF-DENIAL

Self-denial does not lie in the surrender of some questionable desire, or in the excision of some pleasant or offensive habit. It is not the cutting off of a few branches from the tree of self, but it is the laying the whole tree low. Self-denial is not the restraining of some frills of worldliness, but it is the drying up of the fountain and laying all the channels bare. Christ elaborates and explains the principle by describing it as the casting off of the things of this Earth.

PATIENCE

We need patience that will clear and quiet the atmosphere so that everything may be seen in a true light, without exaggeration or prejudice, and will bear the wrongs of others kindly and without resentment.

PRAYER

Prayer will help patience and go far beyond a mere helping. Prayer will create conditions, give success to the right, bring good out of evil, and give victory over defeat. There is much sin in politics and much corruption. Politics is not the school of virtue, nor are those whom it puts to rule over us in these days the terror to evildoers that they ought to be; but politics will never be purified nor righteous rulers put in office by impatient and prayerless political partisans.

We are met with the statement that the case is too far gone for prayer to reach. If this be true then are we wholly gone, for there is no cure for evils that can go beyond prayer, for prayer goes as far as God can go. Matters had gone very far into the fathomless depths of corruption when Nero was on the throne and Felix was his representative. Paul met this condition, not as a partisan or with severe denunciation, but as a Christian by earnest exhortation:

> *That first of all, supplications, prayers, intercessions, and giving of thanks be made for all men; for kings, and for all that are in authority; that we may lead a quiet and peaceable life in all godliness and honesty.* (1 Timothy 2:1-2)

SPIRIT REPRESSION
Spiritual Repression
May 12, 1892

HOLY GHOST RELIGION IS SYMBOLIZED BY FIRE

Utterance is not religion, but a vigorous religion must be expressed. The light is to be put on a candle stand, not under a bushel basket. Holy Ghost religion is symbolized by fire, but the symbol finds shape and expression in tongues of fire. The gift of utterance and its diversity and power was a marked, if not the main feature of the primitive Church. The Apostolic Church depended more on its witnessing functions than on any other force to propagate the gospel. True spiritual operations stir the great deep of the soul. God's presence is a mighty awakener, and this awakening must find expression.

God kindles the flame in the heart, but He touches the lips that they may give utterance to the inflamed heart.

HEAVEN IS THE MODEL

Heaven is the pattern after which our religion is to be modeled and it is neither silent nor drowsy. Heaven is all life, all voice. The Apostle Paul moved under the propulsion of the purest and strongest standards, and yet he can scarcely pen his weightiest principles without bursting out with the spontaneous utterances of thanksgiving and praise. The most casual glance into the Apostolic Church reveals the stir and expression that marked it. The expression was exuberant, noisy and exhilarating, but it was the noise and exuberance of an overflowing life. The expression may have violated fashionable or frigid taste and sometimes it exceeded religious order. The primitive Christian poured out the pent-up fullness of his spirit-stirred life to comfort, exhort, and to edify, and in doing so received a blessing and gave a blessing. These expressions were not mere verbiage nor shadowy effusions; profound principles and the full current of a mighty life were back of the expressions, creating and demanding them.

We are no advocates for noise; there may be much noise with no background of spiritual feeling and no foundation of granite principle. We are not pleading for mere talk and nothing but words. Talk is cheap. Words may abound like leaves and may serve but to hide the barrenness of heart religion. We are averse to studied or stereotyped utterance. These are distasteful and hurtful to every sentiment of piety but true spiritual life must find utterance for the divine experience that makes its heart's saddest, sweetest history and brightest hopes.

EXPRESSION IS THE LAW OF SPIRITUAL LIFE

Expression is the law of spiritual life, and necessary to its continued and vigorous declaration with clear expression, for the suppression of opinion is declared to be injurious to both reason and sincerity. To repress abates the vigor of the thought-creating power, and also adulterates the fountain of purity. Men must have opinions, and those opinions must be expressed or men will cease to be men. Religion must have life and feeling, and these must be expressed if religion is to retain any life or vigor or be anything more than a royal mummy. The Christian who habitually represses the spiritual emotions which are God-created in his soul will soon be shorn not only of these sweet, life-giving feelings that nerve and clarify the soul, but the principles from which these emotions spring will be like a tree stripped of its leaves and roots and left to decay and death.

SPIRITUAL REPRESSION

Spiritual repression is one of the diseases which is afflicting Christians of this day. The disease is found in various stages from its incipiency to its most malignant form. In most cases, it is chronic and of such long and customary standing, that in many places it is regarded as the healthy condition. Our seasons of revival bring us back to original spiritual conditions and give us a glimpse of what ought to be our everyday life. But the revival itself is becoming by its rareness abnormal and its illustration of spiritual principles is regarded as exceptional. The revival passes and the spiritual wave recedes to its low watermark.

The Christian movement is modeled after a primitive style. It had much of this spiritual utterance, the product of its faith and love. With them, as in the early Church, there was the spiritual expression in a marked way. Their spiritual life was too vigorous to be repressed, out it must come by inherent force. To repress spiritual life or stifle its utterance belongs not to Christian tradition or to its ethics. "What we have seen and felt with confidence we tell." The Church was divinely framed to afford channels for the communication and contagion of spiritual principles and the emotions kindled by them. The class meeting, the love feast, the happy and confident outbursts of her new converts, the spontaneous and joyous singing, the hearty and stirring amen giving spiritual unity and impulse; the simplicity, freedom and spontaneity of her meetings, the rich and varied experience detailed by her votaries; all these gave constant and practical opportunities to cultivate and perpetuate the gifts of spiritual expression. Fellowship, freedom and increased spirituality were the fruits of this expression as well as the soil from which it sprang.

DECLINE FROM THIS ORIGINAL STATE

We have declined from this original state and our institutions are no longer distinctly spiritual, nor are they vitally spiritualizing. Church business, the machinery of a great ecclesiasticism engages time and strength; other things and other gifts and agencies have been substituted in a measure for the direct and all-powerful operations of the Holy Ghost so that our eyes are not set on Him nor our hearts filled by His presence, so as to make our methods instinct with His life. Our quarterly meetings are largely routine and secular, our average love feasts dry and tasteless, and our class meetings degenerate or obsolete. Church music, formal, pretentious, often worldly and always non-devout, has replaced our joyous, soul-moving singing. Our spiritual courage is too timid or our spiritual lungs too weak to articulate an amen. The process of spiritual repression has dried up our spiritual rivers and deadened our spiritual fires. We plead for the genuine article, no quackery, no substitute nor shadow do we want; not the drill and order of the program, not the effusion of sentiment nor the spurts and jerks of a galvanized life, but the quickening of the Holy Ghost to give volume and expression, form and voice. Dumbness is not one of His gifts. Silence never reigns where the Holy

Ghost does. We need to be filled with the Holy Ghost to cure our spiritual lockjaw, to flood our spiritual dryness, so out of us according to the promise, there shall flow rivers of living water, spontaneous, irresistible, refreshing and free.

ABOUT PRUDENCE
Christian Discretion
May 26, 1892

In one of the battles of the American Revolution, General Lee was ordered by General Washington to open the attack, which for some cause he failed to do. General Washington reprimanded him by inquiring what untimely prudence prevented him from carrying out the orders of his superior? "I know of no man," said Lee, "who has more of that rascally virtue than yourself."

Prudence often stands in the way of courage and degenerates into hesitating timidity. It does not rank high as a Christian virtue because of its timid nature; it's weighing of conditions and circumstances too much, and is always careful. A virtue that has a horror of making mistakes, and is ever balancing contingencies and conditions and moves with timid steps, cannot be the companion of faith, which while neither rash nor presumptuous, faith never counts or regards conditions and never acts timidly.

Neither God nor Christ estimates worldly prudence highly. Christ rejoices with gratitude that God has left it out of the list of His favorite virtues. We have this record: *"At that time Jesus answered and said, I thank thee, O Father, Lord of heaven and earth, because thou hast hid these things from the wise and prudent, and hast revealed them unto babes"* (Matthew 11:25).

Prudence is too cool and calculating for the uses of an earnest piety. It separated many of Luther's early friends from him. Wesley exclaimed, "God deliver me and all that seek Him in sincerity from what the world calls Christian prudence!"

IMPRUDENCE

Imprudence is the cry that is raised against earnestness and zeal. Christ was charged with being beside himself. Paul laid himself open to the same charge from the prudent, timid ones. Imprudence comes in as a grievous charge against those who are striving to execute the discipline of the Church. To execute its laws, as executed they ought always to be, exposes one to the charge of imprudence. The execution of discipline stirs up strife, creates friction, and the wise ones are ready to say discipline must be executed, purity protected, and the law honored; but there was rashness in the administration. The charge of imprudence is the penalty always adjudged against the enforcer of discipline, but the fearless soldier sentinel will not hesitate in the discharge of duty, even in the face of such a mild penalty as that of being charged with rashness.

SPIRITUAL LEADERSHIP
Spirit-led Leaders
June 2, 1892

SPIRITUAL LEADERSHIP IN THE CHURCH

The Church is very sensitive to the touch and control of its leaders. No looking glass shows greater fidelity in giving back the features of the face than does the Church in responding to the men and principles that dominate it. Pauline principles prevailed while Paul governed. The only way to get rid of Pauline principles was to renounce the man Paul. Every mastering spirit in the Vatican has left his impression on the Roman Church. A spiritual leadership results in a spiritual church. A worldly or non-spiritual leadership begets the same. The Church will follow its leaders, or change them. Spiritual leadership is the inauguration of spiritual times, the pledge of God's favor and the prophecy of true and large prosperity. Spiritual matters go greatly awry when non-spiritual leadership directs. Religion has perilous sailing when unskilled hands are at the helm, or ignorance, treachery, or weaknesses are at the prow. It was a sad day for God and His people when children were princes and babes had rule.

By spiritual leadership we do not mean simply the headship of strong men who hold and control spiritual matters with a forceful grasp. An earthly diadem has never encircled more of the greed of place, the greed of gain, or the greed for self, than has the tiara of churchly popes. Neither do we mean the control of those who by hook or crook get to the front in ecclesiastical things and dabble in spiritual affairs.

CHARACTER DETERMINES LEADERSHIP

The character of the men who lead determines the leadership. If the men are worldly, the leadership will be so. Men of affairs, mere materialized men, dazzled by the secularities of the Church advance ambitious men. Lovers of money or lovers of fame will never rise to the heights of spiritual leadership. They may see these sunny heights far away, but they are dim and shadowy to their sight. Spiritual leadership is the gift and function of men in whom the Holy Ghost has planted the fullness of matured spiritual principles; men to whom spiritual principles are the most real, the most potent, the most conspicuous things with all else held in secondary esteem. This leadership in principle, policy, and method is nothing more and nothing less than the presence and power of the Holy Ghost leading at every point and quickening in every way.

FAITH, HOLINESS, AND PRAYER

Spiritual leadership regards faith, holiness, and prayer, as the only true church forces. Forces so mighty and engaging as to discount or retire all else is exceedingly jealous lest other worldly forces should seek to rival or replace these. Spiritual leadership belongs to men whom the Holy Ghost has transformed and who learn all their principles and plans from being constantly closeted with God. All their efforts and schemes are but the execution of the results of this counseling. This leadership comes not to the front by personal desire or personal force nor by the pressure of a canvas; but God needs them, God puts them there.

JOHN WESLEY

Mr. Wesley is an illustration of spiritual leadership. A scholar, poet, philosopher and theologian; but neither one nor all these gave character to his leadership. Philosophy despised him, poetry ridiculed him, theologies rejected him, and scholarship scorned him. They forgot or despised his natural or acquired talents in the fierceness of the spiritual struggles that put him to the front. None of these native gifts colored his leadership or controlled his career. He reproduced in his life the spiritual principles God had mightily radiated in his heart. He preached them without a stint, with the truest loyalty and projected them on the world with the power of the Holy Ghost. His poetry, philosophy, scholarship, and preaching ability had many rivals, doubtless many superiors, but in his submission to God, his singleness of aim, his lack of worldliness, his prayerfulness and his faith; these had no superior, scarcely a rival, and by these and into these he led his followers. A spiritual leader he was as distinguished from an intellectual, theological, scholarly, or ecclesiastical one.

APOSTLE PAUL

Paul was a spiritual leader. He could have been a leader in politics, social reforms and Grecian culture, with great thoughts, schemes, and ambitions, but his sound conversion and spiritual fullness and meekness cured him of these illusory, pretentious and vague vanities. He had no force to waste on other interests, no taste, and no talent for other calls. God's Kingdom with its exhaustive solicitudes and demands silenced and sobered him, and taxed to the utmost all his powers. His heart grew faint with its throbbing for men, but broke to lead them only to the Cross. He trod the land of song, of history, of philosophy; he looked on the places where the world's empire trembled on the decision of a battlefield, without feeling a thrill from these immortal and classic scenes or events. Paul came into place not by a pressing ambition to be first in honor or power. God elected, commissioned, and thrust Paul into leadership. He directed the Church in her narrow, unworldly, yet broad and worldwide way. Paul followed in the footsteps of Christ, breathed His spirit, championed His doctrines, was crucified to the world and trampled all secular and worldly aids and aims underfoot. He relied solely on the Holy Ghost, always prominent and stressing that reliance, always at the front, leading the charge against the world, the flesh and the devil. Such was Paul in his spiritual leadership, and such are the leaders who follow him as he followed Christ.

The Church is no enemy to brains or learning. It offers no premium to fools, only fools for Christ's sake. We have not divested its true leadership of all human force, either native or acquired; this native energy and these acquisitions are dominated, hidden and surcharged with the opulence and impregnation of spiritual forces. Fletcher was a genius.

Carvosso was a man of the soundest judgment. Bramwell was no mean scholar, but Fletcher led as a saint and not as a genius. The leadership of Carvosso was not that of a man of mere affairs and uncommon sense, but a leadership of the most practical, pervasive, and intense holiness. Bramwell's scholarship was lost in the marvelous force of his faith and prayers and the eminence of his holiness and spiritual power.

The Church may have great men who can preach great sermons, church lawyers and historians, church editors, graceful writers and popular preachers; men who can plan great Church movements and execute them, men who can represent us in social or ecclesiastical circles; but none of these are the essential qualifications for spiritual leadership. None of these elements can project or continue Christianity true to its God-ordained mission.

FOUNDATION OF SPIRITUAL POWER

Church leaders may rank high in mental endowments and have all the learning of the schools. They may excel Paul or Wesley. But if they are not preeminent in spiritual power, the very thing that made Paul and Wesley what they are for God and for the world, they cannot be the true successors of these godly leaders. Men can grasp all the principles of Church advance by the philosophy of a strong intellect, but can neither master nor project these principles except by the grasp and energy of a strong faith. They can declare the philosophy and facts of the Christian movement, but cannot reproduce them even in miniature. They can pursue some favorite study for days and nights and not grow weary, but their spiritual nerve cannot bear the strain of one hour's wrestling with God. They can stir themselves up to take hold of great religious movements, but cannot stir themselves to take hold of God. Nothing is so erratic, so blind, and so pernicious as genius, worldly wisdom, and brain force, when foisted into spiritual leadership.

WORLDLINESS

The world is coming into the Church at many points and in many ways. It oozes and pours in. It comes in with brazen front or soft, insinuating disguise. It comes in at the top and bottom, and percolates through many a hidden way. Our only protection and rescue from this worldliness comes in our intense and radical spirituality. Our only hope for the existence and continuance of this high, saving spirituality under God, is in the purest and most spiritually aggressive leadership in the Church. This type leadership knows the secret of power, the sign by which she has conquered, and has conscience, conviction, and courage to hold her true to her symbols, true to her traditions, and true to the hidings of her power. We need this leadership; we must have it.

By the perfection and beauty of its holiness, the strength and elevation of its faith, the potency and pressure of its prayers, the authority and spotlessness of its example, the fire and contagion of its zeal, the singularity, sublimity, and lack of worldliness of its piety, it may influence God and hold and mold the Church to its heavenly pattern. Such leaders! How mightily they are felt! How their flame arouses the Church! How they stir it by the force of Pentecostal presence! How they embattle and give victory by the conflicts and triumphs of their own faith! How they fashion it by the impress and importunity of their prayers! How they inoculate it by the contagion and fire of their holiness! How they lead the march, in great spiritual revolution! How the Church is raised from the dead by the resurrection call of their sermons! Holiness springs up in their wake as flowers at the voice of spring, and where they tread the desert blooms as the garden of the Lord. The Church demands such leaders along the whole line of official position from the lowly to the superior. How feeble, aimless or worldly are our efforts; how demoralized and headless for God's work we are without them.

LEADERSHIP, A GIFT OF GOD

The gift of this leadership is not about power. They are God's gifts. Their being, presence, number and abilities are the tokens of His favor. The lack of these gifts is a sure sign of His disfavor and the presage of His withdrawal. Let the Church be on her knees before the Lord of Hosts that He may more mightily endow the leaders we already have all along the line.

THE PASTOR
Pastoral Care
July 14, 1892

The Church has always needed pastors and always will need them. We do not underrate the necessity of preaching. It's vital importance to the maintenance and spread of the gospel cannot be exaggerated; but the functions of a pastor in visiting and seeing to his flock are of equal importance. There can be neither opposition nor separation between the preacher and pastor; they are one. Preaching and pastoral care and declaring the gospel and personal oversight belong to the same person. Their functions are of the same divine office. They are so united they stand or fall together. They are interdependent. The efficiency and true success of the one depends on the efficiency of the other.

The charge has been made against the Church that it does not afford the conditions for a Christian pastorate. This is not true. It does afford the conditions for a successful pastorate, but it demands greater energy, industry and great study and work to secure these ends. The preacher who will give his mornings to prayer and study and his afternoons to visiting in the homes of the people will meet the conditions of a faithful pastorate and secure its best results. If the preacher allows the fact he will be with his charge but a limited time to abate his diligence, relax his industry, and unstring his mental and spiritual forces, then he will fail; but if he will allow his limited time to secure the legitimate ends of putting all his spiritual energies and industries into play because his time is short, then he will afford the strongest incentives to faithful pastoral work. We need inquiry and stirring along the line of pastoral work. We are failing at this point, and to fail here is to emasculate our ministry. Though we preach like angels, without painstaking, tender, personal, pastoral care, the preaching will come to naught.

THE WORK OF THE CHURCH
Two Priorities
September 29, 1892

The time has come when fundamental truths must be often and strongly stated. The materializing trend is so strong it will sweep away every vestige of the spiritual and eternal if we do not watch, work, and speak with sleepless vigilance, tireless energy and fearless boldness. The attitude and open declaration of much of the religious teaching we now bear is the same strain and spirit that characterized Unitarian, Jewish or rationalistic utterance half a century ago. The American Israelite sets forth the main object of the Jewish church in this language:

> The main object of the Jewish church today is not so much to save individuals out of society, as to save society; not to save men out of a community so much as to save men and manhood in the community; the

world, not the individual, is the subject of redemption. This was the endeavor of the prophets long before the Christian era, and this view of the duty of the workers for the redemption of the world is gradually being adopted to a greater or less degree by all sects of all creeds.

IDENTICAL THINKING FROM PROFESSED CHRISTIANS

We would not transfer this statement to our columns if it were not identical in idea with very much that we have seen from professed Christians, and from not a few church leaders. Advanced thinkers and discoverers have elaborated the same idea. They seem not to realize their true condition, which is one of going back and not going forward. This backward step entombs religion in the grave where Judaism has been buried all these centuries. It may well accord with the idle dreams of the rabbis to think of regenerating the world and ignoring the individual. Superlative nonsense of this kind belongs to the school of Jewish learning and Jewish blindness; but for a Christian with the history of his church before him, crowned and crowded as that history is with the fruits of a vigorous spirituality, to hold such views is strange and to one unacquainted with the blindness and perversity of the human heart, it would seem impossible.

The phrase "to save the world" has a pompous sound. It is acceptable for the church to apply itself to bettering the temporal surroundings of the individual and improve his sanitary conditions; to lessen the bad smells that greet his nose, to diminish the bacteria in his water and to put granite in the pavement for him to walk on instead of wood or brick. All this sounds fine and agrees well with a material age and becomes practical in operation and evident and imposing in results. But does this agree with the sublime dignity and essential aim of the church? Do we need any church to secure these ends? Councilmen of common talent, an efficient street commissioner and the ordinary vigilance of the average policeman will secure these results in their best way. It needs no Church or Bible, no Christ, no personal holiness to secure these ends, and this is the point to which all this vaunted advance tends. If the ends of the Church are directed to those results which can be as well or better secured by other agencies, the Church will soon be regarded as a nuisance and a thing to be abated.

The purposes of the Church of God rise in sublime grandeur above these childish dreams and philosophies. Its purpose is to regenerate and sanctify the individual, to make him holy and prepare him by a course of purifying and training for the high pursuits of an eternal life. The Church is like the seine cast into the sea; the purpose is not to change the sea so much as to catch the fish out of the sea. Let the sea roll on in its essential nature, but the net catches its fish. No bigger fools would ever be found than fishermen who were spending all their force trying by some chemical process to change the essential elements of the sea, vainly hoping thereby to improve the stock of the fish they had not and never could catch. By this method personal holiness would be impossible, and Heaven would be stricken from creed and life and hope.

THE SINGULAR AIM OF THE CHURCH

Sometimes we hear the expression spoken by men who ought to know better, that the Church has been too single in her aim, too exclusively addicted to the spiritual and the heavenly. A caveat is entered against this condition, and a demand for an enlargement of her aims to take in Earth as well as Heaven, and to minister to the body as well as the soul. With such declarations we have no sympathy, for they betray our trust. We believe that the Christian movement under God has alone more for the temporal weal of the people than all the sanitary, social, or political organizations or reforms put together. The Colliers of England are to this day the monuments of the temporal advance that followed the Church as a spiritual force. The happiest, most contented and thriftiest people are those who have been the recipients of the mightiest spiritual influences. Temporal advance and betterment follow the wake of every profound spiritual movement as inevitably as the waves follow the mightiest ocean vessel. The church which concerns itself the most with getting its people spiritual does the most for their temporal good. The religion that puts the most of Heaven in the hopes and hearts of its people will do the most to bless and alleviate their stay on Earth.

THE CHURCH MUST HOLD TO HER SINGULAR PURPOSE

Instead of being caught by the deceitful glare of materialized ends, the Church must hold herself more rigidly to the great purpose of her being "to spread scriptural holiness over these lands." We will consecrate ourselves to religion. Let others follow the task of bettering communities; we will apply ourselves to the lowlier task of converting the individual. Let other organizations devote themselves to getting ready to live; let us devote ourselves in getting them ready to die. Let others insanely try to make a Heaven on Earth; we will spend our force in winning men to a real and eternal Heaven. For he who has the fullest preparation to die has the best preparation to live, and he who devotes himself to Heaven, where Christ and God, the angelic and glorified hosts are, will be the best devotee to bless Earth and do good to men.

DECAY OF SPIRITUAL INSTITUTIONS
Materialism
January 26, 1893

LOSS OF SPIRITUALITY IN THE CHURCH

The loss of spirituality in the Church may be tested by the decay of its institutions. This decay may be seen in the death of these institutions or in their transformation. A spiritual institution may collapse or it may be so transformed that every spiritual element is eliminated. The transformation of spiritual institutions is the most popular, the most delusive and the most damaging thing that can befall the Church. Fashion, changed times, feeble piety, these lay hold on the spiritual church and while the original name and machinery are retained, change in the whole life of the institution can occur.

WATCH NIGHT SERVICES

Dr. Rigg, President of the English Wesleyan conference, issued a New Years letter to the Wesleyan Church at their watch night service, a letter that forecast well for a revival of spirituality in that church. The letter is eminently spiritual and timely. The special occasion that called forth the letter is past, but the principles which underlie this appeal are enduring and deserve serious thought by everyone concerned for the return of spiritual power to the Church. It is admitted on all hands there are great changes in our love feasts, class meetings, camp meetings, watch nights and revivals; they are not the same in spiritual being or spiritual manifestations as they used to be. The people seem to accept this as a matter of course, attributing the change to the superficial causes of changed conditions. They are not willing to admit what ought to be so evident, that these changes are owing to the loss of spirituality and the institution

279

has really changed from being a religious one to a worldly one with a thin veneer of religion on it. The principles to which we are committed and propose to discuss in this article, find their illustration in the watch night service as presented by Dr. Rigg. Of the old spiritual watch night service he says:

> The elder members of our church are never likely to forget the watch nights of forty or fifty years ago. Three hours were not considered too much to give to its solemnities. The closing of the year suggested a review of the past and an anticipation of the future, not only for time but for eternity. The mysteries of life and death and the disclosures of the Judgment Day always gave a deep coloring to the addresses and to the prayers. The vows of the past were recalled and renewed in a spirit of anticipation of the solemn service of the coming Sunday. The memories of those who had been taken during the year were often brought to the minds of the assembled congregation; the special characteristics of the year as affecting the whole nation were not forgotten. At the same time the voices of Thanksgiving with the rich melody of heartfelt songs of praise, bursts of congregational psalmody full of faith as well as holy solemnity were interspersed throughout the service, clothing it with a character of lowly and grateful triumph as well as deep consciousness of weakness and failure. The watch night service was a great seed time. The soul-stirring preachers of that time preached some of their mightiest sermons; they were the choicest local preachers, men of no common gifts assisted them, taking their due part in the service; prayers were poured out full of passionate confession, adoration and entreaty.

WATCH NIGHT SERVICES OF THE PAST
COMPARED TO THE PRESENT

The watch night thus observed could not fail to be a mighty spiritual force. Into the prepared soil of such an occasion the imperishable seed of the gospel was cast. The aim of such an occasion was not a pleasant observance to which the frivolous and fashionable were drawn by the charms of novelty or for the social pleasures of a worldly occasion under the thin guise of religion. The old watch night was intensely spiritual; it drew the spiritual and repulsed, the prayerless; everything was eliminated from it but spiritual aims, spiritual agencies, and spiritual results. Dr. Rigg contrasts this institution in its spiritual vigor with its modern representative into which so many vitiating elements have been allowed to come. He says:

The watch night of today is different from that which I have described. Other churches borrowed from us the custom of religiously celebrating the last hour of the year. In so doing, they adapted their services to the tastes and character of their congregations, sometimes even lending to the hour a note of festivity in harmony with the fashionable keeping of New Years Eve. We have borrowed something from the churches around us. The duration of the service has been abridged by at least one half, sometimes by more. Its grand character of solemnity has to a large extent disappeared. Within the now allotted space it would be difficult for effects of religious conviction and emotion to be produced such as seldom failed to accompany the services of the older time. The service, in some places at least, is in danger of becoming an observance kept up more as an ancient relic and a long established custom than because of any real heart of religious earnestness belonging to it. I ask

281

in all frankness, are our modern times in this respect better than the times of old?

Dr. Rigg also asks this pertinent question:

Is the habit of keeping with much prayer and solemn meditation, appointed seasons of devotion and self-examination passing away from the Church, and henceforth to be counted as one of the peculiar characteristics of the most earnest and at the same time extreme section of Anglo-Catholic High churchmen?

Therein lays the solution of the whole matter. So much of the world has come into our churches, we have become content with a carnal piety that covets no great spiritual gifts, and utters no groans for spiritual perfection, but is content with a poor, dying rate. These seasons of intense devotion and spiritual uplifting have no interest for us, but rather repulsion and we must take these institutions and dilute their spirituality that they may be tasteful.

THE OLD-TIME CAMP MEETING

The old camp meeting will afford an illustration of the same truth. Originally it was an occasion of great spiritual power. It was a meeting of spiritual forces for a general and deadly assault on sin. The directors of the meeting went there to worship God. It was a withdrawal from the world, from business, and from home for spiritual union and edification, and the results told upon all the regions round about.

THE MODERN CAMP MEETING

The modern camp meeting is a cross between a modern revival and a picnic. It is a pleasant occasion with just enough religiousness in it so as not to make it unpleasant to worldly tastes, with enough of the picnic to enlist all the pleasure seeking, the flippant, and the carnal; a place where the Sunday newspaper finds a ready sale and is eagerly read by the preacher who is to please the motley throng up to the hour he enters the pulpit, Sunday at 11 A.M. Tennis and croquet flourish on the grounds, athletics are part of its edifying program. The modern camp meeting, the place where the world and religion meet in happy wedded harmony, covers two Sabbaths that the boarding tent may be a source of profit, at the bar where cigars, ice cream, and other fashionable Christian commodities are sold on Sunday to help pay the current expenses, and where the church's percentage from the railroads may be largely enhanced by Sunday excursions.

An institution of this kind is called a camp meeting, resembling the old ones in nothing but in name and in tents. A success in everything else except in saving sinners and edifying saints. The reason of its failure in these inconsiderable items as it judges them, is charged to changed conditions and changed times; but the camp meeting is declared a success because of the number of tents, the genteel folks who were there, and the quiet orderliness of the occasion, the recreation and the generally good time that it afforded. An institution of this kind, baptized by the world and run by the world, often violating the decencies of religion, is called a camp meeting and proposes in name and purpose to be the successor of the grand old spiritual institutions that planted the Kingdom of God in Pentecostal storms of wind and fire, and smote the empire of hell to its foundations. It is not a successor but an imposter, a counterfeit, and a fraud; and because it does not do the regenerating and sanctifying work of the genuine camp meeting, we say that work cannot be done and we are to accept the results of the modern institution as the first and best fruits of the new dispensation and the results of the happy and long-prayed union between the flesh and the spirit.

The Christian Register, a Unitarian paper, says:

> Unitarians may not have been as prompt as their
> Methodist brethren in adopting the camp meeting;
> but when they did adopt it, they made some important
> improvements upon the original pattern and now it
> is a regular annual feature in the Unitarian calendar.

The perverse spiritual conditions which made the camp
meeting possible to the Unitarians depraved it from its high
nature and declared its unfitness for its original spiritual uses;
our modern revivals have also been depraved by the infusion of
worldly and non-spiritual elements into them. They are not to
be compared as spiritual factors with the revivals that marked
the planting of Methodism in England and which marked its
career in this country. The spiritual decay in these institutions
is to be accounted for by the feeble spiritual forces that direct
them. Dr. Rigg declares himself thus:

> It is my conviction if these services were observed in
> the ancient spirit and if the whole fellowship of our
> church, our class meetings and quarterly visitations
> were also kept up as in early times, we should not feel
> the need of seeking to create new and special seasons
> for humiliation and intercession, but should have as
> our frequent experience "times of refreshing from the
> presence of the Lord" bringing with them "showers of
> blessing" and an increase in our numbers from year to
> year such as would fill our hearts with thankfulness,
> accessions of truly converted and spiritually renewed
> members of the church and children of our Father in
> heaven.

We believe this to be true. If we will renounce the world
and get down in earnest, simple minds, and most prayerful

faith, seeking the Lord, and administer these institutions with the same unworldly and strong spiritual principles as those which characterized our fathers, we would have the same magnificent spiritual results.

A GROWING EVIL
Evaluating by Financial Standards
February 16, 1893

He who would save the Church must be eagle-eyed and maintain strength of vision. This is more especially true of those churches noted for their spirituality because against these the assaults of Satan will be the most insidious, artful and unceasing. The angels are called watchers and the prophets are watchmen. The preacher is akin to the angels and the successor of the prophets, and is committed by every consideration to sleepless vigilance. The most pernicious and potent evils steal into the Church unawares. The tares were sown while men slept.

CHURCHES CLASSIFIED BY MONEY

We are brought face to face with the fact that churches are being classified by the money they pay. Money is becoming a potent factor in the items of making a church attractive. The large salary paid is the first item in the right hand column of credits. A poor salary is the chief debit to its discount. Appointments are rated as first, second, third and the rating item is the salary. This new rule of declination scarcely estimates the holiness of the people, the spiritual possibilities of the field, the opportunities for labor, and the endurance or denial. The highest salary fixes the superlative degree and the lessening number of dollars fixes the declining scale. This evil is not imaginary in its existence or in its dire results. The evil is widespread, potent and disastrous. It is too strong to be corrected by church sentiment; it creates a sentiment that defies or silences authority.

THE PERNICIOUS EVIL OF EVALUATING A CHURCH BY ITS MONEY

The preacher must be supported in a generously Christian way. To do this is a solemn duty; to do it well is a fine trait of a growing piety. But to make this liberality a lure for the preacher and by it put the mark of first class on the church is to turn the grace of God into lasciviousness and degrade the ministry. To classify a church by the money it gives is a most pernicious evil, subversive of the gospel and at war with every spiritual instinct. Such an estimate is in open conflict with the example and teaching of Christ and opposed to the character of the saints who laid the granite principles of His system deep in the foundations of the world. There was neither a high salary nor low. It was an eternally unknown quality. To these apostles money played no part. The urgency of a divine call and a heavenly mission pressed them out, the love of Christ constrained them and the need of perishing humanity fired and strengthened them to labor and suffer. The thought of how much money they were to receive would have degraded their spiritual manhood and revoked their commission.

The preacher who pauses to weigh the salary he is to get or judges the goodness of his field of work by the money it paid last year, has yet to learn the first lesson in the self-denying school of the itinerancy and is not worthy of having his name on the roll of the men whose lofty principles and sublime self-crucifixion enabled them to plant and train Christians to be a sin-destroying and world-conquering force. It is in the very heart of the Christian system to call the preacher and leave the matter of his support as a secondary and after consideration which is to play no part as an inducement or a motive.

EVALUATING CHURCHES BY MONEY HANDS THE KEYS OF GOD'S KINGDOM TO MATERIALISM

To classify churches by the money they pay is to deliver the keys of God's kingdom to materialism and not to the purity and power of the true apostolic succession, therefore, making mammon enthroned in the church and not God. Nothing could dishonor God more surely than this. Nothing disembowels the gospel more effectually. Nothing could be more foreign to the animating spirit of the church, and nothing strikes a deadlier blow at its spiritual life. If anything but the archangel's trump could stir the grave of former church leaders with resurrection power or resurrection indignation, this would do it. Their prophet's eye saw this evil from afar, and they hedged and buttressed, warned and invoked against it. If anything can palsy the arm of the Church, crown her with ashes, and incriminate her by an adulterous connection with the world and cause her life blood to run poison through all her veins; it is that her ministry no longer seeks with self-denying zeal for fields which no tiller's hand has ever touched. Places where the poor, the imprisoned, and brokenhearted sigh for relief. Places where weariness and reproach are to be borne for Christ and all things of gain despised so that large revenues of glory may be secured to Him.

SELF-INDULGENT THINKING

However, the thinking is to turn away from these lowly services and waste places that self may be indulged, salary obtained, and ease and reputation secured. The downgrade of a preacher has been reached when he estimates his ministry, not by the number of sinners saved or the number of saints helped heavenward, but by the amount of money raised, the number of fashionable or wealthy additions to the congregation and the reputation and indulgence which a large salary accords. If these worldly views were confined to the few, even then the conditions would be contagious and the disease would eat like gangrene; but we fear they are wide-spread and growing and everything and everybody will be caught in the flood. Large salaries attract the preachers, draw the transfers, dazzle, bewilder or enslave the authorities, and command the best talent and as a consequence, small salaries and hard work lose their inspiration, and fall by comparison into neglect with the odor of degradation on them.

THE INEVITABLE RESULT

The inevitable result of classifying churches by the salary they pay is the classification of preacher by the salary he receives. By this rule spirituality, edifying gifts and fidelity will not only be ignored they will be discounted, for these are unpopular virtues and money will never put a value on unpopular and slow sale virtues.

The itinerancy will be a woeful sufferer. Nothing but a name and a corpse will remain, its ties of brotherhood will be rigid and as cold as ice, and its heroism and fortitude will live only in the past. Self-denial, humility and holiness will be unknown graces. The itinerant preacher will no longer be a mark and marvel, one whose highest ambition is to be first in sacrifice, the chief in all lowly labors, and counting not even his life dear so that his ministry may be approved of God, But his ministry will degenerate into a worldly one, seeking reputation on every popular or sensational wave, laying everything under tribute to please the popular ear, and keep himself in place and increase his notoriety. Trimming and lightness will be his stock in trade; cowardice, covetousness and worldliness his essential characteristics, a ministry for sale already sold to the highest bidder. Preachers will no longer be under authority as soldiers ready to march at a moment's order; no demands to make, no favors to ask, seeing in the call of hierarchal authority the call of God and duty; but money will call them, its voice once heard drowns all other voices. Money will demand the preacher and enslave him; he will be but a servant of its bidding. Money rule will recognize neither the Holy Ghost nor the spiritual church body; it will have no law but its lusts, yield to no authority but its pride, power and interest.

A first class church by money estimates must have a first class preacher; first class by the most worldly values. It will have him if in the market, and if not in the market it will make a market for him. Every spiritual estimate and attribute of the ministry will be depraved. The graces of a less showy, but unworldly ministry will be despised; poor and weaker churches will be overlooked or their needs carelessly met; centralization will prevail, extremities paralyzed and the whole connection will be ransacked and demoralized to satisfy the clamorous tastes and lusts of these first class churches. They will be but ecclesiastical brokers, mediators between a subsidized ministry and an imperious church, notary publics to put their names and seals to the yearly contracts.

CONGREGATION EVALUATED BY
FINANCIAL ABILITY

Another result from this baneful money classification of churches is estimating every man who joins the church by his financial ability. Money has become the staple of the church and a man's bank account is the only measure for his soul. The amount of saving power the man brings to the church is not reckoned, the strength of his faith, the richness and miracle of his conversion, the preciousness and power of his prayers, the holy loveliness of his life, these are small items; but the amount of money and social influence he brings and the increase in finances is the main thing. Good men rejoice that a sinner has

289

repented, and the angels are thrilled that a soul is new born to Heaven. A first-class church joins in the harmony moved by the fact its bank account will be increased and it will be better able to maintain its position to make its demands. Out of the dispensation of grace and of the Holy Ghost such a church goes into the dispensation of the world and of mammon.

RELIGION IN BUSINESS
Application to Life
February 23, 1893

"My business is one thing, and religion another," said a pretended religious man when the preacher sought to bring the spirit and law of the New Testament to bear on and control his business. Few men, perhaps, would so candidly confess they had divorced religion and business, but it is done on practically every hand. The Bible knows nothing of this divorce. With the Bible, business and religion do not belong to two different and opposing realms. They spring from the same fountain, though they may flow in different directions, they are actuated by the same spirit and may perform different functions and secure different ends. John Wesley has words of wisdom on this point. He says:

> Without question the same purity of intention which makes our alms and devotion acceptable must also make our labor or employment a proper offering to God. If a man pursues his business, that he may raise himself to a state of figure and riches in the world, he is no longer serving God in his employment and has no more title to a reward from God than he who gives alms that he may be seen, or prays that he may be heard of

men. For vain earthly designs are no more allowable in our employments than in our alms and devotion. They are not only evil when they mix with our good works or with our religious actions, but they have the same evil nature when they enter into the common business of our employments. But as our alms and devotions are not an acceptable service but when they come from a pure intention, so our common employment cannot be reckoned a service to Him but when it is performed with the same piety of heart.

DO ALL TO THE GLORY OF GOD

This means to purify the man; then whatsoever he does, whether at his office, in church, in his prayer closet, worshipping God, or selling and buying, he will do all under the mastery of the great principle, to the glory of God.

The failure to enforce the vital principles so strongly asserted by John Wesley and so clearly and strongly declared in the Bible is one cause of our feeble spirituality and our failure to be aggressive in God's cause. We are urgent for men to give and we stand as paltry beggars at the doors of the thrifty and wealthy Church members, pleading in vain for money enough to make religion appear in a respectable garb, however, a wiser and more religious duty is ours, and that is to enforce the religious way of making money. If we could secure this, the giving would be spontaneous and liberal. The most difficult end to secure is to get money to go out in right ways when it has come in by wrong ways. We need a wedding between business and religion, and the offspring of such a marriage will be frugality, thrift, and cheerful, ungrudging giving.

GOOD AND BAD PRINCIPLES

Covetousness and religion cannot go hand in hand. Bad business principles and good religious principles are never joined. Until we rid our business of its worldly and low features, and elevate it to the purity and dignity of motive enjoined in God's word, it will be a continuous snare and hindrance to religion. Worldliness is the great sin of the modern Church. Worldly motives and worldly aims in business is a wide door through which the world enters unhindered into the Church. The Church that allows its members to divorce business and religion makes a suicidal mistake. The Church can raise no poorer crop than a crop of millionaires.

HARD LESSON
Holy Spirit Dependence
February 23, 1893

TOTAL DEPENDENCE ON THE HOLY SPIRIT

The urgent absolute necessity of the power and presence of the Holy Ghost in the work of the ministry is one of the vital and initial truths of religion. The first and last element of success in God's work is dependence on the Holy Spirit. This dependence on the Holy Spirit must be absolute, concentrated, and absorbing, for in that way there will be no drawing of faith from any other instrument or agency and will dishonor them and put them in the background. This first lesson is a fundamental lesson without which all others are worthless, and all other revealed truth is vain and helpless. It is the most difficult to learn. It is the lesson the Church must ever learn anew and is always forgetting.

We are always prone to substitute other energies for this divine energy. The Church is always filling the place of this omnipotence by its manufactured potencies. Preachers have the rarest knack of leaving the Holy Ghost out of their reckoning, or if they do reckon Him, it is so that some grasping and conspicuous earthly agency may become the channel of His operation and the powerful ally to fill up His lack of conspicuous and self-assertive display. In one of our leading churches the pulpit had been filled for four years by a popular pastor. To begin at the beginning and remove the rubbish and lay the foundations deep and strong, the new pastor preached on the Holy Ghost and his people told him they had not so much as heard there was any Holy Ghost.

The Christian at work gives this incident:

A preacher of much experience said the other day he had not been relying as much as he ought to have done on the presence and power of the Divine Spirit in his pulpit efforts and prayer meetings. He sought forgiveness from God for his own pride, independence and self-assertion, and determined to cultivate henceforth as much as possible an inner consciousness of the absolute need of God's grace and immediate help, together with a humble, yet confident, expectation of the Spirit's influence. With these feelings of renewed consecration he entered upon the week of prayer at the opening of the year, and with the happiest results. His people seemed to catch the same feelings; the interest in God's requirements and promises began to spread. There was revival first in the hearts of professing Christians where all true revivals commence. And now many of the unconverted, and hitherto uninterested are gathering every evening into the sanctuary to join in its prayers and hymns with a prospect of a considerable ingathering of souls.

This case is representative. The Church and the ministry unconsciously get into a condition of grieving and quenching the Spirit by transferring faith from God, the Holy Spirit, to material and other agencies. Learning, talent, popular gifts, executive ability, and an organizing force are conspicuously relied on in the preacher, and by that process the Holy Spirit is retired. Social position, money, church organizations, and churchly activities, are put to the front and the Holy Spirit is grieved. Many a church like Sardis has a big reputation for strength, piety and works while it is dead. A name to live and yet dead because other agencies had been stressed and made prominent and the Holy Spirit had not been sought and trusted to the discredit of all else.

SENSITIVITY OF THE HOLY SPIRIT

The Holy Spirit is the most sensitive of all beings; His warmth the easiest chilled, His presence the readiest to retire, and His love the quickest grieved. He must not only be sought with all other dependencies renounced, but His presence must be vigilantly appreciated and tenderly and warmly cherished. He will tolerate no rivals, He enters into no confidences, and He seeks no worldly allies. He has all power to secure all the divine ends. His arm needs neither Aaron nor Hur to support it; but *"his right hand and his holy arm, hath gotten him the victory"* (Psalm 98:1). In what baneful hour did we forget the lesson our fathers knew so well, *"Not by might, nor by power, but by my spirit, saith the LORD of Hosts"* (Zechariah 4:6). The Christian at work sets forth a great truth which we must lay to heart:

> The same sermon preached in this living consciousness of the Spirit's aid and guidance may be the instrument of converting many hearers, but when preached with sinful intellectual pride and vain human self-reliance, it may fall dead or at most reach only the hearer's admiration for rhetorical excellence and eloquence.

We have no defense for ignorance, we are neither its advocates nor apologists; but we are suffering far more at present from the pride and self-sufficiency of learning than we are from the lack of culture. We have lost much more by our material advance than we have gained. We are poorer by our wealth than we were in all our poverty. Self-sufficiency in the preacher or in the Church bars the operation of the Holy Ghost.

A RELIGIOUS VIEW
Not a Social Church
March 16, 1893

There is a strong demand for the Church to be social, entertaining, pleasant, and attractive in its spirit. That it must be kind and brotherly is one of the first truths of religion. Heartiness is not gushing and brotherliness may be the reverse of gossip. This fact must always be supreme, the Church and its meetings are consecrated to worship. Lightness or the social freedom of conversation does not become it. Nothing so quenches the spirit of worship as gossip; the hallowed sober spirit of worship cannot abide in such an air. Friends should be recognized, brethren warmly grasped, and strangers welcomed, however, all this can be done without unbending the spirit of God's house. Spiritual civilities are but incidental to the house of God. To worship God is the main object of the occasion; to commune with Him, and not to see and enjoy friends, must be the consuming desire of the hour.

DEMAND FOR A SOCIAL CHURCH

There is complaint the Church house is not socially a warm place, and the demand is made that this defect be patched up by broadening the lines of Church agreeableness by shaping it after the fashion of a club or making it a mere meeting of persons in the interest of friendliness. All these devices will not only fail, but they will so alter the functions of the Church its divine ends will be forgotten. If the Church is kept up to a normal spiritual heat, these casual ends will be secured most effectually. The attempt to regulate these minor matters without securing greater spiritual life is the foolishness of the man who tries to get the plumage of a rare bird by shooting at its feathers. Shoot the bird and you get feathers, bird, and all. The difficulties that bar universal friendliness and brotherliness are too many and great to be broken down by anything but religion in its purest form. The Christ life reproduced is the only life that produces this universal brotherhood, and this strong brotherhood of grace will produce all the little decencies and trivial traits of the tenderest brotherliness. Where there is so much complaint and quackery about this matter, it is refreshing to find one who takes a religious view of the whole subject. *The Presbyterian* records this instance:

> A lady in humble circumstances the other day in conversation with the wife of the minister expressed herself in a very sensible manner about churchgoing. She said in substance: "When I go to church, I do not expect people to speak to me, nor do I wish to be spoken to simply because I attend it; neither do I want my pastor to feel he must always be speaking to me, lest I feel slighted and become offended. I go to church because I like to go and because of the good I get.

This is the religious view of this whole matter. We do not believe the church is hearty enough in its communion with saints because it is sadly deficient in the Christ heart. But we do not believe in turning the church into a place for social cheer and a place to do the agreeable in chatter and gossip.

To make the church meeting a center of social attraction, general effusiveness and converse is to deprave it. To appoint committees to do the agreeable or for the pastor to break his neck to get to the front door to go through a general handshaking and hold a powwow with those leaving at the end of the service is too professional to be hearty, too impersonal to be sincere, and too voluble and distracting to be spiritual.

FELLOWSHIP IN CHRISTIAN CHARACTER

We do greatly need fellowship in our Christian character. This fellowship is the cement of mankind. It will not only make our seasons of worship glow with the sweetest and strongest brotherly sympathies, but our whole lives, business, home, and church, will give out these tender ties that will link us to humanity and attract humanity to us and to our Christ. However, these divine attributes will never be found by tinkering at, or even overhauling the old ship of Zion and refashioning her after the popular, but low and delusive views of a social brotherhood. Men will never save men; and men will never be brothers to men on the plane of a humanitarian brotherhood. They must rise to the exalted plane of a divine brotherhood modeled by the life, death, and intercession of the divine man. A church where God is recognized as "a consuming fire," and worshiped "acceptably with reverence and Godly fear," affords the only heat that can weld humanity into this divine brotherhood.

PASTORAL CARE
The Necessity
April 20, 1893

If we were to emphasize one of the urgent needs of the Church we would state that need to be pastoral care. Pastoral care to be exercised fully and responsibly as a vital part of the pastoral office. The time never has been nor will it ever come when the Church does not find in the loving, painstaking, and diligent pastor the sources of spiritual vigor. The time never has been or will ever be when the lack of this pastoral care will not result in spiritual decay. In this demand for pastoral care we do not abate one iota the necessity of faithful, strong, scriptural preaching. The pastor and preacher are not two men, but one. Preaching and pastoral care are two functions of the same office and their duties pertain to the same vocation. Preaching is the vitalized declaration of revealed truth in public ministration. Pastoral care is dealing with the individual by personal contact.

TO PREACH OR TO PASTOR

Preaching is shooting at the flock; pastoral care is the singling out a bird and following it, wounded or unhurt, into its hiding place, and fixing gun and bead and charge on it. The functions of preaching and pastoral care in the ministry are inseparable to its success. Preaching cannot be done with efficiency without strict pastoral care. Pastoral care will be vain and insubstantial without faithful preaching. God has joined the two and no man can put them asunder. No way has been discovered by which a flock of sheep can be trained and developed in self-help as to dispense with the office of the shepherd. The bulk of the people will no more keep walking in the way to heaven without the pastor's personal oversight than a flock of sheep will keep walking in the right way without the oversight of the shepherd.

PERSONAL PASTORAL CONTACT

We do not need less vigor and fidelity in the pulpit but we do greatly need more fidelity outside of it; more of the teaching from house to house, more of spiritual, personal, private contact with the individual. The pastor or church which does not fix its eye on the individual will not affect the mass. Fidelity to the one is that which makes fidelity to the many. Direct and fearless preaching in the pulpit does not take on the character of courage and fidelity until it has been supplemented by kindly, open warnings to the individual. A prominent Methodist man who had fallen into great trouble when wishing to be rich by enlarging his business made this declaration to an old pastor "he was the only man who had ever said anything to him personally about his soul." This makes a point at the defective place in many a popular pastorate.

A preacher may gain pulpit reputation and wholly ignore and degrade the work of the pastor. Pulpit reputation and saving souls are often opposite poles. No man can edify the saints and perfect them in holiness without pastoral care. Training and pastoral care are functions that cement the force of the preacher. The preacher's faithfulness in pastoral care makes and measures the aggressive force of the Church.

MINISTERIAL VOWS INCLUDE PASTORAL CARE

The Church is so vitally concerned that its preachers be pastors, it charges them in the form of a solemn vow at their entrance into the full fellowship of the itinerant's self-denying labors that they will visit from house to house. Mr. Wesley declared he knew no branch of the pastoral office that is of greater importance than this. By repeated experience we learn though a man preach like an angel, he will neither collect nor preserve a society which is collected without visiting them from house to house. For what avails public preaching alone, though we could preach like angels? Every traveling preacher must instruct them from house to house. Till this is done, and that in good earnest, the man will be little better than other people. Our religion is not deep, universal or uniform; but superficial and uneven, and it will remain so until we spend half as much time in this visiting as we now do in talking uselessly.

It will not do for a preacher to say he has no taste or talent for the pastor's work. A preacher has taken a solemn vow to do it; under the pressure of a solemn oath, and under the pressure of duty and accountability more solemn than any oath, he is bound to do it. To say he has neither taste or talent for this most important function of his vocation is to acknowledge total unfitness for the work. The taste ought to be cultivated by him and the talent acquired or he should quit the work. It is almost, if not wholly, a crime to continue in a work so fearfully responsible without taste or talent for its vital functions, and make no effort to remedy the defect. No man can take hold of the Church for God who does not exercise the pastoral function. Preaching, though ever so impressive and charming, without it being backed by the pastor's personal oversight will lose its force and charms on many a soul by the time the benediction is pronounced. Pastors are the preachers whose words endure. Pastors can only take hold of a people for God. Pastors are the shepherd Saviors of God's flock. Only pastors can lay the foundations of God's temple, enduring and strong. The Word of God is demonstrated and shared through the actions of God's people, the Church. *"And they continued steadfastly in the apostles' doctrine and fellowship, and in breaking of bread, and in prayers"* (Acts 2:42-47).

PRAYING FOR THE HOLY GHOST
Spiritual Growth
April 23, 1893

Mr. Mills, the evangelist, said in his opening service in this city "that we were not to pray for the Holy Ghost; that to do so was an error, harmless but still an error. The Holy Ghost was in the world, and we were not to pray for Him." That the Holy Ghost is in the world as God is in the world is true. That the Holy Ghost is in the world as Christ is in the world is true. And it is also true there is nothing predicated of Him being in us and in the world that is not predicated of God and Christ being in us and in the world. The Holy Ghost was in the world in measure before Pentecost, and in the measure of His operation then, He was prayed for and sought for, and the principles are unchanged. The truth is, we can pray for any good thing from God, for He is the sum of all good to us. The truth is we seek after the Holy Ghost just as we seek after God, just as we seek after Christ, with strong crying and tears and we are to seek always for more and more of His gifts, and power and grace.

The truth is the presence and power of the Holy Ghost at any given meeting is conditioned on praying faith, and if a statement like that of Mr. Mills does not work damage it is because the faithful ones have not so learned Christ. It may be replied that Mr. Mills succeeds, and his success proves his theory. But his success is despite his theory, and because the major part of those working in his meeting neither believe nor act on his theory. Mr. Mills does have a widespread religious movement, but to secure an enthusiastic and general religious movement by the concurrence of all churchly forces and by the tactics of a skilled leader is one thing, and to have the presence of the Holy Ghost with searching, convicting and converting power on the individuals is quite another. There may be a widespread sensation awakened in religious matters by these secondary agencies which never is and never can be precipitated upon the individual conscience in saving power.

GIFT OF THE HOLY GHOST

The gift of the Holy Ghost is one of the benefits flowing to us from the glorious session of Christ at the right hand of God; and this gift of the Holy Ghost and all the other gifts of the enthroned Christ are secured to us by prayer as the condition. The Bible by express statement as well as by its general principles and clear and constant intimations teaches us that the gift of the Holy Ghost is connected with and conditioned in prayer. Christ declares this general principle: *"If ye then being evil know how to give good gifts unto your children, how much more shall your heavenly Father give the Holy Spirit to them that ask him?"* (Luke 11:13).

When the Holy Ghost came on Christ at His baptism, He was praying. He told His disciples He would secure the Holy Ghost for them by praying to God. The descent of the Holy Ghost on the day of Pentecost was preceded by many days of intense prayerfulness. A few days after Pentecost the disciples were in an agony of prayer, *"and when they had prayed, the place was shaken where they were assembled together; and they were all filled with the Holy Ghost"* (Acts 4:31). This incident destroys every theory that denies prayer as the condition of the coming of the Holy Ghost after Pentecost, and confirms the view that Pentecost, as the result of a long struggle of prayer, is illustrative and confirmatory that God's great and most precious gifts are conditioned on asking, seeking and knocking, through importunate prayer. Paul prayed that the Christians in Ephesus might be strengthened by the Holy Ghost and filled with all the fullness of God. The apostolic prayer was for the *"grace of the Lord Jesus Christ, the love of*

God, and the communion of the Holy Ghost" (2 Corinthians 13:14) to be with the saints.

We do not call attention to this important doctrine to simply correct an error, but to enforce a great truth. We would urge the seeking of the Holy Ghost. We need Him, and we need to stir ourselves up to seek Him. The measure we receive of Him will be gauged by the fervor of faith and prayer with which we seek Him. Our ability to work for God and pray to God and live for God and affect others for God will be dependent on the measure of the Holy Ghost received by us, dwelling in us, and working through us. The power of the Holy Ghost is evidenced by souls being saved, disciples being made, and the presence of joy and peace in our lives.

PASTORAL VISITATION
Pastoral Care and Visitation
May 4, 1893

Pastoral care and pastoral work find their best expression in pastoral visitation. That is what it means to go after the people, to go after them where they stay. Archbishop Leighton said: "Were I again to be a parish minister I must follow sinners to their houses, and even to their alehouses." The people must be sought after; we must go to them before they will come to us. As alluring as Heaven is we would never have gone there if Christ had not come after us, where we are.

Not to see and know the people in their homes is not to see and know them at all. No iron rule can be laid down as to how often the preacher ought to be in the homes of his people. He ought to be there so frequently they will feel the blessing and force of his coming; be there often enough to know the ways of the home life; often enough to be a welcome and familiar visitor, a cherished friend and a wise and holy counselor; often enough to remove strangeness, establish confidence, win love, and to know the spiritual character of the home and individual life.

PASTORAL VISITING IS TIME WELL SPENT

It will take time for pastoral visiting. It will take conviction and conscience and will. It will take more than these; it will take a system, something of routine with much regularity. A list ought to be made of the homes to be visited, and these classified and allotted to their day; four or five afternoons each week should be devoted sacredly to this purpose, and if the scriptural and disciplinary injunctions to redeem the time "by spending no more time at one place than is absolutely necessary" be followed, it will be surprising how many families can be visited. A membership of one thousand can be visited easily in eight weeks and leave plenty of time for special visits to the afflicted. This is not theory; the writer has put it into practice over and over again. That we have not time to do this is a deception.

PASTORAL AUTHORITY
Pastoral Oversight of the Church
May 11, 1893

CONTROL IN THE CHURCH

The Church must be controlled. Law is to be enforced, rules are to be observed, order to be maintained, purity secured and discipline enforced. To accomplish these ends which are necessary to spiritual being and well-being, authority must be lodged somewhere. The New Testament clothes the pastor with authority. He has the right of exercising spiritual power. He is placed at the head to govern. Obedience and guidance are elementary to the Church. Rule and authority are essential to the ministry. The Church is an organization, a school and a kingdom. The organization must have a head, the kingdom must be governed and the school ruled. The apostles ruled and they came with the rod as well as with love. Government is inherent in the word pastor; his position is one of direction and control. He must lead and hold, teach and direct, preach and govern.

PASTORAL OVERSIGHT

The Bible is explicit in its directions about the relation of pastor and people. He is charged to take the oversight; his right to rule is not only recognized, but his relation is so authoritative he is held responsible for the laxness and defection of his people. He has so many wide opportunities for influence; fidelity to his relation secures him to so many constraining forces that he is held to a very strict account for the integrity of the church. In Christ's letter to the seven churches in Asia, while the church is held to account, the responsibility and accountability rest primarily and immediately on the pastor who is termed the angel.

SPIRITUAL AUTHORITY

This spiritual authority is over the individuals and they are charged to obey them who have the rule. The pastor is not the manipulator of ecclesiastical machinery; he does not run his church as he does his clock, oiled, cleaned occasionally and wound up regularly that it may run itself in a way as material and mechanical as the clock. The pastor's authority is personal and it presses on the individual. He is to look after each and see that each is in line and time. He is to make diligent inquiry and search out conditions or failures; he is to apply remedies, precepts, comforts, the rod, food or love, as the case demands. He must see to it results are secured. His sermons are not lectures; his connection has no reference to hire or salary. He is there to meet the duties of the highest and holiest relationship. He has the care of souls. The laws of spiritual life are committed to him; obedience is to be secured, penalties enforced and authority upheld. He has no arbitrary irresponsible authority; he is no lord over God's heritage. The authority springs from the pastor's relation to God and to God's people, spiritual and unrestrained and accepted on the part of each. The pastor is to rule with diligence and the people are to obey gladly.

FAILURE OF PASTORAL AUTHORITY

The church becomes feeble and languishes in its spiritual life without unity and order because of the failure of pastoral authority. This divinely instituted authority is not felt. It is the backbone of the church. This spinal column in many a church is dislocated or dissolved. The pulpit study with its rhetoric, sermon making, social gad and gab, or laziness have swallowed up or dissipated this authority. The church must have the pressure, the molding and the reverent fear which come from a God appointed ruler. This authority flowing through the rich, loving, firm personality of the man, flowing through his example, his prayers, his faith, his preaching and exhortation, his pastoral care, pastoral work, and pastoral visitation must press on the church at a thousand points and on the individual through every channel.

This function of authority so necessary to the well-being of the church is almost lost. Protestant recoil from priestly rule and tyranny has carried us to the other extreme. But this recoil is not the main trouble; the main trouble is the world and mammon rule in the church; these despise authority and will not submit to control. With the laxity of discipline and decay of authority in the home, society and state, the Church taking its cue and reaping the fruits of home, social and political lawlessness.

DECAY OF PASTORAL AUTHORITY

The change which has come over the pulpit is another source of decay of pastoral authority. It often surrenders its function of training to be a caterer to curiosity, pleasure, sensation, or a mere entertainer instead of being the throne of authority, the mouthpiece of God's law and God's gospel. The pulpit, the rival of the theater in its popularity, sensation, pleasure and carnality, is the deathblow to pastoral authority. The pulpit of God demands obedience, wins reverence, and creates authority. But the theater has no right to govern, the opera cannot enforce rules and entertainment can neither command nor win obedience. The ministry stands alone in elevation and divinity; its aims and nature unique, to save from sin and discipline for Heaven. It must govern, or it is nothing. It lays down rules and announces laws. It proclaims duty and demands obedience. It speaks for God. Its authority is divine. It must rule in its sphere hearts, consciences and lives. The efficiency of this government has everything to do with the vigor, growth and stability of the church. No rule is anarchy; a weak rule is feebleness, disorder and decay. A vigorous rule is a resurrection call, everything is quickened and freshened; tonic, iron, and buttresses are in it.

The Church needs pastors, pastoral care, pastoral work, pastoral visitation, and pastoral authority. Pastors we must have, clothed with all the sacrifices, courage, and heart of the Good Shepherd, combined with His firm, constraining and restraining authority. Wicked or weak rulers are the curse of the home, country, and Church. The demoralizing and despoiling forces pouring into the Church were never stronger, and weakness in her rulers now runs rampant.

THE DIVINE BUSINESS
Business of the Church
June 15, 1893

The Church of God has a business to which it is committed. That business is the divine one of saving and sanctifying souls. The only business of the Church is to win men to Christ by saving them from their sins and preparing them for Heaven. It is not the business of religion to preserve an institution but to save a soul. It is not the business of the Church to collect money and increase and aggregate its material resources, but to promote holiness. All else is incidental, and accidental. To turn these accidents and incidents into the main thing is the grievous error into which the Church is ever prone to fall; a trap laid by Satan in his wiliness and by which he has caught and debauched ecclesiasticism of every order, creed, and age. When a Church puts emphasis on its money and materials, when its wise men and lenders spend the time of the convocations in disbursing and managing its material assets, it is on the high road to a hard and lifeless ecclesiasticism.

LIFELESS ECCLESIASTICISM

All Church history testifies to this fact, as the Church increases in material resources the tendency is to decline in soul saving power. Nothing restrains spiritual operations so greatly as filling the time and strength of Church agents and agencies with its secondary and material ends. To make these operations first in intention and interest not only detracts from the spiritual efficiency of the Church, but destroys that efficiency. The churches that have saved the people from their sins and perfected the saints have given themselves to this object, made it first, and the incidentals have followed naturally, necessarily, and in full supply.

A COMMON DANGER FOR A
SOUL WINNING CHURCH

It is the easiest and most common thing in the world for a soul winning church, full of zeal and power, with its preachers all aflame for God and His cause, to degenerate into a conservative ecclesiasticism. It will grow as a club grows, by accretions and not by life. It will have influence; social, financial and fashionable. In many ways and by many parasites, it will have the semblance of life, everything of life but its root, heart, and fruit. Its preachers will be sweet sermonizers, good, popular and pleasant preachers. Its leaders may be great philosophers, great divines, elegant scholars, splendid orators, in all things gifted, in all things rich, only poor and without gifts in the divine art of saving souls and sanctifying saints.

The trend from soul saving to ecclesiasticism shows its first and strong symptoms among the leaders and preachers of the church; spiritual decay begins at the top. Signs of spiritual decay:

- When the preacher is no longer the leader in holiness
- When his preaching no longer proceeds from the influence and presence of the Holy Ghost
- When his preaching no longer stands as a censor over the sins and lives of his people
- When great and gracious seasons of spiritual fructifying no longer spring up from his ministry, the fatal disease has invaded and prostrated his spiritual energies.

JOHN WESLEY

The leaders of great spiritual movements have been apostles in the soul saving art. Wesley was mighty in his soul saving gifts. As a man of affairs, a splendid orator, or an ecclesiastical statesman, he would not have outlived his day and the movement set on foot by him would have perished within the limits of Oxford; but his transcendent gifts in getting men to forsake sin and putting them on the stretch for the highest heights of holiness gave him the world as his parish, and sent the movement through all that parish instinct with divine life. Asbury and McKendree would never have rooted Methodism in America by their Episcopal prerogatives, dignities, or itinerancy; if they had not had the best gifts for soul winning and if they had not been graduates in that divine art, their many goings and labors would have been as traceless as the writing on the sandy shore of the ebbing and flowing sea.

ECCLESIASTICAL CHURCHES ARE GROUNDED IN WORLDLINESS

A church whose leaders and preachers are not trained experts in the business of soul saving and soul sanctifying, will be rooted and grounded in worldliness. A church such as this will prosper after a fashion, but it will be after the fashion of the world. It will have additions, as the lodge or clubs have additions. It will have influence, as society, fashion, and money, as the world has influence; but the spirit of repentance and holiness will be as strange to it as the flowers of June to the Arctic regions. We fully endorse the statement, "The greatest of all possible ecclesiastical calamities is when the policy and administration of churches are controlled by men who either have never possessed or have lost the divine art of bringing sinners to Christ."

After Wesley's death, Wesleyanism lost the art of soul saving and sanctifying because its leaders lost it. It takes no prophet to see that the Church is losing by degrees the divine business of making men holy. Additions we have, but who is so blind as not to see a majority of these additions are chaining us to members whose veins never felt the pulsation of a true spiritual life.

DIVINE ART OF SOUL SAVING

The art of soul saving is a divine art, but easily lost. It is the only art in which the Church ought to glory. If we lose it, we lose our all, and we will lose it if our leaders lose it. Great preachers they may be; learned and eloquent statesmen and philosophers they may be, but the worst of all calamities is on us if they cannot pierce the soul with penitential grief, introduce the joy and power of the new birth, and edify to perfection the saintly soul. The Church's great leaders have been great soul winners and great sticklers for holiness in its most perfect form. Let us stand by our history, tradition and succession.

A PRESCRIPTION
Worldliness Cure
July 27, 1893

THE SICKNESS

From all sources, we hear statements in regard to the overflowing worldliness in the Church. The symptoms of this worldly evil are numerous, unmistakable, and alarming. We are surprised the evil is so clearly seen by men of different shades of spiritual opinion and experience.

THE CURE

The cure of worldliness is the one crying demand of the well wishers to the Church. Honest and earnest pastors declare it is the first essential to any spiritual and healthy progress in the Church. Can it be cured is the question we hear asked? Cured it can be; for this disease there is the Balm in Gilead.

PASTORS LEAD IN THE APPLICATION
OF THE CURE

If the pastors will set about in a firm, self-denying, kindly way, it can be done. The preacher must set about seeking God for a great personal blessing on his own soul until he has a conscious experience of the Holy Ghost; a new commission like Isaiah had, and like Peter had on the day of Pentecost. Whether it is called a first, second or third blessing, he must have it, distinctly, consciously, and powerfully, until he knows what it is to have a broken and contrite heart. He must be pure in spirit, mourning over sins, all sins, sins everywhere, with a knowing, hungering and thirsting after righteousness. To this there must be added all phases of self denial; habits which pertain to ease and self indulgence must go. God must be sought early before the day dawns, sought with the whole heart and not letting up until they are filled with all the fullness of God. The daily paper, the new theological book with its mixture of good and bad ideas, truth and error, must be laid aside, and the Bible read in their stead; read, studied, prayed over and wept over. The whole time the preacher is laid out conscientiously, prayerfully, and fully for God by "being diligent, never unemployed; never trifling but deeming this time best employed when communing and interceding for self and his people. Much of his time should be spent in reading the Holy Scriptures and such studies as help his knowledge of the Scriptures. He must lay aside the study of the world and the flesh.

If the preacher thus filled with God and God's Spirit, as a personal, conscious, full, indwelling, purifying, quickening power, will preach the Word of God out of his heart, be *"instant in season, out of season; reprove, rebuke, exhort with all longsuffering and doctrine"* (2 Timothy 4:2), and will follow this up by personal admonition, he will find a marvelous change worked. Friction, stir and opposition there will be, for the vile juices are being cast out and inflamed. Let the preacher rid himself of all forms of the disease of worldliness, malignant or mild, positive or negative. When the physician has cured himself, he will be able to cure his people.

FAITH CURES—GOD CURES
God-centered Faith
July 27, 1893

It seems to be a most difficult matter to get men to think along Bible lines. Correct views are pressed to an extreme when all their correctness is swallowed up. These extreme views beget other extreme views. True doctrine is seen only in its caricature and the truth is rejected from fear there may be some error in it. Good men, anxious to avoid the error of one extreme, embrace an error equally pernicious at the other.

FAITH IS NOT INDEPENDENT OF GOD

Faith and faith cures are so presented that God is left out of the account. Faith is accredited as an independent thing, a kind of fetish to be worshiped; a thing self existent and all powerful; an end and not a means; a Lord and not a servant. Faith is so presented that God becomes subordinate and impersonal.

GOD-CENTERED FAITH

Faith is a mighty factor when it centers in God. We are fully converted to the fact we do not exercise that faith in God which duty and privilege demand. The gospel would spread far more rapidly, and God's hand in material as well as spiritual matters would be far more evident and powerful if we had stronger faith. But the efficiency of faith and all its energy lies in the fact that it centers in God. It is not a blind, impersonal, independent energy. But faith is strong and powerful because of God's promise and power behind it. It reposes its trust in the God of all goodness, wisdom, and power, and what it secures must flow from and be qualified by God's supreme wisdom and goodness.

FAITH AND DISEASE

Faith has been pressed to such an extent in curing diseases that many good people have been alarmed or disgusted into the rejection of the great and consoling truth that God deals with our bodies. We must admit from a New Testament point of view, God does give special dispensations to individuals, *"dividing to every man severally as he will"* (1 Corinthians 12:11). We could scarcely deny without going in the face of the facts and grieving God's spirit that the marvelous work of Mueller in England or of Francke in Germany was the result of a special endowment of God's spirit of faith for a special work. These results came as truly from faith as the deliverance of Daniel from the lions' den or of the three Hebrew children from the fiery furnace.

However, the doctrines of God's dealing with our bodies may be damaged by fanatical views on the one hand or rejected by a timid or rationalistic unbelief on the other, it is a Bible truth of great comfort that God *"forgiveth all thine iniquities; who healeth all thy diseases"* (Psalm 103:3). Our body is sacred to Him. In His book, all its members *"were written which in continuance were fashioned when as yet there was none of them"* (Psalm 139:16). Jesus Christ bore our sickness as well as our sins. His earthly life, so largely taken up with relieving the wants of the body, was not an abnormal condition or a mere episode in His history. He is *"the same yesterday, today and for ever"* (Hebrews 13:8). His curing so many bodies, which is the flesh, was not simply symbolic of the fullness and richness of the spiritual reliefs He bestows, but also declares the truth

He bears the sickness of our bodies as well as the sickness of our souls at His Father's right hand; the divine revelation that *"he forgiveth all thine iniquities, he healeth all thy diseases"* (Psalm 103:3) is the basis of prayer and faith for diseases of body as well as of soul. Therefore the New Testament prophet cries out, looking at the saints in all ages stricken with sickness: *"Is any among you afflicted? let him pray"* (James 5:13). We believe those who use prayer but reject the means of doctor and medicine are fanatics. We also believe those who use doctor and medicine without resting the case by faith and prayer in God are without faith.

THESE TIMES
Materialism
September 7, 1893

THE AGE OF MATERIALISM

The people of this age, especially the American people, have been living too fast. Too many fortunes have been made too suddenly, and all forms of evil induced by high living and much money spending have come in on us. A moneyed civilization has brought in materialism, luxury, speculation, falsehood and fraud. The evil results are its only cure. The prostration of all our industries, the dissipation of our fortunes; all our gloom, despondency and loss, will lead to the arrest of many a wild and wayward course, until we search in our hearts and learn of the vanity of earthly good. Cardinal Gibbons gives some good advice in a recently published book. It is so pertinent to these times that we copy his five rules to govern conduct. They are so full of sound common sense and the next best thing to religion, and so important an adjunct. They are:

315

1. Cultivate a spirit of industry, without which all the appliances of organized labor are unavailing. A life of patient industry is sure to be blessed with a competence if it is not crowned with an abundant remuneration. The majority of our leading men of wealth are indebted for their fortunes to their own industry. Take an active, personal, conscientious interest in the business of your employer, and the more you contribute to its success the better he can afford to compensate you for your services. He will be impelled to requite you with a generous hand.

2. Foster habits of economy and self-denial. No matter how modest your income may be, always live under it. You will thus protect your liberty and business integrity and guard yourself against the slavery of debt.

3. While honestly striving to better your condition, be content with your station in life and do not yield to an inordinate desire of abandoning your present occupation for what is popularly regarded as a more attractive vocation. A feverish ambition to accumulate a fortune which may be called our national distemper is incompatible with peace of mind.

4. Sobriety will be an angel of tranquility and will comfort yourself and your family.

5. Above all, let religion be the queen of your household. When the evening of life has come and your earthly labors are drawing to a close, it will cheer you with the bright prospect of an eternal Sabbath.

DISCIPLINE CAN BE ENFORCED
Authority
September 28, 1893

We hear it said discipline cannot be enforced in the Church. If this be true, then we are in a hopeless condition as far as spiritual prosperity is concerned. The church which cannot enforce its discipline is almost worthless as a soul-saving, sin-destroying force.

DISCIPLINE REQUIRES FAITHFUL PREACHING AND TENDER REPROOFS

We believe with all our heart there is scarcely a church within our bounds which cannot be brought into a state of good discipline within the limits of a four years pastorate. Most faithful preaching after the simplest and most direct New Testament style will be necessary. The great gospel facts, with all their serious and eternal results, will have to be applied over and over again to the consciences of the church members until they are impressed, awed, and sobered into thoughtful arrest. A constant stream of reproofs and rebukes with all tenderness, doctrine and long-suffering must be poured in upon their willing or unwilling ears.

FIDELITY, COURAGE, LOVE, PASTORAL CARE, AND OVERSIGHT

Fidelity, courage and love in the pulpit must be accompanied by the most painstaking pastoral care and personal oversight. In private, in person, in the home and from house to house the pastor must follow, watch, and work, until every member and the farthest extremities of the membership feels the impulses and the weight of his authority and aims. A pastorate that incorporates the principles of the good shepherd, who gives his life for the sheep will strengthen the diseased, heal the sick, bind up the broken, bring again that which was driven away and will save the lost most surely and effectually.

SEVEN CHURCHES OF ASIA

The seven churches of Asia whose backslidden apostasy called for the indignant and fiery revelation and protest of Jesus Christ, could have been saved and brought back to the strictest discipline. Their condition was not hopeless, and if their "angels" had been faithful their condition doubtless would have been much happier. It is our deliberate opinion a pastorate can bring any church to that spiritual condition where they will illustrate in heart and life the New Testament lifestyle. It has been done many a time, and can be done again.

The New Testament does not provide for a backslidden or low state of piety, or for an undisclosed church. Guilt and the blood of souls will be on the hands and consciences of the leaders, both preachers and laymen, if our churches are allowed to fall below and stay below this soul saving standard.

SATANIC DEVICES
Wiles of Satan
September 28, 1893

SATAN WORKS IN THE GUISE OF AN ANGEL

Satan carries on his biggest business in the guise of an angel. The Church is ever ready to adopt his shining devices. They seem so fitting to secure proper ends. The elect are almost deceived by his devices. The feeble saints fall into his traps by the scores. The worldly Christians are the pressing advocates of Satan's saintly ways.

SATAN'S WAYS ARE INSIDIOUS

Satan's ways are never to do evil outright, but to do evil under the guise of good. His master device is not to destroy the Church organization, but to pervert it; this is his wiliest scheme. He will be happy to let the machinery of the Church remain in perfect order if he can direct its aims. One of his wily schemes is to turn the Church into an entertainment monger. If he can do this his happiness is complete. His first step is to turn the service of praise into an entertaining musicale; then the pulpit for entertainment. The whole occasion of worship becomes pitched on the low designs of entertainment and his end is gained.

To one ignorant of Satan's devices his success along this line seems marvelous. No more dire apostasy is to be found anywhere than in those churches given over to the entertainment business.

SATAN PROMOTES THE SECULAR AND WORLDLY

The fashion these days is to widen the Church to take in all forms of secular and worldly things; to widen so as to take in Satan also, for he never stays out when the world comes in. The fact the entertainment business in the Church seems so innocent and such a little thing and is so much the custom, does not lessen its destructive forces; for it is the things which seem so small and innocent with which Satan does his deadliest and most delusive work. There are few churches which have escaped this snare. In nearly every church the whole or part of its worship has been debauched to the ends of entertainment. In fact, the current is so strong in that direction, it is almost irresistible. The pastor who stands against it is usually swept away with an avalanche or voted to be an idiot or an old fogy.

The Bible idea of a church is to worship God; church should be a place where all the grave and reverent virtues are called into exercise, mercy and grace are to be sought, pardon,

319

sanctification and edification, are to be secured. Nothing can be more foreign to the place and the occasion than entertainment and nothing more pervasive to the ends of worship. This idea of entertainment floods the church with an ocean of frivolities and foolishness, rather than what God intended it to be.

PROFANE FRIVOLITY

All this profanity is the result of admitting Satan under the angelic guise of innocency to direct the Church. If the pulpit had not debauched its sacred functions to please, if the praise of God had not been debauched by fashionable church music, if the choir and the preacher had not taken a hand in the entertainment, then the whole force of the church life would not have been given up to this profane frivolity.

These results are the native outcome of following satanic devices in running the church. The entertainment business is one of the world's ruling forces and Satan has his hand on it. He inspires and directs it to secure his ends. The church remains pompous, proud and fashionable, but God is not in her. The last and greatest calamity of downgrade has been reached; she is declaring she is *"rich and increased in goods and have need of nothing; and knowest not that thou art wretched, and miserable, and poor, and blind, and naked"* (Revelation 3:17).

SAINTS WANTED
Saints and Earthly Work
November 30, 1893

THE GREATEST NEED FOR EARTH

If Heaven were to advertise its greatest need for Earth, it would be for saints. This world needs saints more than anything else. Christianity is a dry, dull work, much ado about nothing if it is not made real and illustrated by holy living. To the world, Christianity is a foolish mystery and its Bible a sealed book. To make Christianity omnipotent or even potent, it must be enforced by holy living. It must have open Bibles in the shape of saintly lives. The living, ever present, all convincing epistles written by God's own hand on human hearts and shining out with embellished letters in human lives are the Bibles which are greatly needed now.

We need real saints, formed after the fashion of the New Testament and the 13th chapter of First Corinthians. There are plenty of saints in Heaven. The garments of sainthood glitter even more than Heaven does. Every person you meet there glitters. Earth needs saints though, too; but many of our earthly manufacturers of saints seem to have failed, or at least quit the business. Some of these saint making institutions, chartered for that sole purpose, have been turned into a more popular, more worldly, or more paying business. Saint making is a slow, unprofitable business. They are needed because of their worth and utility. They are precious for their rareness as well as for their intrinsic value. They seem like angels visits, few and far between.

The Church did not have the exclusive right, but did have an original and liberal grant for the business of saint making and she did a fine work when her machinery was new and her artisans fresh and skilled. She does not seem to succeed so well now. New hands and old machinery make havoc often of the producing powers. If the supply has diminished, the demand has increased and is urgent. We do not want the gravestone or calendar saints, nor the pictured or historical ones. We need living saints for present, practical uses.

We want grown saints, not baby saints, as Paul termed the Corinthians. The world will never be saved by the nursery saints. We want saints who will influence and shine. Baby saints may be sweet, but they can neither shine nor impress.

Saints are holy folks, positive folks. They have nothing of the namby-pamby about them. They hate sin and love God. They are divorced from Earth and wedded to Heaven. They are fighters and soldiers by profession. Their spoils are won in conflicts; their characters formed on the battlefield by facing the foe. They are formed out of hard material, but capable of high polish. They are brave talkers, but braver doers. They stand up and confess for their Lord on all proper and test occasions, but they have more than they profess; feel more than they say; and they bear their testimony in doing, denying and dying as well as in speaking.

THE VALUE OF SAINTS

These saints are of great value in all churchly places. A large number can be utilized in positions of Church leadership, the lower and the higher places. Saintly timber is not bad timber to make leaders of the Church which was brought into being and fashioned by leaders of the saintly type; pastors they were by divine right and by the imposition of divine hands. It is a great benediction to have a saint in the leader's chair ordering and tempering the local church. Only saints know the secret of the Church; none but saints can direct its machinery skillfully. Things go so smoothly when a saint is at the helm. If things do not go smoothly the helmsman keeps his head and heart calm in the roughest places. One feels so safe in the hands of saints.

TRUE SAINTS

True saints will do for general secretaries, editors and presidents of colleges. The missionary cause should only be touched by saintly hands. Saintly prayers and saintly sympathies are its projecting forces. A religious newspaper shines with no dim light, speaks with no uncertain sound, forms no alliance with the world and gives no quarter to sin when a saint sits in the editor's chair. Cultured and gifted these all may be, but saintship ought to be first. It does not soil gifts and culture to have a little first class saintship mixed with them. The preaching eldership is a good place for a saint to shine in.

SAINTS IN THE PULPIT

Richard Baxter said, "Blessed are the people who have a saint for a pastor." It is of immense value to have saints in our pulpits. They are so unselfish and meek, they charm; their deliverance of God's Word is gracious and drops like honey. They have such a keen polished edge they almost seem to apologize for their caustic and searching qualities. These saintly pastors so bless our homes by their presence, prayers and sympathies; they are such shining examples; their lack is an irremediable loss. Give us a large supply of saints of the best quality to fill all the churches, and then we will never lack the finest saintly finish.

A good quantity of saints can be used in church stewardship. Financial ability they may have; liberal giving as well as liberal assessing may be their characteristics, but their chief characteristic ought to be their saintship, fashioned in the Christian mold "of solid piety, who both know and love the Church doctrine." These saintly stewards are of the manifold grace of God as well as of finances. A goodly quantity of saints are needed in our homes to establish family worship, train children and servants for Christ, put a halt on all undue and feverish home excitements, and on all worldly tendencies, and to form, by their saintliness, the sober, sweet, heavenly influence of a Christian home. These homemaking saints must be patient, gentle, firm and wise, with heavenly wisdom. Female saints are preferred because they are generally of sweeter tone and of a richer and more delicate mold. A few of these female saints can be used to attend woman's missionary meetings, not for the novelty of addressing mixed assemblies, not to create a mere sentiment toward pagan woman, but to cultivate faith and a self-crucifying love to Christ and to teach by example economy, frugality, and self-denial, as the basis of action; and to show how a saintly woman can, by faith, prayer and holy living do much for Christ in all womanly ways.

A large supply of saints can be used to fill the pews. The atmosphere of God's house scents so freshly and sweetly of Heaven when the pews are filled with saints. Saints come to God's house with such a reverent tread and with so many holy longings. They are prayerful and quieted in God's presence and clamor with intense desire for the sincere milk of the Word. They are there for worship and not to be entertained; to be probed, not to be pleased; they come with meek hearts and not with itching ears. An elect number of male saints are needed for business. We want to marry business and religion and to blend righteousness with trade. Give us a quantity of the most sterling stuff to be in stores, offices, banks and everywhere.

HOW THEY MADE THEM
Becoming a Saint
December 7, 1893

We do not for a moment think that the business of saint making is the peculiar right of any time or place. We do think, however, that the primitive Church had remarkable gifts which the Church in after ages lost. We do believe in the days of Wesley and under his direction, saints were formed with singleness of aim, with wonderful facility, and with remarkable perfection. We would not cover the past with a false glamour, neither would we detract from the present; but it does seem to us the business of saint making does not flourish among us as it did in Wesley's day. He had such a rare knack of holding the Church to its one business of saint making that he would not even allow it to go into the church making business that lies so near alongside of it and which so many great churchmen seriously and most ruinously mistake for the same business.

THE FOCUS OF SAINT MAKING

The principal idea in saint making is to turn all the spiritual forces to the one end of making the individual holy; not simply to save him from sin, but to implant in him an eternal hatred of sin and to transfigure him into such beauty he will be in no mean way the reproduction of the Holy God.

The Church was chartered to make saints of the first class order. Its birth idea was "to spread scriptural holiness over these lands." Saint-making is quite a different thing from church making or running the machinery of a church after it is made. It takes great spiritual power to make saints, and spiritual power was the main feature, we might say the only feature of the early Church.

JOHN WESLEY AND ADAM CLARKE

Fortunately we are not left to fancy or to doubt as to their way of conducting the divine business. John Wesley and Adam Clarke were two of the great and skilled leaders of the Methodist movement. We have a graphic description of the way they did it in a letter from Adam Clarke to John Wesley. This description takes us back to the days when Methodism was in full vigor of operation under the eye of its divinely appointed and blest leaders. The occasion was a great revival. Dr. Clarke had appointed a special prayer meeting for those who were the most earnest in seeking God. He had put much stress on this special meeting for special prayer and had informed Mr. Wesley of it, and refers to it and the results thus:

You perhaps remember the account I gave you of the select prayer meetings which I had just then established for those only who had either attained or were groaning after full redemption. I thought as we were all with one accord in the same place, we had room enough to expect a glorious descent of the purifying flame. It was even so; great was the grace that God caused to rest on us all, and your five or six were able to testify that God had cleansed their souls from all sin. This coming abroad, for it could not be long hid, the change being so palpable in those who professed it, several others were stirred up to seek the same blessing and many were literally provoked to jealousy.

Dr. Clarke informs Mr. Wesley of a mutual acquaintance who it seems had not attended the meeting, but who was much affected by what he had heard. He questioned Dr. Clarke closely about the meeting. He was satisfied, convicted, and confessed that it was "a lamentable thing that those who have begun to seek God since I did should have left me so far behind; through the grace of Christ I will begin to seek the same blessing more earnestly and never rest until I overtake and outstrip them, if possible." This man was honest in his inquiries and set about at once seeking for "all the fullness of God." Dr. Clarke describes his effort and success:

For two or three days he wrestled with God almost incessantly. He came into my room with great apparent depression of spirit. Earnest inquiry was evidently impressed on every muscle of his face. "How shall I receive the blessing, and what are its evidences?" were nearly the words with which he accosted me. I gave him all the direction I could, exhorted him to look for it in the present moment, and assured him of his nearness to the Kingdom of God. He returned to his room and after a few minutes spent in wrestling faith his soul was fully and gloriously delivered. He set off to the country, and like a flame of fire ran over all the Societies in the island, carrying the glorious news wherever he went. God accompanied him by the mightily demonstrated power of His Spirit, and numbers were stirred up to seek, and several soon entered into the promised rest.

We see in this process how carefully these souls crying after more of God were nursed, encouraged, and directed by these church leaders. This prayer meeting and its outpouring were but the first tokens, and Dr. Clarke, like a wise and watchful pastor, took advantage of these spiritual tokens and so arranged that the meeting took on an enlarged form. He says:

I now thought it was requisite to be peculiarly workers together with God, and therefore appointed a love feast. Such a Heaven opened on Earth my soul never felt, and my eyes never saw before. Many glorious love feasts I have had the privilege of enjoying in England and Ireland; but this one exceeded all, and was beyond anything I can describe. Several were filled with pure love and some then and since have, together with a clean heart, found the re-removal of inveterate bodily disorders under which they had labored for a long time. This is an absolute fact of which I have had every proof which demonstration or any other kind of evidence could afford or rationality demand.

There were on some occasions some eccentricities and bastard births. These frequently are the attendants on great spiritual movements. The Wesleyan leaders though, were spiritually wise, strong, discriminating and they cut off with Pauline insight and firmness these parasites or false shoots. Of this meeting Dr. Clarke says:

One thing was very remarkable in this love feast, there was no false fire; no, not a spark that I could not wish to have lighted up in my own soul to all eternity; and though God wrought both on bodies and souls, yet everything was under the regularity of his own Spirit, and fully proclaimed its operation alone.

He also gives the gracious results. To speak within compass I think there are not less than fifty or sixty souls which, in the space of less than a fortnight, have entered into the good land; and many of these are established, strengthened, and settled in it. Still this blessed work goes on, and daily we receive good news from town and country.

One gracious fruit of this revival was to destroy false doctrinal views. Nothing gives a greater impetus to sound doctrine; nothing gives it a deadlier blow than a wonderful outpouring of God's spirit. It leads into all truth and illumines it and discovers all error. This description of an old-time, genuine meeting declares:

This speedy work has given a severe blow to the squalid doctrine of sanctification by or through sufferings, which was before received by many to the great prejudice of their souls. For more than a year past I have been obliged to attack it in public and private; and though through the help of God I sufficiently proved its absurdity, yet several would believe their own way, notwithstanding all I said; but now these palpable evidences overpower all prejudices.

It had the effect, too, to destroy another phase of wrong equally destructive to the work of genuine grace; that is hard, legal, partisan views of full salvation. The statement Dr. Clarke makes of this gracious effect is in these words: Several who had long been adept at making Procrustes' bed are now redeemed from every particle of sour godliness.

Mr. Wesley replies to this letter:

The account you send me of the continuance of the great work of God in Jersey gives me great satisfaction. To retain the grace of God is much more than to gain it; hardly one in three does this. And this should be strongly and explicitly urged on all who have tested of perfect love. If we can prove that any of our local preachers or leaders either directly or indirectly speak against this, let him be a local preacher or leader no longer because he that could speak thus in our congregations cannot be an honest man.

An incident like this gives us our spiritual bearings. We may drift. We will drift unconsciously and this taking our spiritual bearings is absolutely necessary for safety and for satisfaction. If we are not familiar with this work of taking reckoning, and not much given to it, we will drift far away from our chartered course.

CHRIST AND DISCIPLINE
Learning Obedience
February 22, 1894

The attitude of Christ to the seven churches in Asia Minor is one of discipline. In the Apocalypse He reveals himself to make the matter of discipline more emphatic? In the first chapter of the Revelation by St. John we have the Christ of Discipline. In many other forms He revealed himself during

His earthly life but He comes back to us in a new and terrific light in this disciplinary revelation of himself. Fiery indignation, a fiery conquering tread, unsullied purity, full orbed glory, insulted majesty, terrific threatening, a double-edged sword, are all revealed in His attitude to these representative churches.

HE THAT HATH AN EAR

That these seven churches are represented is clear from the striking and seven times reiterated call, *"He that hath an ear, let him hear what the Spirit saith unto the Churches"* (Revelation 2:7). The condition of these churches is sadly suggestive. They were established by apostolic hands, nurtured by apostolic example, faith and zeal; and yet before a century expired from the birth of Christ and while at least one apostle who had nurtured them was living, they are in such a malignant condition of decline Christ feels bound to make His personal reappearance to rectify and save.

THE DISCIPLINE PRINCIPLE

Only one of these churches maintained the vigor and purity of its virgin faith. Another was true, but weak. Two were thoroughly worldly; one of these was full of churchly activity, "a name to live but dead." The other was dead in name as well as in fact. Two of the remaining three were debased in doctrine and in morals. The other had declined in the purity and ardor of its first love.

The bonds of discipline had been loosed. The vital point of their failure was found in the lack of the trained and soldierly principle of "overcoming." Discipline has this conquering principle in its keeping. The divine call to each of these churches is to restore this principle which protects purity, gives power and insures victory. Failure at this point was failure all along the line. With discipline relaxed the whole spiritual nerve becomes flabby and vicious; love declines, doctrine becomes corrupt, morals debased, and the world comes in like a wild, desolating flood.

REVELATION OF CHRIST

Christ is a revelation to these churches, for all churches and for all times. He sets forth the demand that He makes of His universal Church. Whiteness of head and heart, conspicuous and crowning, is His first and great demand. He must have absolute purity in doctrine and life. His majesty, truth and eternity are appealed to in support of this demand for purity. His fiery eye and fiery feet are against all enemies or false or weak friends who would remove the wall of discipline which protects this purity. Christ here appears indignant and aroused. It is the indignation of a general who finds his army demoralized or the indignation of a husband in the presence of the infidelity of his bride. How flaming are His eyes! What fury in His glowing feet! How fierce and sharp His two-edged sword! How fierce and exacting the noonday splendor of His brightness! How His fiery eye, fiery tread, and two-edged sword reveal the fierce, relentless opposition He has to evil and evildoers in the Church! How His countenance, as the sun shining in His strength, images the brightness and purity which His glorious and full presence in the Church produces, shining away the night and death of bad doctrine, bad living and dispersing the poison of the world! His right hand tells of the mighty power and fearfulness of His grip on the preachers, and locates the seat of authority, responsibility and accountability.

STANDARD OF HOLINESS

Discipline had fallen so low in these churches that the preachers and people lost the standard of holiness and were wholly ignorant of the true condition of things. In fact, they were facilitating themselves on great prosperity; they were large in numbers, influential in wealth and social position and stood high in worldly exhibits and activities.

We have before us in this revelation, and the attitude of these churches, an object lesson of how lax discipline is the great enemy of righteousness and holiness. Feeble love, lax morals, wrong doctrines and worldliness all come out of this Pandora's Box.

In the system of Christ, the preacher is primarily responsible for the condition of the church. Christ in this revelation recognizes that elementary principle, and so the "angel" (the preacher) is first addressed, and through him the church also is addressed and held to its responsibility. It is the business of the preacher and the church to put away these evils. Failing to do this, they are held accountable for the results. The preacher and the church must rid themselves of complicity with all wrong and wrongdoers or else Christ will rid himself of them. *"I will remove thy candlestick out of his place except thou repent"* (Revelation 2:5), He says to one of them. To another, *"Repent; or else I will come unto thee quickly, and will fight against them with the sword of my mouth"* (Revelation 2:16). Of the offenders in Thyatira He declares:

> *And I gave her space to repent of her fornication; and she repented not. Behold, I will cast her into a bed and them that commit adultery with her into great tribulation, except they repent of their deeds. And I will kill her children with death; and all the churches shall know that I am He which searcheth the reins and hearts; and I will give unto every one of you according to your works.* (Revelation 2:22-23)

To the active, reputable church workers in Sardis He says:

> *Remember therefore how thou hast received and heard and hold fast, and repent. If therefore thou shalt not*

watch, I will come on thee as a thief and thou shalt not know what hour I will come upon thee. (Revelation 3:3)

For the lukewarm in Laodicea He has this penalty: *"So then because thou art lukewarm and neither cold nor hot, I will spew thee out of my mouth"* (Revelation 3:16). These are toxic statements from the Great Head of the Church for these lax, almost licentious times when the nature of church discipline is lost sight of, and its enforcement charged as a folly or a crime. In Christ's attitude there is no trace of squeamishness, policy, weakness or cowardice which discounts or ignores discipline or fears to hold firm reins or to visit penalties on the incorrigible. What a rebuke the attitude of Christ to these churches gives those apologists for a worldly church, who ignore, defame, or denounce the enforcement of discipline.

SET ON FIRE
Firing Up the Preacher
March 1, 1894

An intelligent layman, a professional man, said to us: "Our preacher is a good man, a sound, practical preacher and clear in his statements of the truth; but he needs to be set on fire." We do not hesitate to say one of the greatest needs of the pulpit today is that the preacher needs to be full of zeal and holy fire.

THE SYMBOL OF SPIRITUAL GRACE

The tongue of fire is the symbol of all spiritual grace. The tongue of fire lies at the foundation of all the powerfully aggressive, richly edifying, powerfully persuading, and sweetly drawing forces of the pulpit.

The flame which fires the preacher's tongue must be the flame from Heaven. No Earth kindled flame will do the work of preaching the gospel. It must be a flame that will not only quicken but purify; and while it is put to great heat, it must purge from every stain of passion.

A Heaven-inflamed ministry is our great need. The Methodist Times, London, declares it to be "the greatest need of British Christianity," and makes this strong appeal: There has never been a successful or permanent religious movement that did not owe its initiation and establishment to mighty and passionate preaching. And there never was a time when the pulpit was potentially so effective and so attractive as today. When will Christians realize the significance of the fact that the spiritual and divinely instituted symbol of Christianity is not a crucifix, sword, or pen but a "tongue of fire?" The tongue ever has been and ever must be the main instrument of such a voluntary and rational religion as true Christianity. What we want then above everything else is preaching, but preaching of the right sort. It goes without saying that it must be passionate preaching. A cold tongue, a calm tongue or a dry tongue, is worse than useless. It must be a tongue "of fire." We have had too many essays in the pulpit.

DR. BUNTING

Real preachers are not schoolmasters or academic professors. It is all rubbish to talk about an "instructive ministry" which does not inflame the imagination or fire the heart. All real preachers, that is to say prophets, have always had tongues "of fire" even when their temperaments were philosophical and their tendency logical and didactic. Think of the great Dr. Bunting. He was not a rhetorician or a rhapsodist; but he sobbed and he wept in the pulpit in Grosvenor Street,

Manchester as he pleaded passionately with what was then the wealthiest and most fashionable congregation to forsake their sins that very hour. How wrong it is to say some men cannot plead earnestly and intensely, but must be cold, calm and reserved. Who exhibits an unimpassioned temper when his house is on fire, when he is discussing home rule or, when his blood is up at a committee meeting? There is latent in every heart and an inexhaustible fund of enthusiasm and emotion that is raised to a white heat when we are possessed by "the passion for souls," and are baptized with the Holy Ghost "and with fire."

BAPTISM OF THE HOLY GHOST

Without the baptism we are weak as other men. We may instruct, please, or amuse; but we shall never persuade our hearers to submit themselves to Christ. Even when by the grace of God, in answer to believing and expectant prayer, we have received the baptism of fire; we must use our brains, the whole of our brains, if we mean to do real and permanent good. It is a fatal mistake to rely upon mere physical vigor or upon the passing magnetic influence of sanguine youth. It is a deadly error to preach old sermons when they have ceased to fire our own souls.

This one thing the ministry is ever forgetting. We are constantly being directed to other sources of power, and we ultimately loose the power to change from a weak church that cannot equip its army to defend sin in its midst.

THE GOOD SHEPHERD
Qualities of a Pastor
March 8, 1894

The shepherd and the sheep is a favorable figure in the Bible. *"The LORD is my shepherd"* strikes a sweet, responsive note in the Christian experience. The Bible gives us many pictures of this pastoral relation, of the shepherd's tenderness, courage, vigilance and self-denial. These are not chance pictures. It was no accident the patriarchs, Moses and David, were shepherds. They were figures of Christ the Great Shepherd; they were also types of what His under shepherds should be.

THE GOOD SHEPHERD

In the tenth chapter of John, Christ draws the character of the good shepherd in strong contrast with the heartless stranger shepherd and the spirit of the hireling. The good shepherd governed his sheep by example, by voice and by rod. Government, feeding and safety were one, and the good shepherd controlled, pastured and defended them. The good shepherd had authority over them because he belonged to them. His sympathy, presence and love were ever with the sheep. The good shepherd's heart is with his sheep. The sheep yielded to the mastery of the shepherd's rod because they had yielded to the mastery of his heart. They listened to his voice because his heart spoke through his voice. The sheep followed his person because his heart shined through his person. All this and more too may be said of the good spiritual shepherd.

THE STRANGER SHEPHERD

The stranger shepherd did not belong to the sheep. The sheep did not belong to the hireling. There was no sense of ownership in either case. The good shepherd belongs to the sheep, and the sheep belong to him. A double ownership is attached. The stranger shepherd did not know the sheep. The hireling does not love them. The good shepherd knows and loves his sheep. The stranger cannot rule the sheep. The hireling can only drive or beat them. The good shepherd can rule them; he leads rather than drives; he wins but never beats. The stranger shepherd has no heart in the matter. The heart of the hireling is in the hire. The good shepherd is all heart; hire and salary have no place. It was no accident Christ the Good Shepherd had not where to lay his head. The taint of money would have discrowned His Messiahship

THE GOOD SHEPHERD AND THE COUNTERFEIT

The eternal distinction between the shepherd and all phases of the counterfeit lies in the statement, *"I am the good shepherd: the good shepherd giveth his life for the sheep"* (John 10:11). He stakes everything on the relation, subordinates all things to it and surrenders all things for it. What is money, reputation, ease or popularity? All are nothing. The sheep are everything. Their safety absorbs heart, head and hands; fills every waking moment and colors every sleeping one. The good shepherd gives his life for the sheep, not to maintain his reputation or protect the sheepfold, but for the sheep. It is not creeds, or sects, or opinions, that the spiritual shepherd gives his life for, but for men. The whole being is to go out to save men, not to preach so many sermons or collect so much money, but to save men. The very essence, contact, and whole soul of the good shepherd centers in that lofty, self-denying, courageous, manly principle, *"He giveth his life for the sheep."*

The salvation of the sheep is the shepherd's ruling passion. For this he is wasted and worn, "In the day the drought consumed and the frost by night, and sleep departs from the eyes." The good shepherd has given himself to the sheep. They have mastered him. No man can take hold of men till they have mastered them. No man can take hold of a generation for Christ who does not give his life for them. No man can be a good minister whose life does not flow in its richest, reddest, fullest streams through that ministry. The ministry must not be outside of the man nor merely taken on by the man, nor merely a part of the man; it must be the whole man, made after the purest and noblest pattern. What sacrifice! What toil! What suffering! What surrender! What conflicts endured! What enemies faced! What losses in the "giving his life!"

One of the saintly and sainted, Pastor Baxter, who, impressed his church for God by the simplicity and holiness of his character and his abundant labors, when questioned as to a new literary work, replied: "When God put me in the work I gave myself to it, and I have not had time for literature or scholarship since." When Newton was asked how he made his discoveries he answered: "By always thinking about them." This is the secret of success, to give ourselves to it. Christ gave himself to His work, and had no time for other things. To 'get' is the language of the stranger shepherd and the hireling. To 'give' is the language and law of the good shepherd. "May a physician," says Baxter, "in the plague time take any more relaxation or recreation than is necessary for his life when so many are expecting help in case of life or death? Will you stand by and see sinners gasping under the pangs of death and say, God doth not require me to make myself a drudge to save them? Is this the voice of ministerial or Christian compassion, or rather one of sensual laziness and diabolical cruelty?"

STUDY GUIDE

BIOGRAPHY OF E.M. BOUNDS

1. How did E.M. Bounds learn "new and higher lessons" from God?

2. What were some of his careers?

3. To what Protestant denomination did Bounds belong?

What was the "something else" that Bounds experienced at a brush-arbor meeting?

4. Why did Bounds refuse to sign the Oath of Allegiance to the federal government?

5. What happened to him as a result of not signing the Oath?

6. Why did the men to whom Bounds ministered as a chaplain call him "the walking bundle"?

7. What Civil War battle was known as "the Gettysburg of the West"?

8. Where did Bounds help to establish a Confederate cemetery?

9. What was the primary goal of Bounds when he became pastor of Franklin's Methodist Episcopal Church?

10. How did he endeavor to achieve this goal?

11. How many children did E.M. Bounds and his wife, Emma, have?

12. Of what publication did Bounds become the editor?

13. Why did he leave this position?

14. How did Bounds spend the last nineteen years of his life?

15. What was the legacy that Bounds left to the Church?

16. How many books on prayer did he write?

VOLUME I: ON MISSION

A CALL TO PRAYER

1. Why is this age known as the Missionary Age?

2. What contrast did Dr. Olin give regarding missionary giving and faith?

3. What is another name for "the spirit of missions"?

4. What is the primary need in the work of missions?

5. What will prayer for missions and missionaries accomplish?

REVIVAL PREACHING

1. When is the time to plant the great doctrines of the faith in people's minds?

2. On what was the best revival with which God ever blessed our ministry based?

PLANS, WORK, CONSECRATION

1. To what "fatal mistakes" does Bounds allude at the opening of this chapter?

2. Which question that was raised by the Apostle Paul struck the keynote for his entire life of service?

3. How does Johann Wilhelm Neander describe the greatest achievements by the greatest men in behalf of humanity?

4. How does Bounds define *consecration*?

THE MOURNER'S BENCH

1. What does Bounds mean by "the mourner's bench"?

2. What are the effects of the mourner's bench experience?

A SERIOUS MATTER

1. What is the time of our greatest peril?

2. How does Satan accomplish his "master work"?

3. What is one possible fault in public education?

AN ANOINTED CHURCH

1. What does the power of the Holy Ghost do for the Church?

2. How does the anointing of the Holy Ghost come to us?

3. How does Bounds define *unction*.

4. What does the anointing give to the Church?

THE REVIVAL

1. What is true revival?

2. How does a pastor sow the seeds of revival?

THE PRAYER MEETING

1. Give two of Bounds' metaphors for prayer meetings.

2. What is the objective of the prayer meeting?

3. What happens at a true prayer meeting?

4. What is the effect of prayer meetings upon Sunday services?

WHERE THE REVIVAL BEGINS

1. Is the Church no longer revival oriented?

2. How should we promote revivals in our churches?

3. Where does revival begin?

4. In what ways do some preachers hinder revival in their churches?

SERIOUS BUSINESS

1. What happens to the Church without revival?

2. How can we prepare for revival?

A SELF-DENYING MINISTRY

1. How does Bounds define *self-denial*?

2. What is the only way to keep the great facts of revelation alive in the hearts of the people?

3. Upon what is the spiritual success of a ministry dependent?

4. What is the cure for bodily afflictions and political and social issues?

THE CHURCH FOR GOD

1. How can the immense resources of the Church be used for the Christianization of the world?

2. What does Bounds mean by "taking hold of the Church"?

THE CHURCH HELD FOR GOD

1. What is the charter mission of the Church?

2. What must a preacher have if he wants to take hold of the church for God?

3. How does Bounds define the kind of courage a preacher needs?

4. How does a preacher hold the church for God?

A TYPICAL MOVEMENT

1. What must direct all our movements?

2. What does Bounds have to say about the most successful missionary movements?

GOD REVEALED IN US

1. What does the revelation of God do in our lives?

2. Of what is the life of Mrs. Jonathan Edwards a good example?

OUR FIGHT AND WEAPONS

1. Against what do we, as believers, wage war?

2. In what sense is it accurate to say that the Christian is a soldier?

3. Who said, "Give me 100 preachers, who fear nothing but sin and desire nothing but God. Such alone will shake the gates of hell and set up the Kingdom of Heaven upon the Earth"?

THE SPIRIT OF CHRIST

1. What are the elements of a Christ-like spirit?

2. Why is zealousness required to do good works?

3. How do we obtain a Christ-like spirit?

GUARD THE HOME

1. What are the three primary foes of the Christian?

2. Describe the true Christian home.

A STRONG CHURCH

1. What are the elements of church strength?

2. What is the measure of a church's strength?

3. In what ways is the Church affected by material progress?

4. Contrast the pious church with the worldly church.

5. In what does the Church's strength lie?

CHRIST ON DISCIPLINE

1. In what sense is discipline a basic principle of Christianity?

2. What does Christ say about discipline?

THIS WINTER

1. What are the two species of revival to which Bounds refers?

2. What are the characteristics of the two species of revival?

3. How does Bounds describe true revival?

4. In what sense are revival and entertainment in opposition to each other?

HINDRANCES TO THE REVIVAL

1. What does the lack of preparation for a revival prevent?

2. What is the spirit of revival?

3. In what way is too much singing a hindrance to revival?

4. What does the indifference of church leaders cause?

WITNESSING VERSUS BOASTING

1. What is the foundation of true witnessing?

2. In what way does boasting resemble witnessing?

3. How does Bounds define *witnessing*?

4. Why is witnessing necessary for spiritual development?

5. How do we still the enemy and the avenger?

HOLDING VERSUS SAVING

1. What is the difference between saving and holding?

2. What is one main cause of the evils of the entertainment business?

THE CAMP MEETING SEASON

1. Describe the old-time camp meeting.

2. What was the spirit of the old-time camp meeting?

AN IMPORTANT DISTINCTION

1. What distinction does Bounds make between sensational preaching and preaching that creates a distinction?

2. What do we learn from Paul's preaching to Felix?

THE AGGRESSIVE POWER

1. In what do the aggressive forces of the gospel lie?

2. What is accomplished by the teaching of spiritual principles?

3. In what way is this process like the planting of seeds?

4. How does Bounds describe the successful pastor?

THE CHURCH PREPARED

1. What kinds of revivals are discussed by Bounds in this chapter?

2. What hindrances to revival does he discuss in this chapter?

THE REVIVAL

1. In what sense is revival the sign of soul-saving revival?

2. How does revival show the revelation of God's power and glory?

THE PRELIMINARY WORK

1. What is the preliminary work that is necessary for revival?

2. What does Dr. Cuyler recommend?

A WORKING CHURCH

1. What does the church at Sardis show us?

2. In what are the elements of genuine revival found?

3. What are Finney's chief points in this section?

WORKED UP, PRAYED DOWN

1. What's the difference between a "worked up" or "prayed down" revival?

2. Define a "prayed down" revival.

3. What is the role of "effectual, fervent prayer"?

A GREAT DANGER

1. What does Bounds mean by "seeing with spiritual eyes"?

2. What did Bounds see as being the imperative duty of his hour?

THE CHURCH PERPETUATED

1. What are some of the great evils that have come against the Church?

2. What did John Wesley recommend with regard to the perpetuation of Methodism?

AFTER THE REVIVAL

1. To what does Bounds compare the true revival?

2. What is the most important work of a church after revival?

VOLUME II: OUR SPIRITUAL WALK

CHRISTIANITY, CONSERVATIVE AND AGGRESSIVE

1. What are the roles of salt and light?

2. What does Bounds mean by saying, "Christianity is both conservative and aggressive"?

PRAISE GOD

1. What does the spirit of praise accomplish?

2. Should we shout God's praise?

3. Should we sing God's praise?

4. What does praise produce?

5. What do songs of praise illustrate?

6. Whose hymns does Bounds consider to be John Wesley's sermons in rhyme?

7. What is the object of praise?

HEAVEN

1. What must permeate our service on Earth?

2. To what should the Christian life be in responsive harmony?

3. What is the city whose builder and maker is God?

4. What does meditation upon Heaven do for us?

FASTING AND CHRIST

1. How does fasting relate to the teachings of Christ?

2. What is the spiritual value of fasting?

MAKING OUT A CASE

1. What are some of the hidden fountains of piety?

2. What does Bounds mean by *defective piety*?

WORLDLY PRUDENCE

1. In what sense might prudence be considered a cowardly virtue?

2. What is true Christian prudence?

3. What is the difference between worldly prudence and Christian prudence?

ELEMENTARY PRINCIPLES

1. Why is conviction of sin necessary?

2. What happened to the Rev. Wilbur Fisk after he submitted himself to God?

3. What is the anointing of the Holy Ghost?

4. What happens when we draw near to God?

DECAY OF REVERENCE

1. What are the effects of a lack of reverence in a worship service?

2. What are the causes of a lack of reverence in a worship service?

3. According to Bounds, what is pantheism?

4. How does Bounds contrast the unmixed gospel with the highly seasoned gospel?

A LESSON FROM ELI

1. What are the two great fundamental principles that are cited by Bounds in the beginning of this chapter?

2. What do we learn from the life of Eli?

3. How does failure to govern the family dishonor God?

THE SOCIAL VERSUS THE SPIRITUAL

1. What is one major cause for spiritual decline with the church?

2. What happens when we substitute social forces for spiritual ones?

3. What is the difference between social life and true spiritual unity?

4. How did Bounds feel about societies in the local church?

5. What were his views regarding fairs, festivals, and parties?

6. On what should a church be founded?

ARRESTED DEVELOPMENT

1. How does personal piety grow?

2. What does Bounds mean by "spiritual arrest"?

3. What is sanctification?

4. What are the causes of spiritual arrest?

5. Describe the process of perfection.

THE PRESENT EVIL WORLD

1. How does apostasy begin?

2. What did Dr. Mendenhall have to say about worldliness and apostasy?

THE MODEL STEWARD

1. Contrast the good steward with the bad steward.

2. How does Bounds describe the model steward?

3. What should the relationship between the pastor and the model steward be?

HOME KEEPER

1. Describe the atmosphere of the Christian home.

2. What, according to Bounds, is the woman's responsibility?

3. What is the high calling of a home keeper?

4. In what ways is the Church indebted to women?

CHRIST AND THE OLD TESTAMENT

1. What did Christ think of the Old Testament Scriptures?

2. In what ways is Christ connected to the Old Testament Scriptures?

3. How did Christ use the Scriptures?

TOTAL DEPRAVITY

1. What is meant by the total depravity of mankind?

2. What are the jewels of our faith?

3. What is the death blow to self-righteous pride?

HOW THEY CAME INTO IT

1. How is saintly character formed?
2. What do intense fellowship and prayer do for us?

CHRIST'S DYING TESTIMONY

1. In what ways are the Old Testament and the New Testament connected?
2. How did Christ view the rejection He experienced from the Jews?
3. What do we learn from Judas Iscariot?
4. How does Jesus' death fulfill the Old Testament?
5. What happened on the Road to Emmaus?

THE MAN

1. How does God regard personal purity?
2. How are personal purity and materialism in opposition to each other?

DISCIPLINE OF EXAMPLE

1. What is Bounds' definition of *discipline* in this chapter?
2. What is the pastor's role?

FRAMES

1. What does Bounds mean by "frames" in this context?
2. To what satanic snare does Lady Maxwell refer?

WAKING UP

1. What is the job of the Christian press?

2. What paralyzes all vigilant and zealous effort?

TESTIMONY VERSUS BOASTING

1. Upon what should we depend in giving testimony to our faith?

2. How does Bounds describe spiritual wisdom?

CHRIST AND DISCIPLING, PART 1

1. What is the object of Christ's training school?

2. What are the foundational principles to which the Church must strictly adhere?

3. In what ways did the Wesleyan Movement promote holy brotherhood?

CHRIST AND DISCIPLING, PART 2

1. Why is purity in the Church important?

2. What do we learn from the example of Christ cleansing the Temple?

3. What extreme measures are demanded in order to have purity in the Church?

4. What happens when discipline decays within a church?

THE STRANGER

1. What three different characters are portrayed in the Parable of the Shepherd and the Sheep?

2. What is the problem with the stranger shepherd's heart?

THE MODERN IDEA

1. What effect has rationalism had on the Church?

2. How does corruption put on incorruption?

3. What is the role of the Resurrection of Jesus Christ in all of this?

SELF-DENIAL

1. What is the taproot of Christianity?

2. What is the great hindrance to religion?

3. What does the lack of self-denial lead to?

FAITH

1. What is the effect of the emasculating idea of faith that Bounds describes?

2. What do we learn about faith from the Earl of Shaftesbury?

VOLUME III: LEADERSHIP GOD'S WAY

THE LEADERSHIP OF FAITH

1. What is the distinguishing factor that should be present in church leaders?

2. How does Bounds characterize faith in this chapter?

3. How does prayer aid faith?

4. How is faith brought into leadership?

5. What does Bounds mean by the leadership of faith?

AN OLD REMEDY

1. What does the "old *Discipline*" do for the Church?

2. What is "the remedy for the evil"?

3. What is the focus of the *Methodist Discipline of 1798*?

THE LEADERSHIP OF HOLINESS

1. Why can't a church rise above its leadership's control?

2. What is the first principle of purity?

3. What was the giant evil in the Church of Bounds' day?

4. What is the role of holiness within the Church and its leaders?

PAUL'S GLORYING

1. How was Paul able to glory in tribulation?

2. What was Hannah More's attitude toward suffering?

DRIVING OUT EVIL THOUGHTS

1. Does everyone experience evil thoughts?

2. How does one get rid of evil thoughts?

3. What is the effect of praying in spirit and truth?

CHRISTIAN PERFECTION

1. Is Christian perfection attainable in this life?
2. What is the role of holiness in attaining to perfection?
3. How does Bounds define Christian perfection?
4. Should change be gradual or instantaneous?

DUTY

1. What is the meaning of "duty"?
2. Should freedom and love be exalted above duty?

THE TRUE RELATION

1. What is the true relation of the Christian to Heaven?
2. What is Heaven?
3. What should our view of Heaven be?

SPIRIT REPRESSION

1. By what is Holy Ghost religion symbolized? Why?
2. What is the law of spiritual life, according to Bounds?
3. What does Bounds mean by "spiritual repression"?
4. How does spiritual repression affect us?

ABOUT PRUDENCE

1. What is the difference between worldly prudence and Christian discretion?

2. What effect does imprudence have upon our Christian lives?

SPIRITUAL LEADERSHIP

1. How does Bounds view spiritual leadership?

2. What is the role of character in determining leadership?

3. What is required in the life of a spiritual leader?

4. In what ways does John Wesley's life exemplify spiritual leadership for us?

5. How did the Apostle Paul demonstrate spiritual leadership?

6. What is the foundation of spiritual power?

THE PASTOR

1. What is the relationship of preaching to pastoral care?

2. Why is pastoral care important?

THE WORK OF THE CHURCH

1. What two priorities does Bounds point to with regard to the work of the Church?

2. What should the singular aim of the Church be?

DECAY OF SPIRITUAL INSTITUTIONS

1. How does materialism bring about decay?

2. What were some of the differences between watch night services of the past and those that took place in Bounds' time?

3. What are the differences between old-time camp meetings and present-day ones?

A GROWING EVIL

1. What is wrong with churches being classified by money?
2. What are the results of evaluating a church by financial standards?

RELIGION IN BUSINESS

1. Do religion and business belong to two opposing realms?
2. What is the great sin of the modern church?

HARD LESSON

1. What, according to Bounds, is the first and last element of success in God's work?
2. What will bar the operation of the Holy Ghost?

A RELIGIOUS VIEW

1. Why should a church not become a social church?
2. What does Bounds say is the cement of mankind?

PASTORAL CARE

1. How does Bounds define pastoral care?
2. What is the distinction between preaching and pastoral care?

PRAYING FOR THE HOLY GHOST

1. Upon what is the presence and the power of the Holy Ghost at any given meeting conditioned?

2. What is "the gift of the Holy Ghost"?

3. What is the evidence of the power of the Holy Ghost?

PASTORAL VISITATION

1. In what do pastoral care and pastoral work find their best expression?

2. What does visiting in homes help the pastor to understand?

PASTORAL AUTHORITY

1. What is the responsibility of the pastor?

2. From what does the spiritual authority of the pastor spring?

THE DIVINE BUSINESS

1. To what business is the Church of Jesus Christ committed?

2. What is a common danger that is found in soul-winning churches?

3. In what are ecclesiastical churches grounded?

4. In what sense is soul-saving a divine art?

A PRESCRIPTION

1. What is the cure for worldliness in a church?

2. What are the symptoms of worldliness in a church?

3. What is the pastor's role?

FAITH CURES—GOD CURES

1. What is the difference between faith and God-centered faith?

2. What kinds of people are fanatics, according to Bounds?

THESE TIMES

1. What does Bounds recommend to overcome materialism?

2. Do you think we are more or less materialistic today than people were in Bounds' times?

DISCIPLINE CAN BE ENFORCED

1. What does discipline require?

2. What do we learn from the Seven Churches of Asia?

SATANIC DEVICES

1. How is Satan frequently disguised?

2. Why do we need to be aware of Satan's schemes?

SAINTS WANTED

1. What is the greatest need for Earth?

2. What is the value of saints?

3. Who are the true saints?

HOW THEY MADE THEM

1. How are saints made?

2. What do John Wesley and Adam Clarke teach us about this important subject?

CHRIST AND DISCIPLINE

1. What was Christ's attitude toward the seven churches in Asia Minor?

2. What does Bounds mean by "the discipline principle"?

SET ON FIRE

1. What does the tongue of fire symbolize?

2. What is the baptism of the Holy Ghost and what does it do for us?

THE GOOD SHEPHERD

1. What are the characteristics of a good shepherd?

2. What is the distinction that Bounds makes between the Good Shepherd and all others?

INDEX

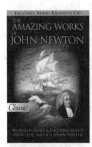

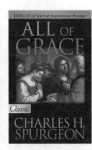

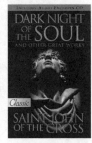
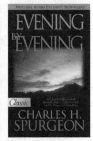
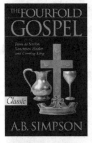

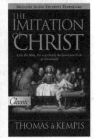

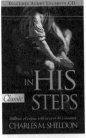

INCLUDES AUDIO EXCERPTS CD

IN HIS STEPS

Classic

Millions of copies sold in over 45 countries

CHARLES M. SHELDON

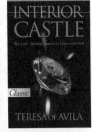

INCLUDES AUDIO EXCERPTS CD

INTERIOR CASTLE

The Soul's Spiritual Journey to Union with God

Classic

TERESA OF AVILA

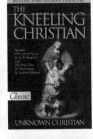

INCLUDES AUDIO EXCERPTS DOWNLOAD

THE KNEELING CHRISTIAN

Classic

UNKNOWN CHRISTIAN

MADAME JEANNE GUYON

Classic

EXPERIENCING UNION WITH GOD THROUGH INNER PRAYER & THE WAY AND RESULTS OF UNION WITH GOD

MORNING BY MORNING

Classic

CHARLES H. SPURGEON

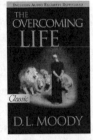

INCLUDES AUDIO EXCERPTS DOWNLOAD

THE OVERCOMING LIFE

Classic

D. L. MOODY

THE PILGRIM'S PROGRESS IN MODERN ENGLISH

Classic

JOHN BUNYAN

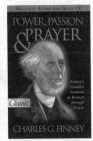

INCLUDES AUDIO EXCERPTS CD

POWER, PASSION & PRAYER

Classic

CHARLES G. FINNEY

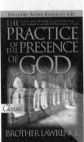

INCLUDES AUDIO EXCERPTS CD

THE PRACTICE OF THE PRESENCE OF GOD

Classic

BROTHER LAWRENCE

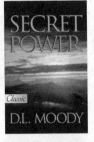

SECRET POWER

Classic

D. L. MOODY

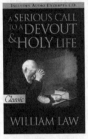

INCLUDES AUDIO EXCERPTS CD

A SERIOUS CALL TO A DEVOUT & HOLY LIFE

Classic

WILLIAM LAW

THE SOVEREIGNTY OF GOD

Classic

A.W. PINK

INCLUDES AUDIO EXCERPTS DOWNLOAD

SPURGEON ON PRAYER

Classic

CHARLES H. SPURGEON

TABLE TALK

MARTIN LUTHER

Classic

INCLUDES AUDIO EXCERPTS DOWNLOAD

TORREY ON PRAYER

Classic

THE POWER OF PRAYER & THE PRAYER OF POWER

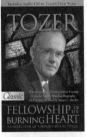

TOZER

Classic

FELLOWSHIP OF THE BURNING HEART

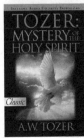

INCLUDES AUDIO EXCERPTS DOWNLOAD

TOZER: MYSTERY OF THE HOLY SPIRIT

Classic

A.W. TOZER

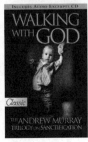

INCLUDES AUDIO EXCERPTS CD

WALKING WITH GOD

Classic

THE ANDREW MURRAY TRILOGY ON SANCTIFICATION

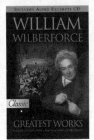

INCLUDES AUDIO EXCERPTS CD

WILLIAM WILBERFORCE

Classic

GREATEST WORKS

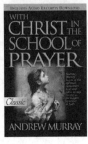

INCLUDES AUDIO EXCERPTS DOWNLOAD

WITH CHRIST IN THE SCHOOL OF PRAYER

Classic

ANDREW MURRAY

DR. DARREL KING researched, compiled, and edited this material. He was born in Missouri and attended Missouri Baptist College and Luther Rice Seminary. He has pastored in the St. Louis and Atlanta areas. Dr. King served with the World Literature Crusade, teaching Change the World Schools of Prayer, and served with the Home Mission Board SBC in Prayer for Spiritual Awakening. He currently is Director of the E. M. Bounds School of Prayer in Conyers, Georgia.

9/6/20
9/21/21 Con

Pure Gold Classics

CHRISTIAN CLASSICS

A classic is a work of enduring excellence; a Christian classic is a work of enduring excellence that is filled with divine wisdom, biblical revelation, and insights that are relevant to living a godly life. Such works are both spiritual and practical. Our Pure Gold Classics contain some of the finest examples of Christian writing that have ever been published, including the works of John Foxe, Charles Spurgeon, D.L. Moody, Martin Luther, John Calvin, Saint John of the Cross, E.M. Bounds, John Wesley, Andrew Murray, Hannah Whitall Smith, and many others.

The timeline on the following pages will help you to understand the context of the times in which these extraordinary books were written and the historical events that must have served to influence these great writers to create works that will always stand the test of time. Inspired by God, many of these authors did their work in difficult times and during periods of history that were not sympathetic to their message. Some even had to endure great persecution, misunderstanding, imprisonment, and martyrdom as a direct result of their writing.

The entries that are printed in green type will give you a good overview of Christian history from the birth of Jesus to modern times.

The entries in red pertain to writers of Christian classics from Saint Augustine, who wrote his *Confessions* and *City of God*, to Charles Sheldon, twentieth-century author of *In His Steps*.

Entries in black provide a clear perspective on the development of secular history from the early days of Buddhism (first century) through the Civil Rights Movement.

Finally, the blue entries highlight secular writers and artists, including Chaucer, Michelangelo, and others.

Our color timeline will provide you with a fresh perspective of history, both secular and Christian, and the classics, both secular and Christian. This perspective will help you to understand each author better and to see the world through his or her eyes.